C000083919

CASEBOOK

Shakespeare
Early Comedies

A CASEBOOK

EDITED BY

PAMELA MASON

MACMILLAN

First published 1995 by
THE MACMILLAN PRESS LTD
Houndmills, Basingstoke, Hampshire RG21 2XS
and London
Companies and representatives
throughout the world

ISBN 0–333–42658–4 hardcover
ISBN 0–333–42659–2 paperback

A catalogue record for this book is available
from the British Library

Printed in Malaysia

CONTENTS

Part 4: *Love's Labour's Lost*

Critical Comment before 1950
ROBERT TOFTE (1598), p. 189 – CHARLES GILDON (1710),
  p. 190 – SAMUEL JOHNSON (1765), p. 190 – GEORGE
  BERNARD SHAW (1886), p. 190 – WALTER PATER
  (1889), p. 192 – HARLEY GRANVILLE BARKER (1927),
  p. 193 – JOHN PALMER (1946), p. 195

ACKNOWLEDGEMENTS

The editor and publishers wish to thank the following for permission to use copyright material:

Ralph Berry, '*The Comedy of Errors*: The Subliminal Narrative' in *Shakespeare and the Awareness of the Audience*' (1985) pp. 30–45, by permission of Macmillan, London and Basingstoke; Muriel Bradbrook, 'Dramatic Role as Social Image: A Study of *The Taming of the Shrew*', *Shakespeare Jahrbuch*, XCIV (1958) pp. 132–50, reprinted in *Muriel Bradbrook on Shakespeare*, Harvester Wheatsheaf (1984), by permission of Simon and Schuster; Harold Brooks, 'Two Clowns in a Comedy (to Say Nothing of the Dog): Speed, Launce (and Crab) in *The Two Gentlemen of Verona*', *Essays and Studies*, XVI (1963) 91–100, by permission of The English Association; and 'Themes and Structures in *The Comedy of Errors*' in *Early Shakespeare*, Stratford upon Avon Studies 3, ed. J. R. Brown and B. Harris (1961) pp. 55–71, by permission of Edward Arnold; James L. Calderwood, '*Love's Labour's Lost*: A Wantoning with Words', *Studies in English Literature*, 5 (1965), pp. 317–32, updated version included in James L. Calderwood, *Shakespearean Metadrama*. Copyright © 1971 by the University of Studies in English Literature and the University of Minnesota Press; David Daniell, 'The Good Marriage of Katherine and Petruchio', *Shakespeare Survey*, 37 (1984) 23–31, by permission of Cambridge University Press; Philip Edwards, an extract from *Shakespeare and the Confines of Art* (1968) pp. 37–48, Methuen and Co., by permission of Routledge; Inga-Stina Ewbank, ' "Were man but constant, he were perfect": Constancy and Consistency in *The Two Gentlemen of Verona*', *Shakespearian Comedy*, Stratford upon Avon Studies 14, ed. M. Bradbury and D. Palmer (1972) pp. 31–57, by permission of Edward Arnold; Bobbyann Roesen [Anne Barton], '*Love's Labour's Lost*'; *Shakespeare Quarterly*, 4 (1953) 411–26, by permission of Shakespeare Quarterly; Gāmini Salgādo, ' "Time's Deformed Hand": Sequence, Consequence and Inconsequence in *The Comedy of Errors*', *Shakespeare Survey*, 25 (1972) 81–91, by permission of Fenella Copplestone [Salgādo]; Cecil C. Seronsy, ' "Supposes" as the unifying theme in *The Taming of the Shrew*', *Shakespeare Quarterly*, 14 (1963) 15–30, by permission of Shakespeare Quarterly; Stanley Wells, 'The Failure of *The Two Gentlemen of Verona*', *Shakespeare Jahrbuch*, XCIX (1963) 161–173, by permission of Bohlau-Verlag.

Every effort has been made to trace all the copyright holders but if any have been inadvertently overlooked the publishers will be pleased to make the necessary arrangement at the first opportunity.

GENERAL EDITOR'S PREFACE

The Casebook series, launched in 1968, has become a well-regarded library of critical studies. The central concern of the series remains the 'single-author' volume, but suggestions from the academic community have led to an extension of the original plan, to include occasional volumes on such general themes as literary 'schools' and genres.

Each volume in the central category deals either with one well-known and influential work by an individual author, or with closely related works by one writer. The main section consists of critical readings, mostly modern, collected from books and journals. A selection of reviews and comments by the author's contemporaries is also included, and sometimes comment from the author himself. The Editor's Introduction charts the reputation of the work or works from the first appearance to the present time.

Volumes in the 'general themes' category are variable in structure but follow the basic purpose of the series in presenting an integrated selection of readings, with an Introduction which explores the theme and discusses the literary and critical issues involved.

A single volume can represent no more than a small selection of critical opinions. Some critics are excluded for reasons of space, and it is hoped that readers will pursue the suggestions for further reading in the Select Bibliography. Other contributions are severed from their original context, to which some readers may wish to turn. Indeed, if they take a hint from the critics represented here, they certainly will.

A. E. DYSON

NOTE ON TEXTS

In the editorial matter all Shakespeare quotations have been standardised to the New Penguin editions:

The Comedy of Errors, ed. Stanley Wells (1972)
The Taming of the Shrew, ed. G.R. Hibbard (1968)
The Two Gentlemen of Verona, ed. Norman Sanders (1968)
Love's Labour's Lost, ed. John Kerrigan (1982)

INTRODUCTION

LABELLING *The Comedy of Errors, The Taming of the Shrew, The Two Gentlemen of Verona* and *Love's Labour's Lost* as Shakespeare's Early Comedies contains the seeds of the slighting disparagement so often accorded to the four plays. There has long been the assumption that 'comedy' is less worthy of serious attention than 'tragedy', but it is the epithet 'early' that has caused most trouble. For too long it has been the cue for critics to group the individual plays as apprentice pieces and consider them primarily as preparation for Shakespeare's later, greater work. This approach can occasionally be illuminating: G. Wilson Knight relates *The Comedy of Errors* to Shakespeare's late plays and J. R. Brown forges a fascinating link between *The Comedy of Errors* and *The Merchant of Venice*, arguing that both show possessiveness and greed transmuted into generosity and trust. However, generally and unsurprisingly, the early plays suffer from being forcibly yoked to *Twelfth Night, Much Ado About Nothing* or *The Tempest*. The tenor of many critical articles has been of disappointment that the earlier aspires to the later and fails.

There are a few obvious similarities between the four plays. They all test (but in very different ways) the boundaries of theatre's codes and practices. It may also be argued that they provide evidence of the superiority of the female mind. But predominantly they have been seen as sharing flaws and failure and the word 'experimental' has been too frequently wielded in a pejorative or dismissive sense. Criticism which has sought to establish a generic notion of 'early comedy' has been relatively uninspired. There are some distinguished exceptions to this assertion, but it is surprising (and disappointing) how frequently one or more of the plays is excluded from discussions advertised as exploring Shakespeare's comedies. *The Comedy of Errors, The Taming of the Shrew* and *Love's Labour's Lost*

15

have all variously had their champions, but *The Two Gentlemen of Verona* remains the Cinderella of the group. Of those critics who deal with all four plays, H. B. Charlton considers Shakespeare's comic method in the historical context of English, Italian and classical comedy. E. M. W. Tillyard offers a straightforward account, play by play. His chapter on *The Comedy of Errors* is sharply perceptive in its appreciation of the play's depth of humanity. In individual chapters on the plays Alexander Leggatt offers lucid and sensitive analysis of the variety of Shakespeare's comic art. Ruth Nevo also considers all four plays in her vigorous discussion of 'comic transformation'. She argues a chronological line of development, seeing the early comedies as a 'gallimaufry of experiments': *The Comedy of Errors* and *The Taming of the Shrew* as 'two early farces', *The Two Gentlemen of Verona* 'interesting but abortive' and *Love's Labour's Lost* 'subtly counterpointed'. Her individual chapters are consistently stimulating and throughout her discussion is illuminated by the conviction that the plays offer 'an unceasing experiment of the imagination upon dread and upon desire'. Of the writing that deals with the four early comedies as a group Anne Righter's section in *Shakespeare and the Idea of the Play* entitled 'Shakespeare Early Comedies: Shadows, Dreams and Plays' (1962) is a most persuasive and sensitive account. She weaves thematic links between the texts, exploring particularly Shakespeare's fascination with the 'character of dramatic illusion'.

However, the decision to allow each of the four plays its own identity and give each its own place within this volume derives from the strength of those critical approaches which have allowed each play its intrinsic, individual quality. The organisation of this Casebook endorses R.S. White's verdict that 'no other group of plays in the canon so firmly defies categorisation' (*Shakespeare Survey*, 37, p.1).

The Comedy of Errors

It might once have seemed outrageous to describe *The Comedy of Errors* as a polished play. However, its slick theatrical flair is

the early studies in this volume. The other extracts are important stepping stones in the play's critical history. Coleridge was the first critic to see the play as farce and Hermann Ulrici the first to present a more serious philosophical view of the play. G. R. Elliott's essay explores the play's 'comic horror' and has proved highly influential.

The articles included in the modern studies explore more fully different strands in the critical discussion of *The Comedy of Errors*. Harold Brooks offers a careful, detailed analysis of the themes and structures of the play. He makes a strong case for the extraordinary skilfulness of Shakespeare's craftsmanship. The play's preoccupation with time is explored by Gāmini Salgādo as reflecting a complex pattern of confusion and uncertainty. Ralph Berry argues that the layered source material is emblematic of a rich exploration of experience. His psychoanalytic study discusses ways in which the play explores ideas of identity and deep fear.

The Taming of the Shrew

Recent criticism of *The Taming of the Shrew* has been turbulent. Debate about its textual relationship with the somewhat different version entitled *The Taming of a Shrew* has been upstaged by the vigour of the argument about gender and marriage. There is now a danger of Shakespeare's play being interpreted as a one-issue play with critics and directors feeling it necessary to indicate their allegiance to one side or other or perch precariously on the ironic fence. The play is more complex and in particular its construction more subtle than that debate might sometimes allow. Attention has frequently been drawn to the characteristic Shakespearean themes of disguise, appearance/reality and the play's overt sense of performance, but we are also presented with issues of social conformity and transgression.

Lucentio and Tranio rapidly become audience to 'some show to welcome us to town'. The self-conscious theatricality of the inhabitants of Padua reveals a shallowness of purpose. Wealth and appearance hold sway and Katherina is excluded

by the value system her father operates. Bianca is the 'treasure'
who must have a husband, while Katherina has been encour-
aged to regard herself as of little value. Petruchio reveals his
contempt for this society:

> Go to the feast, revel and domineer,
> Carouse full measure to her maidenhead,
> Be mad and merry, or go hang yourselves
>
> (III ii 223–5)

setting himself and Katherina apart from a celebration informed by drinking and crudity. The guests' response confirms
his scepticism. The ease with which replacements are nomin-
ated 'to supply the places at the table' reveals the gulf that
separates Petruchio and Katherina from Paduan society. It is
ironic that the disguised Tranio should have complained at the
wedding about Petruchio's 'unreverent robes' and urged him to
'put on clothes of mine' – clothes which in fact belonged to
Lucentio. Petruchio challenges convention through dress
('to me she's married, not unto my clothes') and urgently
removes Katherina from a society in which she has become
trapped by her reputation.

The shift of location to Petruchio's house provides a further
perspective upon the social world. Katherina retains a lingering
allegiance to Padua and its values. She likes the hat not least
because it is fashionable ('gentlewomen wear such caps
as these') but Petruchio sets out a higher priority (''tis the
mind that makes the body rich') and his denunciation of worth
based upon fine clothes reflects the extent to which Padua is
giddy with the fashion. On their return Katherina and Petruchio will present a united challenge to the established social
values.

Lucentio's cliché-ridden speech which opens the last scene is
punctured by Petruchio's 'Nothing but sit and sit, and eat and
eat'. Unsettled, the others close ranks in an attempt to exclude
and isolate Katherina and Petruchio. The widow is immediately on the offensive and both she and Bianca seek to enhance
their own status as wives in contrast to the shrewish Kate.
Their husbands console themselves with their confidence that

Petruchio 'has the veriest shrew of all'. The wager reveals less about obedience; more about the disparate levels of communication between the couples.

Katherina and Petruchio leave to consummate their marriage with a refreshing directness and an implicit contempt for the others: 'Come, Kate, we'll to bed'. They have something to which the others cannot aspire ('we three are married, but you two are sped'). Once again Katherina and Petruchio will turn their backs upon a society which has been exposed as shallow and superficial. The play ends with no harmonious, celebratory, all-encompassing dance, but rather the very clear affirmation of the strength of an emotional truth which transcends the petty, conventional bounds of wooing and wedding. The other characters fail to understand what they see. Tranio earlier had referred to Petruchio's household as a 'taming school' and in the closing moments Hortensio and Lucentio take refuge in the tired and discredited judgement:

> *Hortensio*: Now go thy ways, thou hast tamed a curst shrew.
> *Lucentio*: 'Tis a wonder, by your leave, she will be tamed so.
> (v ii 186–7)

As in *A Midsummer Night's Dream* characters go through a dream experience which is subliminal and brings them to a point of recognition previously unattainable. Curtis describes how Katherina 'knows not which way to stand, to look, to speak, / And sits as one new-risen from a dream' (IV i 171–2). As Petruchio forces her to come to terms with reality he won't let her sleep. In the Induction Sly sleeps, is transformed and wakes, but believes he is still sleeping. No, he's told, the past was a sleep, this is reality. In his deluded persona he watches a play – 'a kind of history' – and yet in the fiction he finds a truth: a reality far more vivid, more real than the reality of those watching. Though it is tempting to find a correlation between Sly and the audience it is more illuminating to see the Sly scenes as the theatrical metaphor and the 'play' as truth – to turn the frame inside out. That is why we lose sight of him. He becomes absorbed into the play as it reaches out to embrace us too.

Early criticism of *The Taming of the Shrew* reflects interest in the play's construction. Johnson praises the plotting as does Hazlitt, who also commends its 'downright moral'. Their comments are reproduced here as are pieces deriving from performance. Henry Morley's account of Samuel Phelps' interpretation of Sly reveals an interest in characterisation in an area of the play more usually considered solely in terms of structure. G. B. Shaw's comments were prompted by his decision *not* to go to see Garrick's *Catharine and Petruchio*, explaining that he preferred Shakespeare's. His vehement denunciation of Katherina's last speech perhaps paved the way for Mary Pickford's wink in the 1929 film version. Margaret Webster is credited with being the first critic to put the case for an ironic reading (in 1942) and her argument is reproduced below. In the Modern Studies section the relationship between the different strands of the play is explored by C. C. Seronsy. In a long and detailed article (abridged here) he illustrates the complexities of the three layers of supposition with Katherina and Petruchio at the heart of the play. Muriel Bradbrook locates the play within the context of 'Shrew' literature defining its uniqueness as in no small way related to it being 'Petruchio's play – that is the novelty'. David Daniell writes of the play's 'special sense of theatricality'. While he locates it firmly in the context of Shakespeare's later comedies he also sees it as a text informed by its proximity in composition to the *Henry VI* plays.

The play has predictably attracted the attention of feminist critics but the more interesting responses transcend routine denunciation. In *The Female Eunuch* Germaine Greer offered approval, 'Kate has the uncommon good fortune to find [a husband] who is man enough to know what he wants and how to get it' (p.209). Irene Dash finds 'originality and courage' in Kate, delighting in 'her triumph over Bianca – the triumph of the unconventional over the conventional – of challenging patterns of wooing over the stereotypes'. Coppélia Kahn sees the whole play as a satire on the male desire to subjugate women and the skill with which women manipulate them. This reading sees Katherina's last speech as ironic. Ann Thompson's introduction to the New Cambridge edition offers a well-judged appraisal of the complexities evident in responses to the play. 'The real problem lies outside the play in the fact that the subjection of women to men, although patently unfair and unjustifiable, is still virtually universal. It is the world which offends us, not Shakespeare.' However, in a postscript she adds the personal note: 'In working on the play I have found that my own problem with its overt endorsement of patriarchy does not decrease, though my pleasure in its formal qualities, the sheer craft and detail of the construction, continues to grow' (p.41). The post-modernist, psychoanalytical position is argued elegantly by Barbara Freedman. She states firmly that '*The Taming of the Shrew* is a trap'. The continuing popularity of the play in performance complicates the debate, confirming the play's theatrical vitality and revealing a textual richness that resists closure.

The Two Gentlemen of Verona

The title of *The Two Gentlemen of Verona* directs our attention very firmly. The fierce demands of male bonding is a favourite theme in several of Shakespeare's early plays and one he would return to emphatically with *The Two Noble Kinsmen*. Verona with its euphoniously romantic allure is a favoured location. But perhaps the keyword in the title is 'Two' – the play is structured upon a sense of duality. We are provided with a number of pairs and parallels to complement the pressured partnership of Valentine and Proteus. The duologue with which the play opens is the first of many and it establishes what will be the dominant pattern of ebb and flow. Antitheses, repetition and reflection abound and serve to underpin the sympathy and fellow-feeling of the two gentlemen. The symbiotic nature of their relationship is demonstrated by the way in which the words of one echo or, indeed, seem inevitably to derive from the words of the other. The prompts and cues reflect not only the men's inter-dependence and mutual need, but also their striving for a kind of self-definition which essentially derives from the other self.

Proteus' instinct is towards duplicity. There is only the vaguest hint of any parental opposition to justify his assumption that it is safer to advertise his bonding with Valentine rather than his love for Julia. However, Valentine does not function in any simple way as the constant lover. In conversation with the Duke he reveals an other self of persistence, duplicity and invention which unites him with his alter ego – the fixity of the constant lover Valentine is matched with a protean flux of dissimulation.

Proteus' journey disturbs his emotional equilibrium. Initially he had perceived a straightforward choice between Valentine and Julia and in staying rather than going he had made that choice. Changing his mind to follow Valentine does not lead to a re-establishment of the male bond, for Valentine's love for Silvia has reversed their situations. He has now become the image of his friend in his discovery of a lover's self. In his need for an emotional focus Proteus settles on Silvia as she has become the recipient of the love he had sought to regain. He wrestles in a turmoil that is compounded of contradictions and in pursuit of Silvia he abandons not only Valentine but later Launce.

Julia's pursuit of her lover has led her to be unwilling audience and spectator to the play's central 'love song'. Its lyrics reach out to an unattainable perfection – Silvia 'excels each mortal thing'. The song draws no response from the serenaded woman, only from her unhappy female counterpart. Sitting on stage unacknowledged, Julia's response indicates her fractured self:

> *Host*: How now? Are you sadder than you were before?
>   How do you, man? The music likes you not.
> *Julia*: You mistake; the musician likes me not.
>
>   (IV ii 53–5)

As the Host stumbles to understand her coded words, the musical metaphor emphasises a need for truth, constancy, fixity: 'I would always have one play but one thing.'

This conviction of 'oneness'; this sustained focus is a feature of the women's outlook in the play. It marks a clear distinction between their perception and that of their male counterparts. The women do not know each other and are denied any intimate scene of togetherness. Nevertheless they display an instinctive, intuitive bonding born not of personal friendship but of common cause − a sisterhood independent of acquaintance. In her rejection of Proteus, Silvia focuses more on the abandoned persona of the unknown Julia than on her banished lover. In urging Proteus to 'return and make thy love amends' she gives a voice to the disguised Julia who is witnessing this exchange.

In the only scene in the play between the two women, the steadfastness of Julia's love is contrasted with Proteus' inconstancy, made tangible in the items she carries − two letters and two rings. Julia's 'mistake' with the letter she offers is a moment of revelation − proffered and then withdrawn and as such prefigures a similar moment at the end of the play with the rings. The dialogue in this scene sounds a litany of Julia's name and Silvia's loyalty is to the woman unseen but ever-present. Sebastian's professed knowledge of Julia, 'Almost as well as I do know myself', exploits the emotional subtext of the scene and the account given of the 'pageants of delight' at Pentecost makes explicit a sense of an experienced other self through performance. Julia-as-Sebastian recounts how he was made to 'play the woman's part' with Julia's dress as costume. The role was Ariadne 'passioning/For Theseus' perjury and unjust flight' and such was the effectiveness of that performance that Julia 'wept bitterly'. The moment of self-conscious commentary on the emotional power of performance and theatrical device affirms the empathy felt by both Silvia and the audience:

> Alas, poor lady, desolate and left!
> I weep myself to think upon thy words.
>
> (IV iv 171−2)

This emotional strength complicates our response to the play's resolution. Julia does not betray her woman's self when she faints but wrenches control away from the men and breaks the male contract of exchange. Her giving of the ring to

Proteus is disappointingly interpreted as the confused action of
a wilting woman. 'Out of my neglect' is not true – she did offer
the ring to Silvia and as the audience witnessed that surely we
can credit Julia here with a conscious moment of decision in
deliberately returning Proteus' ring, effecting a moment of
self-assertion and identity. Proteus' prosaic response, 'Why this
is the ring I gave to Julia' fails to give her any hope and she
retreats: 'O cry you mercy, sir, I have mistook' – 'Mistook'
conveys the desolation of abandoned hope. Only when Proteus
persists is there the moment of revelation and affirmation of
self:

> And Julia herself did give it me;
> And Julia herself hath brought it hither.
>
> (V iv 99–100)

'Behold her that gave aim to all thy oaths' might perhaps be
read usefully as a line which could apply to both women to
enable the silent Silvia to stand by (in both senses) Julia.
Proteus' words make sense of such blocking:

> What is in Silvia's face, but I may spy
> More fresh in Julia's with a constant eye?
>
> (V iv 115–16)

A stylised, tightly patterned and choreographed sequence
here – 'Come, come, a hand from either' – might serve the
play well. After the welter of twists and turns, of repetitions,
quibbles, antitheses and paralleling of plot and character, the
heightened awareness of self and other self, after all this
insistence upon duality or 'twoness', the tensions are resolved
and 'oneness' is emphatically asserted: 'One feast, one house,
one mutual happiness.'

Those few critics who have neither ignored nor condemned
The Two Gentlemen of Verona have usually patronised it. Johnson
and Hazlitt conceded that the play contains lyricism and
tenderness despite its structural flaws. Benjamin Victor offered
his solution to the perceived flaws by producing his own version
in 1762. His was a radical response but even in the twentieth
century doubts about the integrity of the play remain. In his
edition Quiller-Couch argued that the difficulties of the last

scene result from a corrupted text. The sensitivity of John Masefield's response is heightened by the generally unsympathetic response the play has provoked.

Although the title of Stanley Wells' essay ('The Failure of *The Two Gentlemen of Verona*') might seem unduly negative, his account reveals limitations rather than failure and he offers a clear appraisal of the play's structural shortcomings. Harold Brooks celebrates the integration of the comic and the serious in the play, capturing in his title the energy and enthusiasm of his approach. Both articles are included in full here. It was possible to include only part of Inga-Stina Ewbank's sensitive and finely-tuned account of the links between *The Two Gentlemen of Verona* and the Sonnets. Although most critics find shortcomings in the play there have been challenges to H. B. Charlton's oft-quoted assertion that Shakespeare's first attempt to make romantic comedy had only succeeded so far that it had 'unexpectedly and inadvertently made romance comic'. Norman Sanders and Kurt Schlueter serve the play well in their introductions to the New Penguin and New Cambridge editions respectively.

Love's Labour's Lost

Love's Labour's Lost charts a journey in which characters are forced to grow up. The King's plan to exalt male bonding and intellectual aspiration at the expense of frivolous pleasures has elements which are pretentious and childish. Directors often choose to present the four men as undergraduates, giving the three years' term a contemporary frame. Were the King alone to make the vow it would be regarded as an act of idiosyncratic commitment. What functions more emphatically is peer group pressure. The King takes the initiative and Longaville and Dumain follow his lead. We are shown a pattern of social behaviour in which individuality is casually suppressed. There is reassurance in imitation, even for Berowne. He speaks out against the detail of the bond but when the King threatens to exclude him: 'Well sit you out. Go home, Berowne. Adieu!' (I i 110), Berowne quickly falls into line.

But the world must be peopled and it is through the people
of the King's world that the nonsense of the Academe is
indicated. What the 'wisdoms' of the men fail to understand,
the 'shallow fools' Dull and Costard (with the assistance of
Jacquenetta) discover. At the beginning of Act Two the Princess and her women stand at the King's 'forbidden gates'. The
Princess is an ancestor of Beatrice in her impatience with
empty courtesy: the men in Navarre (like the men in Messina)
have turned tongue:

> *King:*   Fair Princess, welcome to the court of Navarre.
> *Prin.:* 'Fair' I give you back again, and 'welcome' I have not yet.
>   (II i 90–2)

The Princess is her father's envoy on a political matter of land
and money. Claim and counter-claim await the arrival of the
proof to be provided by 'the packet' due 'tomorrow'. This
opens up a gap of time which the men's fervent interest
appropriates for romance.

The men seek to preserve a distinction between their public
disdain of women and their private desire. This culminates in
the multi-layered overhearing scene (IV iii). For the audience
there is the satisfaction of a patterned stripping away of
pretence. The men's primary allegiances would seem to be to
their public selves. Each one admits the truth only when found
out and no one freely confesses. The delicious piece of plotting
which brings on Costard and Jacquenetta clutching Berowne's
letter is particularly satisfying in the way in which Berowne's
pompous occupation of the moral high ground is undercut by
that most popular stage property. Berowne is desperate to
avoid being found out and tears up the letter – 'a toy'.
Individuality is still suppressed for it is only when the pretence
of each man has been exposed that any of them can feel secure
in his role as lover.

In contrast the women are open and straightforward about
the letters they have received. Their conversation expresses a
sober and unsentimental attitude towards love. Rosaline confirms that Katherine is resistant to love because love 'killed
your sister'. The Princess defines and endorses the appropriate

approach for intelligent women: 'We are wise girls to mock our lovers so' (v ii 58).

The inevitability of death invades the closing moments. The play's artifice of language is underpinned by an emotional truth. It celebrates the illusory power of theatre, yet simultaneously interrogates the genre it inhabits. It transports both the audience and the characters into an escapist world only to jerk them back painfully and unceremoniously to a tough reality. The King's urgent plea: 'Now, at the latest minute of the hour / Grant us your loves' indicates a perspective that is still conditioned by a world of play whose brief interlude is nearly over. The Princess' response voices the substance of a world which has given her a title and denied her a father:

> A time, methinks, too short
> To make a world-without-end bargain in.
>
> (v ii 783–4)

Berowne's complaint 'Our wooing doth not end like an old play' excites us by its dual function within and without the theatrical frame – he is both actor and audience to his own story. In his assumption that Jack would have Jill, Berowne unites fictional contrivance and human desire. In denying both, there is both disappointment and challenge. Berowne and the others have a year to reflect, consider and engage with the realities of pain and suffering before earning the right to return. Armado's last line: 'You that way: we this way' may indicate a division based upon gender or class or a means of marking audience from players. Whatever option is chosen the line demands separation and dislocation. It denies the reassuring comfort provided by the conventional happy ending of actors and audience joining 'hand in hand'.

In 1598 *Love's Labour's Lost* appeared in print and in the same year Robert Tofte recalled a performance he had seen. The relevant stanzas are included here and they reveal touching evidence of the play's emotional power. In contrast Samuel Johnson found some parts of the play 'mean, childish and vulgar' though elsewhere in the text he identified 'many sparks of genius'. Hazlitt expresses contradictory impulses. Though it is the one comedy of Shakespeare's he would part with there is much he would be loath to lose. Shaw is similarly ambivalent in his first published review (included here) of a performance of Shakespeare. Despite the shortcomings of that particular production Shaw is aware of the play's theatrical power. It is undoubtedly productions of *Love's Labour's Lost* which have led the way in the study of the play. Granville-Barker's words proved prophetic.

If any essay can be called seminal then Bobbyann Roesen's (Anne Barton's) deserves that title. She analyses in detail the complexity and subtlety of the play's conclusion. Her essay is included in full here. The richness of the play's language is one of its most striking characteristics and James L. Calderwood's essay explores the ways in which the play shows us 'words so ascendant over matter'. Philip Edwards offers a vigorous rebuttal of those who suppose that 'sweet sentimentalising and sighing are *attacked* by Shakespeare', arguing that Shakespeare is essentially amused by 'the rather extravagant and silly clothes which Desire wears'. Writing within the tradition established by Northrop Frye, C. L. Barber writes sensitively and perceptively on *Love's Labour's Lost* in *Shakespeare's Festive Comedy*.

PART ONE

The Comedy of Errors

CRITICAL COMMENT BEFORE 1950

Gray's Inn Record   (1594)

The next grand Night was intended to be upon *Innocents-Day* at Night . . . The Ambassador [of the Inner Temple] came . . . about Nine of the Clock at Night . . . there arose such a disordered Tumult and Crowd upon the Stage, that there was no Opportunity to effect that which was intended . . . The Lord Ambassador and his Train thought that they were not so kindly entertained as was before expected, and thereupon would not stay any longer at that time, but, in a sort, [were] discontented and displeased. After their Departure the Throngs and Tumults did somewhat cease, although so much of them continued, as was able to disorder and confound any good Inventions whatsoever. In regard whereof, as also for that the Sports intended were especially for the gracing of the *Templerians*, it was thought good not to offer any thing of Account, saving Dancing and Revelling with Gentlewomen; and after such Sports, a Comedy of Errors (like to *Plautus* his *Menechmus*) was played by the Players. So that Night was begun, and continued to the end, in nothing but Confusion and Errors; whereupon, it was ever afterwards called, *The Night of Errors*. . . . We preferred Judgments . . . against a Sorcerer or Conjuror that was supposed to be the Cause of that confused Inconvenience. . . . And Lastly, that he had foisted a Company of base and common Fellows, to make up our Disorders with a Play of Errors and Confusions; and that that Night had gained to us Discredit, and itself a Nickname of Errors.

SOURCE: An entry from *Gray's Inn Record* of 28 December 1594.

Samuel Taylor Coleridge   (?1811)

The myriad-minded man, our, and all men's, Shakspeare, has in [*The Comedy of Errors*] presented us with a legitimate farce in exactest consonance with the philosophical principles and character of farce, as distinguished from comedy and from entertainments. A proper farce is mainly distinguished from comedy by the license allowed, and even required, in the fable, in order to produce strange and laughable situations. The story need not be probable, it is enough that it is possible. A comedy would scarcely allow even the two Antipholuses; because, although there have been instances of almost indistinguishable likeness in two persons, yet these are mere individual accidents, *casus ludentis naturae*, and the *verum* will not excuse the *inverisimile*. But farce dares add the two Dromios, and is justified in so doing by the laws of its end and constitution. In a word, farces commence in a postulate, which must be granted.

SOURCE: Samuel Taylor Coleridge, 'Notes on Comedy of Errors', in his *Shakespearean Criticism*, Vol. I, edited by Thomas Middleton Raysor (1960).

William Hazlitt   (1817)

Pinch the conjuror is also an excrescence not to be found in Plautus. He is indeed a very formidable anachronism.

SOURCE: William Hazlitt, *Characters of Shakespeare's Plays* (1817).

Hermann Ulrici (1839)

... the gradually increasing complication and perplexity, notwithstanding the obvious possibility of a mistake of identity, is not cleared up until the two pairs of twins are accidentally brought face to face. By all this the truth (not more comic than tragic) is most strikingly impressed upon us, that the knowledge and ignorance of man run so nicely into each other, that the boundary line almost disappears, and that the very convictions which we look upon as the most certain and best grounded may, perhaps, turn out to be nothing but error or deception. . . . All are in a moment disturbed by a mere freak of nature, in violating the seemingly most unimportant of her laws, and in neglecting those differences of the outward man by which the senses distinguish individuals. So artificial is the constitution of our world, that the derangement of the minutest of its members is sufficient to throw the whole into disorder.

SOURCE: Hermann Ulrici, *Shakespeare's Dramatic Art: and His Relation to Calderón and Goethe* (1846).

A. C. Swinburne (1880)

In the exquisite and delightful comedies of [Shakespeare's] earliest period we can hardly discern any sign, any promise of them at all. One only of these, the *Comedy of Errors*, has in it anything of dramatic composition and movement; and what it has of these, I need hardly remind the most cursory of students, is due by no means to Shakespeare. What is due to him, and to him alone, is the honour of having embroidered on the naked old canvas of comic action those flowers of elegiac beauty which vivify and diversify the scene of Plautus as reproduced by the art of Shakespeare. . . .

The sweetness and simplicity of lyric or elegiac loveliness which fill and inform the scenes where Adriana, her sister, and the Syracusan Antipholus exchange the expression of their errors and their loves, belong to Shakespeare alone; and may help us to understand how the young poet who at the outset of his divine career had struck into this fresh untrodden path of poetic comedy should have been, as we have seen that he was, loth to learn from another and an alien teacher the hard and necessary lesson that this flowery path would never lead him towards the loftier land of tragic poetry. For as yet, even in the nominally or intentionally tragic and historic work of his first period, we descry always and everywhere and still preponderant the lyric element, the fantastic element, or even the elegiac element.

SOURCE: A. C. Swinburne, *A Study of Shakespeare* (1880).

E. K. Chambers   (1906)

Shakespeare was very much convinced when he wrote *The Comedy of Errors*, of the sound practical truth that indiscretion in the expression of jealousy is by no means a way to remove the causes of jealousy; and that he was careful so to order his play as to give pointed utterance to this conviction. . . .

In so far as it is concerned with jealousy and the ethical problems which hinge upon jealousy, *The Comedy of Errors* has an undeniable claim to the title which it bears. It is comedy in the true sense of a criticism of life, which is at heart profoundly serious, and employs all the machinery of wit or humour, with the deliberate intention of reaching through the laughter to the ultimate end of a purged outlook upon things.

SOURCE: E. K. Chambers, 'The Comedy of Errors' in his *Shakespeare: A Survey* (London, 1925).

John Masefield (1911)

The *Menæchmi* of Plautus is a piece of very skilful theatrical craft. It is almost heartless. In bringing it out of the Satanic kingdom of comedy into the charities of a larger system Shakespeare shows for the first time a real largeness of dramatic instinct. In his handling of the tricky ingenious plot he achieves (what, perhaps, he wrote the play to get) a dexterous, certain play of mind. He strikes the ringing note time after time. It cannot be said that the verse, or the sense of character, or the invention is better than in the other early plays. It is not. The play is on a lower plane than any of his other works. It is the only Shakespearean play without a deep philosophical idea. . . . It is also the first play that shows a fine, sustained power of dramatic construction.

SOURCE: John Masefield, *William Shakespeare* (1911).

G. Wilson Knight (1932)

In *The Comedy of Errors* a tempest is important. We are brought to a world of gold and fun where the tragic work of a tempest is finally remedied by reunions. The sea tempest is here an actual event, the tragic background to a romantic comedy. Aegeon describes, at length, the original tragedy, his words heavy with grief and the turbulence of his misfortunes. . . . Such a tempest is peculiarly Shakespearian. We meet it again and again. Tempests always, as here, tragic, tend to 'disperse', the resulting play to reunite, the people scattered in the tempest. Antipholus of Syracuse thus compares himself to a drop of water seeking for another drop, his mother and brother, in the world's ocean, and so he 'confounds' and loses himself in the 'quest': he is thus without 'content' (I ii 33–40). These are typical thoughts. The ocean is the enemy to love's desire, seeking to engulf the searcher; and 'content' throughout Shakespeare, is an important word.

... we may observe that Aegeon's tragedy 'was wrought by nature, not by vile offence' (I i 34). Such are our tempests often: they suggest the inscrutable enjoiner of fate that drives human barks on to their wreckage. Shakespeare does not only present tragedy in terms of weak 'character'. And we should here observe clearly how the tempest is closely associated with themes of birth – 'a joyful mother of two goodly sons' (I i 50). This happy family, this life-joy of father, mother, and their new-born children, is smashed, severed, 'dispersed' by 'tempest'. So the 'tempest' here is clearly opposed to life, a death force, 'tragic (I i 64). And throughout the action Aegeon's first organ dirge of sea sorrow lingers in our minds, together with the knowledge of his sentence to death. This play is dark with tragedy.

And yet, set against all this, is our gold-imagery, our passages of lyric beauty, our sense of rippling comedy. It is a glorious little play. And, at the close, all is united again, the end is peace, reunion, and pardon, outside the Abbey where Aemilia, Aegeon's wife, has long taken refuge. Aegeon is indeed a tragic figure. But all is quickly now resolved:

> *Aegeon*: If I dream not, thou art Aemilia:
> If thou art she, tell me where is that son
> That floated with thee on the fatal raft?
>
> (V i 347–9)

So this 'wreck at sea' ... is at last remedied. This play concludes in joy, its reunions peculiarly forecasting *Pericles*. ... Both plays show us a story starting with birth, with next the dispersal of a family in tempest, and then a final reunion.

There is there a more intense religious and mythical suggestion. But here, too, it is more than once recognised that this
Ephesus is a land of supernatural mystery:

> Sure, these are but imaginary wiles
> And Lapland sorcerers inhabit here.
>
> (IV iii 10–11)

In this land of gold, merchants, and mystery, all odds are made
even, all sea sorrow finally dissolved in joy and love.

SOURCE: G. Wilson Knight, 'The Romantic Comedies' in his
The Shakespearian Tempest (London, 1932).

G. R. Elliott   (1939)

The 'The' in the title of [*The Comedy of Errors*] may be taken in
a generic sense – that is, as the author's characteristically
modest intimation that he has provided merely one more
species of a well-recognised genus. 'Here', says he, 'are the
Twins of Plautus again; here is the age-old comedy of resemblances.' But time has made the 'The' distinctive: here is
indeed *the* comedy of errors. It is hard to see how the hoary
sport of mistaken identities could be better worked up as the
central theme of a drama.

I think the underlying reason for its success is the fact that
Shakespeare was so thoroughly penetrated by the comic horror, so to call it, implicit in the subject. Real horror attaches to
the notion of the *complete* identity of two human beings. . . . All
normal persons (and especially Shakespeare) set so much store
by human individuality that they shrink from the thought of it
being submerged. And since the amusing, when intense, is nigh
to the serious, there is something shuddery in the close resemblance of persons just when this appears to us intensely
entertaining. . . . *The Comedy of Errors* has a note of real weirdness just when its mirth is keenest.

Another related feature of the play that has also, I think, not been sufficiently appreciated is its structural excellence. Critics have regarded the piece as uninspired because of its comparatively conventional style. But whole form, no less than style, may be the vehicle of inspiration. And the intensity with which Shakespeare gave himself here to the limited but uncanny fun of twinship impelled him to weave his strands into a very close and telling pattern; which, moreover, is often subserved . . . by the very conventionality of the style. I think that in sheer composition this drama surpasses most of his early works and some mature ones. It testifies that this poet, who was later to achieve the most expressive of styles, set his heart at the outset upon achieving wholeness of form.

SOURCE: G. R. Elliott, 'Weirdness in *The Comedy of Errors*,' in *University of Toronto Quarterly*, IX, no. 1 (October 1939).

MODERN STUDIES

Harold Brooks

THEMES AND STRUCTURE IN *THE COMEDY OF ERRORS* (1961)

The Comedy of Errors has its large dramatic design, but is no less remarkable for its controlled detail, unparalleled at this date, except in *The Spanish Tragedy*, outside Shakespeare's other plays. His handling of the lesser units of structure, from the scene downwards, is already sure, and indeed within its conventions brilliant. These units include the scene, a new one beginning whenever the stage is clear; the sub-scene, or *scène* as understood in French drama, a new one beginning whenever the group on stage is altered by anyone leaving or joining it; the passage of dialogue or the set speech, more than one, sometimes, going to make up the *scène*; besides every physical action, whether procession, brawl, or bit of minor business. Fully to appreciate the close bonding of such units in the structure one has to ask what is contributed by every passage as it occurs, and how it is interrelated with others throughout the play. Some illustration is possible, however, by taking a single scene. Act I scene ii will serve, the better as it is not exceptionally highly wrought. Yet even a scene so expository (being the first of the main action) is not allowed to lack the immediate interest that holds an audience. Shakespeare has already the art of fulfilling, and with the economy that secures dramatic compression, three principal requirements of dramatic structure: retrospect, preparation, and immediate interest. By

41

retrospect and preparation the playwright keeps his action moving – the great virtue of dynamic or progressive structure – with the strongest continuity. Further, while he concerns himself with the matter of the present scene, he can add force and meaning to what has gone before, and pile them up for what is to come after, so that, in effect, he is building up several (perhaps widely separated) parts of his play at once. This can be of great value in what I will call the symmetric structure: the structure which by parallel, contrast, or cross-reference, independent perhaps of the cause-and-effect connections of the progressive action, makes us compare one passage or person of the play with another, and so find an enriched significance in both. As for immediate interest, that is indispensable: 'What one requires in the theatre', wrote William Archer to Gilbert Murray, 'is, so to speak, a certain pressure of pleasurable sensation to the square inch, or rather to the minute' – 'pleasurable' being taken in the right sense, this puts it well.

With the first entry and speech of our illustrative scene, there is interest in the appearance of three fresh persons, and some tension: Antipholus the alien is warned that he is in danger of the fate which overtook Egeon in the scene before; a fate summarized in the natural course of the warning. This retrospect, and parallel of situation, link the opening of the main action and that of the Egeon action within which it is to be framed. The link is strengthened by reference to three themes already started in the Egeon episode: risk (and in particular the hazards of Ephesus), wealth and time. Egeon, Antipholus is told:

> . . . not being able to buy out his life
> According to the statute of the town
> Dies ere the weary sun set in the west.

Since these themes will now be developed throughout the main action, the references to them are preparatory no less than retrospective. The theme of moneyed wealth is emphasized by stage-'business': the merchant hands back to Antipholus

> . . . your money that I had to keep,

and he passes it on to his Dromio. The bag of money contains exactly the sum Egeon must find to save his life; and it is to furnish one of the two subjects of the first comic misunderstanding later in the scene, and therefore is implanted visually on the audience's mind beforehand; moreover, it will form a parallel with the gold chain and the purse, other concrete visible properties which carry on the theme and become foci of similar cross-purposes in subsequent Acts. The second subject of the imminent misunderstanding, the summons to dinner by the Ephesian Dromio, is also prepared, and the time-theme touched, in Antipholus' observation:

> Within this hour it will be dinner-time.

Another chief theme of the play is introduced when he is warned to conceal his Syracusan origin; for this concerns his identity. Again, when he bids Dromio depart with the money, Dromio's exit lines:

> Many a man would take you at your word,
> And go indeed, having so good a mean,

foreshadow the suspicion that his master will shortly entertain, while preparing us to recognize it as groundless, a comic error. The rendezvous arranged, at the Centaur, leads to the reunion of master and servant in II ii.

Dromio's jesting exit ends the first *scène*. It is Shakespeare's cue for underlining the promise of comedy: the note of tension at the start has now passed into the background. It is the cue also for Antipholus' direct comment upon Dromio's character, which adds to what has been gathered of his own and of the relations between the two of them. The audience's present curiosity about them is gratified, and its appetite whetted, both together; for the promise of comedy is contained in the informative comment itself:

> A trusty villain, sir, that very oft,
> When I am dull with care and melancholy,
> Lightens my humour with his merry jests,

jests, it is clear, which are very timely. Antipholus' experience of Dromio as a jester is needed to explain his coming assumption that the invitation to dinner is his servant's joke, and his slowly mounting surprise and anger when it is persisted in out of season. The rendezvous with the merchant, 'at five-o-clock', like that arranged in *scène* 1 with Dromio, helps to establish the theme of timing, and the motifs of timely or untimely meetings or failures to meet. It points forward, moreover, to the hour (cp. v i 118) so fateful for Egeon, the hour (though we do not yet know this) of the *dénouement*; somewhat as the mention of dinner-time in *scène* 1 began to make ready for the dinner episode (III i), the play's central pivot.

The *scènes* of three, then two persons, are succeeded by Antipholus' first soliloquy. Here and in the two remaining *scènes*, the immediate interest for the audience strengthens. From the point of view of comedy and the intrigue, *scène* 4, the encounter with the wrong Dromio, is the climax of the whole scene. It is flanked, in the ABA form so frequent in Shakespeare, by Antipholus' soliloquies, which are the imaginative climaxes, and, together with the moment when he strikes (the Ephesian) Dromio, the emotional climaxes too, though there is contrast between his emotion as an exasperated and as a 'melancholy' imaginative man. From the imaginative, introspective man he is, soliloquies (his brother has none) come naturally; his allusion to his 'care and melancholy' has prepared the way for them.

The first of them explains both his special occasion of 'care', and his arrival, contributing by a single stroke to the logic at once of the character and of the plot. He has an aim, fruitlessly pursued: 'to find a mother and a brother'. It is a dull member of the audience who does not refer this back to Egeon's retrospect (narrating much of the dramatist's 'fable', prior to the part enacted), and so conjecture who Antipholus must be. The audience is held, too, by the revelation of feeling. Antipholus' emotional reflections spring from the farewells just exchanged at the end of *scène* 2: 'I will go lose myself', he said, and was commended by the Merchant to his 'own content'. This is the phrase which prompts his soliloquy, where he laments that what would content him is precisely what he cannot get. The idea of his 'losing himself' is taken up in a profound sense, and couched in a fine image commensurate with its thematic importance. The theme of identity is here linked with those of relationship (dislocated or re-established), and of risk. To seek reunion with the lost members of the family, Antipholus is risking his identity; yet he must do so, for only if the full relationship is restored can he find content. And then, hints the image of one water-drop seeking another, the present individual identity will be lost, or transformed, in another way. It is to claim a sinking of identity in the marriage-relation, with the emergence of a new identity, where each is also the other, that Adriana uses the closely similar image in II ii. In the play's harmonic structure, while this soliloquy is thus recalled at that point, in its own place it recalls the situation of Egeon, who on virtually the same quest as Antipholus, has so risked his mortal identity that it is forfeit to the executioner. Antipholus' fear that he is losing himself is full of comic irony. No sooner has he expressed it, than, with the entry of his brother's Dromio, he begins to be the victim of the successive mistakes of identity to which his words are designed by Shakespeare as a prelude, and in the course of which he will come to wonder whether he is beside himself, and has lost himself indeed. The often uproarious comedy arising from these and the other Errors is not my immediate subject; and as regards the *scène* of cross-purposes, I shall make only a few observations, concerned with themes and structure. In the progressive structure of the play, it has two main functions. First, it interests us in Adriana, ready for her entrance in the next scene (II i), and leads to her personal summoning of the alien Antipholus to dinner (II ii). Second, it produces the comic dislocation of relationship between him and his own Dromio when they meet in II ii and Dromio denies the offences he is supposed to have committed here. The present failure of communication and relationship between Antipholus and the other Dromio, resulting from the mistake of identities, is made visible, audible, and tangible by 'business': the blow. Like the theme of relationship, the mistiming theme is brought into close connection with that of mistaken identity. Dromio's impatient mistress, when by strike of clock it was twelve, has 'made it one' upon his cheek; and for him Antipholus is her husband, his master, late for dinner, while for Antipholus Dromio is his servant, returned too soon, and obstinate in ill-timed jest. By Dromio's entrance are initiated the enigmas that beset the characters, and Antipholus is given an aptly enigmatic comment upon it:

> Here comes the almanack of my true date.

The new arrival has the appearance of his Dromio, who constitutes a record of his span from the time of their simultaneous nativities; but by a comic irony, so does the Dromio who has really entered: the comment fits both the false inference from appearance, and the reality itself. Its enigmatic nature conceals, so one finds from the final speech of the Abbess after the *dénouement* (v i 401–7) a further meaning: what approaches with this Dromio is the occasion which will secure Antipholus his true identity through a new date of birth – his true birth into the restored family relationship. That is the metaphor the Abbess employs.

It is by mistaking appearance for reality that Antipholus and his brother's Dromio misidentify one another. The threat to the very self involved in the confusion of appearance and reality is the thought most vividly conveyed in Antipholus' second soliloquy. The soliloquy rounds off the scene, not without certain resemblances to the beginning. Then, the theme of moneyed wealth was given prominence; and there was tension because the Ephesian law spelled danger to Antipholus' goods or life. Now, he is keenly anxious about his money; indeed, that is the motive for his final exit to seek Dromio at the Centaur. And tension rises again with his anxiety; but still more with the profoundly disturbing fears into which it merges, of worse perils than the law's in Ephesus, suggested by its repute as a place of illusions and shape-shifting, of jugglers that deceive the eye, of mountebanks and disguised cheaters, of:

> Dark-working sorcerers that change the mind:
> Soul-killing witches that deform the body.

The lines seize the imagination of the audience at the deep
level where the ancient dread of losing the self or soul is very
much alive. They are highly characteristic of the imaginative
Antipholus, develop the idea in his first soliloquy that his self
is at hazard, and set the pattern for his interpretations of the
strange experiences that befall him henceforward. At present
his sense of those reputed perils of Ephesus, awakened by what
seems the extraordinary behaviour of Dromio, produces the
provisional resolve:

> If it prove so, I will be gone the sooner;

the first sign of the recurrent danger that he will depart before
recognition and family reunion, with the consequent saving of
Egeon's life, can come about. His fears are not cowardice; such
a view of them has been guarded against in *scènes* 1 and 2,
where despite the warning of Egeon's fate, he was determined
to explore the town. The spirit he showed there prepares us for
his acceptance of what will seem to him the mysterious
adventure offered him by Adriana and Luciana: in spite of his
forebodings now, for a time he will be ready to believe that the
mystifications and transmutations of Ephesus may not be all
malevolent.

Every passage in our illustrative scene has thus its functions
both in the scene itself, and in the wider dynamic, symmetric,
thematic, comic structure of the play. Besides this close,
economical texture, there are of course other proofs of Shakespeare's early command of construction in the dramatic medium. He constructs in terms of theatre: he knows, for instance,
the value of business and of devices and episodes which belong
peculiarly to the stage. A famous example is the serenade scene
in *Two Gentlemen*, with its music, its distancing of Sylvia at her
window, and its eavesdroppers – the Host appreciative or
drowsing to sleep, Julia (in male costume) painfully intent. In
The Comedy of Errors, the gold chain seen, the blows seen and
heard, make double the effect they would in narrative. The
asides or semi-asides of the alien Antipholus and Dromio in II
ii, by a sound use of dramatic convention, mark the dichotomy
between their mental worlds and that of Adriana and Luciana

with whom they are in converse. The hilarious and crucial
episode of the rightful husband and his party shut out from
dinner depends for its full impact upon the stage-arrangement:
the parties in altercation are both plainly visible to the audience though not to each other. But the supreme power
manifest in Shakespeare's art of dramatic construction is the
combinative power well indicated by Hardin Craig, who writes
of 'his unequalled [skill] in fitting parts together so that they
[reinforce] one another', and notes that in working upon
materials which often gave him much of his fable ready-made,
his 'originality seems to have consisted in the selection of great
significant patterns'. . . .

   The Comedy of Errors begins and ends with relationship: a
family torn asunder and reunited. Relationship is the motive
that has brought Egeon, and the alien Antipholus and Dromio,
to the hazards of Ephesus; relationship is threatened by the
tensions in the marriage of Antipholus the denizen. The chief
entanglements spring from mistaken identity and mistiming:

> I see we still did meet each other's man,
> And I was ta'en for him, and he for me,
> And thereupon these ERRORS are arose.

The twins appear the same, but in reality are different; those
who meet them are led by appearance into illusion. Repeatedly
one of the persons assumes that he shared an experience with
another, when in reality he shared it with a different one. In
consequence, the persons cease to be able to follow each
other's assumptions, and become isolated in more or less
private worlds. Mistakes of identity all but destroy relationship,
and loss of relationship calls true identity yet more in question;
the chief persons suspect themselves or are suspected of insanity, or of being possessed, surrounded, or assailed by supernatural powers – madness or demoniac possession would be the
eclipse of the true self, and sorcery might overwhelm it. The
alien Antipholus and Dromio fear Circean metamorphosis;
Egeon, that he has been deformed out of recognition by time.
Yet the hazard of metamorphosis and of the loss of present
identity is also the way to fresh or restored relationship.

Antipholus the bachelor desires that Luciana will transform him and create him new; and Adriana's belief that in marriage the former identities coalesce and emerge identified with each other, is true if rightly interpreted. How the possessive interpretation, not relinquished by Adriana till almost the end, is at odds with the free giving and hazarding in which the wealth and debts of love differ from those of commerce, is another central theme, well traced by J. R. Brown. Adriana's envy of a husband's status contravenes principles of order that for Shakespeare and orthodox Elizabethans extended through the whole cosmos. The status of husband, and of wife, Kate's lines in *The Shrew* imply, are related to their places in this hierarchical order:

> Such duty as the subject owes the prince
> Even such a woman oweth to her husband.

Adriana comes to style her husband lord, and they each lay their case, as each has come to see it, before the Duke, reminding themselves and him that the match was first made by his authority. By this point, disorder from the various disruptions of relationship has gone so far in the community, that only the appeals for justice addressed to the Abbess and to him, God's viceroys spiritual and temporal, are capable, the time now being ripe, of leading to a solution.

Not only are the themes organically developed in the action; they are organically connected in themselves. At the centre is relationship: relationship between human beings, depending on their right relationship to truth and universal law: to the cosmic reality behind appearance, and the cosmic order. Trust in mere appearance results in illusion and mistakes of identity, thus dislocating relationship, and so disrupting order: blind conflict and disorder are inevitable when men misconceive true identity and become isolated in private worlds. Besides illusion, there are other factors of disorder: revolt against a wife's place in the cosmic hierarchy is the original source of discord in Adriana's marriage: order is broken, too, by everything untimely. . . .

The development of the action is supported by the use made of the stage-set. Acts II and III are focused upon the Phoenix,

scene of the central crisis. Act IV brings into play the second
domus, the Porpentine, and in accord with the fast-extending
complications has no one focal point: the action is related by
turns to the Phoenix, the Porpentine, and neither. The third
domus, the Abbey, is kept in reserve as the appropriate focus for
the *dénouement*. Dynamic progress is strongly felt in the mounting violence, from the first mere thwack to the drawing of
swords, thrashing with a rope's end, overpowering of 'mad-
men', and elaborate (narrated) vengeance upon Pinch; in the
spreading of error beyond the family to courtesan, goldsmith,
and merchant, until the whole town, at least in Adriana's
fevered fancy, seems involved; and in the darkening conviction
of the imaginative Antipholus that his supernatural experiences
are from the devil. With this explanation, natural to his
melancholy temperament, he has positively encased himself in
error, for it is as coherent as it is fallacious. In like fashion his
choleric brother comes to attribute all his sufferings to a
conspiracy instigated by his wife: both the Antipholi reach the
verge of persecution-mania. Since Adriana also is given her
point of view, which alters before the end, one can say of the
three main persons that although they do not develop in
the sense of being felt to change in character as a result of the
action, their attitudes of mind develop, so that each is felt to
have an inner self. That is, they are not wholly flat characters,
such as might be fitting protagonists of pure farce. They are
simple, but have just enough depth for the play, which Shakespeare, as we have seen, has deepened considerably beyond the
expected limitations of neo-classical comedy.

Even so, in depth and scope he was, of course, far to surpass
it. None the less, it is in its own kind an extraordinarily finished
work. The kind being one that not even Shakespeare could
extend beyond somewhat narrow limits, a less tight form,
exemplified in *Two Gentlemen*, held more promise of *Twelfth
Night*. Yet in recognizing this, one ought also to recognize how
much, in the *Comedy*, he has in fact found room for. Like the
other early plays, it will always be judged by two standards.
One, quite properly, is the standard set later by Shakespeare
himself. But the play should also be appreciated for what it is

in its own right: still actable as a hilarious yet balanced comedy, more pregnant than has perhaps been supposed with Shakespearian ideas.

SOURCE: 'Themes and Structures in *The Comedy of Errors*', *Early Shakespeare*, ed. J. R. Brown & B. Harris (London, 1961), pp. 55–71.

Gāmini Salgādo

'TIME'S DEFORMED HAND':
SEQUENCE, CONSEQUENCE, AND
INCONSEQUENCE IN *THE COMEDY
OF ERRORS* (1972)

In 1938, the highlight of the Stratford-on-Avon Shakespeare season was Theodore Komisarjevsky's production of *The Comedy of Errors*. Between the house of Antipholus and *The Porpentine* a large clock-tower dominated the setting. 'To emphasize the note of farce', wrote the critic of the *Birmingham Gazette*, 'the clock in the tower between the two inns every now and again strikes an hour to which the hands of the clock are not pointing. And the hands gallop to overtake the time.' Other comments, including the producer's own, make it evident that Komisarjevsky considered the play itself to be a poor thing at best, and that therefore the more liberties taken with it the better. The business with the clock may be regarded as a typical instance, another being the weird mélange of costumes from all times and places, presumably to emphasise an Ephesus beyond the range of any time or place. It is therefore mildly ironical that these touches, especially that of the clock, intended as bold and original strokes of production (which indeed they were) should nevertheless be profoundly true to one of the chief concerns of the play, the movement of time and its apparent aberrations.

At about the same time as the production referred to above, G. R. Elliott published an essay on 'Weirdness in *The Comedy of Errors*'[1] in which he drew attention to the element of comic horror which is undeniably present in the play: 'Real horror

52

attaches to the notion of the *complete* identity of two human beings.' . . .

The duplication of identity in relation to time has two aspects relevant to the play. In a general sense, and from the standpoint of the audience, it is a way of distorting and distending time. As such it is for us a fulfilment of one of the functions of comedy, to transcend in some fashion the devouring power of human time, whose movement is always towards decay and death. The matter is not as simple as this however, because this movement, however sinister, is the natural 'given' movement of our world, and Shakespearian comedy, never content to rest in fantasy however much it values it and delights in it, always seeks to establish a viable relationship between the play-world and ours.

For the experiencing agents, on the other hand, duplication of identity which they themselves are unaware of is felt as a dislocation of the ordinary world and of the steady single direction of time as the medium of experience. Apart from observing the signs of decay in ourselves and the world about us, our sense of the flow of time and its direction is given to us by the observable sequence of cause and effect and the progressive accumulation of information. If either of these were disrupted, our sense of time would be deranged, as happens in a very mild way whenever we watch a film sequence run backwards, tapes of races which have just been run, or rather more disconcertingly in certain dreams. A good deal of the action of *The Comedy of Errors* can be fairly described as disruption of the sequence of causality and of the process of storing up information, from the point of view of those involved in it. I send a man off to find out what time the ship sails, and he brings me back a bag of gold. I ask him whether he has put my money away safely and he tells me the dinner is burning. I send for a rope and am brought news of a ship. A servant does what he is told and is beaten for his pains. And so it goes. What you have just seen or heard is denied a moment later. No information, however recently acquired, can be trusted. Of the 1,700 odd lines of the play well over 700 are taken up by characters giving their versions of what has just

happened, and yet no one in the play is able to give a reliable
account of the present or the immediate past. . . .

In terms of 'clock-time', the entire action takes place within
one day, formally marked out by Egeon's couplet

> Yet this my comfort; when your words are done,
> My woes end likewise with the evening sun
>
> (I i 26–7)

at the beginning and by the Abbess's reference to 'this present
hour' in the closing scene. In between, there are more references to the passing of clock-time than in any other comedy.
Phrases such as 'within this hour', 'not half an hour since', 'but
two hours old', 'some hour hence', 'at five o'clock', 'It was two
ere I left him' and so on are scattered thickly throughout the
dialogue. The joke is of course that it is quite impossible to fit
all the various time divisions so precisely referred to in action
within the limits defined by the opening and closing scenes.

The design of the play is not really based on a five-act
structure on the Terentian model. Rather, its eleven scenes
consist of an inner action contained within an outer one to
which it is finally united. The structure of the action corresponds to two different aspects of time. The over-arching
framework, in spite of its threatening implications, is essentially
benevolent. Against a ground of moving accidents by flood and
field, it illustrates the normal workings of the temporal process
in comedy, speaking of the great commonplaces of wedlock,
childbirth, and familial piety and pointing the arrow of our
expectation towards the fullness of time when all disorders are
healed and all divisions settled. It is not fortuitous that this
enveloping action comes to a close in a priory, a place where
harmony and spiritual health both have extra-temporal sanc-
tions.

Within this outer action, however, the main action takes
place in a time gone crazy, twisted, looped, turning in on itself,
not so much the medium of existence as a manifestation of its
perplexities, even, at times, of its horror. To put the matter at
its simplest, the opening exposition scene does not *feel* in the
least like the action that follows. This is not merely because the

matter in hand is more sombre than the later events. It is as much because the tempo and orderly unfolding of the past makes such a strong contrast with the chaos to come. There is all the difference between the measured tempo of sequential development, however distressing the incidents recounted, and the series of false starts, backtrackings, and collisions by means of which the main action is presented. The difference is precisely a difference in the way time unfolds. . . . Tempo, tone, tense and stillness all conspire to place Egeon in a past whose rhythms are discontinuous with the tempo of the main action. An audience's sense of whether time is moving (and at what rate) or standing still while it is listening to the dialogue of a play is very largely a question of whether such dialogue is devoted to the business of the present movement (what is happening before its eyes), or to a character trying to understand what has just happened, or to retrospect. In the main action of the play the two latter functions are constantly juxtaposed; the overarching action is almost exclusively taken up with the former. The 'frozen' time of Egeon's tale contrasts briefly but markedly with the vigorous variety of tense in the Duke's closing words ('would', 'may', 'will', and the imperatives 'try', 'beg', 'borrow', 'live'). The real time of the play has begun to run with:

> I'll limit thee this day
> To seek thy health by beneficial help.
>
> (I i 150–1)

In the next scene, Egeon who has remained a character in a different past is briefly thrust into the play's present in the First Merchant's reference to him:

> This very day a Syracusian merchant
> Is apprehended for arrival here
>
> (I ii 3–4)

This is the only occasion, until the very end when all knots are untangled, that the confused present threatens to come into contact with the ordered past. If Egeon's shadowy identity in the present as 'a Syracusian merchant' were to be given any further definition, the action would have ended before it began.

But it is not, and S. Antipholus looks confidently to the future,
ignoring the past:

> Within this hour it will be dinner time;
> Till that I'll view the manners of the town,
> Peruse the traders, gaze upon the buildings,
> And then return and sleep within mine inn
>
> (I ii 11–14)

We are firmly within the moving moment. The time-bomb with
the crazy clock has begun to tick. The First Merchant's parting
words give us a hint that the inner and outer action will be
completed at about the same time, recalling the Duke's 'I'll
limit thee this day':

> soon at five o'clock,
> Please you, I'll meet with you upon the mart,
> And afterwards consort you till bed-time
>
> (I ii 26–8)

Ironically, the ominous implication of the Duke's words turns
out to be providential, while the genial social promise of the
Merchant's farewell conceals much trouble and confusion. 'I
will go lose myself', says S. Antipholus, using the words in the
first place in their colloquial sense of wandering aimlessly about
the city. But their repetition a few lines later sharply points up
the sense of loss of identity, linked as it is to the potent
Shakespearian image of the water-drop.[2] The point is that both
the literal and the metaphorical senses of the phrase come to
the same thing, as the action of the play demonstrates; it is by
losing himself in the city that S. Antipholus loses his identity.

The notion of steady and regular time is briefly taken up in
S. Antipholus's words to E. Dromio as he sees the latter
approaching:

> Here comes the almanac of my true date
>
> (I ii 41)

but by the very next line, 'What now? How chance thou art
returned so soon?' time's twistings and turnings have begun.
The reference to Dromio is unmistakably ironic, not only
because of the audience's strong suspicion that the false Dromio is not the true date-keeper that S. Antipholus thinks him

to be, but also in terms of the series of pictures of disrupted
time which are the first words uttered by E. Dromio:

> Return'd so soon? rather approach'd too late;
> The capon burns, the pig falls from the spit;
> The clock hath strucken twelve upon the bell;
> My mistress made it one upon my cheek

(I ii 43–6)

Dromio's feeble pun, one of several quibbles on time which we
shall encounter, goes to the heart of the matter. Clock-time
and inward time have already begun to diverge and E. Dromio
tells his supposed master as much: 'Methinks your man, like
mine, should be your clock.'[3] The doggerel lines following the
four I have quoted above, each leaning on the other, pile up
with something of the hectic rhythm of a clock that will not
stop striking.

The action of *The Comedy of Errors* takes the form of a series
of broken appointments, circumscribed by one appointment
that is scrupulously kept (the Duke's meeting at five o'clock
with Egeon). The appointment most frequently mentioned
throughout the play is that of dinner. Dinner, as the principal
Elizabethan meal, marked the chief event of the normal
domestic day. Being usually taken around noon, it divided the
day symmetrically in terms of clock-time. Dinner and the
dinner hour may therefore aptly stand for routine, unhurried
normality, when public and private time kept a congruent
rhythm. It is not surprising that they should figure prominent-
ly in a story which deals with the breakdown of that congruence.

The causal sequence is disrupted when the money that we
saw S. Antipholus hand to his servant a few moments ago
becomes 'sixpence that I had o'Wednesday last'. The act ends
with S. Antipholus reacting, not as one who is trapped in an
unfamiliar dimension of time (which is a metaphysical luxury
reserved for the audience) but, as is more natural, with a
suspicion that he is in an enchanted place. The first two scenes
of the play thus present us with a vivid contrast between the
past and the present. For all its threat, the past is set in steady,
natural time, while the present is wavering and distorted.

With Adriana's 'Sure, Luciana, it is two o'clock', the second act starts with the clock set right again, so to speak. The homiletic exchange between the two sisters on marital obedience, with its smooth and measured movement, is an oasis of calm soon to be disturbed by E. Dromio's arrival, and perhaps Luciana speaks wiser than she knows:

> Time is their master, and when they see time,
> They'll go or come.
>
> (II i 8–9)

She means, of course, that men come and go as they please, but we are soon to see in full swing what the previous scene has already given us strong indications of – a more sinister way in which time dominates the principals in this play.

E. Dromio's recapitulation of the exchange between himself and his supposed master is entirely in terms of the latter's refusal to recognise the time for what it is – the dinner hour. For the audience, hearing the scene they had witnessed only a few moments earlier recreated in capsule form in E. Dromio's vivid snatches of phrase, there is the comic frisson of time telescoped and turned back:

> ' 'Tis dinner-time', quoth I; 'my gold', quoth he;
> 'Your meat will burn', quoth I; 'my gold', quoth he ...
> 'Where is the thousand marks I gave thee, villain?'
> 'The pig', quoth I, 'is burn'd'; 'my gold', quoth he;
>
> (II i 62–3, 65–6)

It is in his apparent failure to recognise the 'right time' that Antipholus's identity becomes a puzzle to his wife, and the servants, in their hithering and thithering and the 'strokes' they collect at either end become veritable travelling clocks being constantly reset. Perhaps E. Dromio's earlier pun ('The clock hath strucken twelve ... My mistress made it one upon my cheek'), feeble as it is, is slightly more pertinent than we had imagined.

> Hath homely age the alluring beauty took
> From my poor cheek? Then he hath wasted it.
>
> (II i 89–90)

Adriana's words not only make her intensely human. With their sudden poignant cutting back to normal processes of time they form a sharp contrast to the unnatural entanglings of the temporal process which we have witnessed and heard of.

The opening lines of the second scene of Act II mark, in the new Arden editor's words, 'a point of rest in the play's mounting confusion' (p. 26, n.). They attempt to impose order on the recent past and place S. Antipholus virtually back at the point where he had said: 'Here comes the almanac of my true date.' As far as he is concerned, the intervening time has been effectively cancelled. If S. Antipholus could resist the temptation for further recapitulation of the events of the half-hour that has gone awry, all would be well, but of course he cannot, and further time-trouble ensues. He accuses S. Dromio of making 'a common of my serious hours' and the conversation moves compulsively into a discussion of the 'right time', focused again upon the crucial event of dinner and lurching on to much quibbling on the power and attributes of Father Time himself. The twin themes of time and identity are completely interwoven in the comic exchange on time and hair. It may be an obligatory set-piece, but if it is, it is in just the right setting. The argument, let us recall, turns on the question of whether or not 'there is a time for all things'. The action of the play forces us to leave the question open, for there does indeed appear to be no 'time' for some of the things that happen in it.

Adriana's entrance and the accompanying change from jerky prose to blank verse harks back once more to an earlier 'natural' time – 'The time was once when thou unurg'd wouldst vow ... How comes it *now* ...' The figure in S. Antipholus's reply –

> ... I know you not.
> In Ephesus I am but two hours old,
>
> (II ii 147–8)

– is no doubt a commonplace but, supported as it is by all the other emphases on time, it plays some part in drawing our attention to a new identity related to a new beginning in time. From the moment of this confrontation, S. Antipholus and his servant abandon all attempts to balance their subjective sense of time against public clock-time. As in a similar situation in

Twelfth Night,[4] the abandonment is signalled in S. Antipholus's
case by a conscious decision to enter the other time of dreams:

> What, was I married to her in my dream?
> Or sleep I now, and think I hear all this?
> What error drives our eyes and ears amiss?
> Until I know this sure uncertainty,
> I'll entertain the offer'd fallacy,
>
> (II ii 182–6)

– while S. Dromio's 'This is the fairy land' puts us in mind of
the most celebrated entry into dream-time in all Shakespeare.
This readiness to yield to the promise of the future, a certain
openness before the hazards of fortune, a willing belief in the
essential benevolence of time, is not merely a precondition of
the development of the comic plot, but also a characteristic of
the Shakespearian comic hero and heroine, especially in disguise, where they always retain a certain freedom of comment
on their assumed roles. Since comedy sees time ultimately in
its aspect of fulfilment rather than of destruction, this faith is
no more and no less than the acceptance by the protagonists
of the world in which they live, move and have their being:

> Am I in earth, in heaven, or in hell?
> Sleeping or waking, mad or well advis'd?
> Known unto these, and to myself disguis'd,
> I'll say as they say, and persever so,
> And in this mist at all adventures go.
>
> (II ii 212–16)

In performance, the words with which Adriana leaves the
stage at the end of Act II, 'Come, come, Antipholus, we dine
too late', would still be in the audience's ears when E. Antipholus appears on the stage for the first time and identifies
himself with the line 'My wife is shrewish when I keep not
hours'. Here he starts out with the 'inner' and 'outer' clocks in
perfect accord; they are never to be so again till the action is
almost over. From the audience's standpoint, however, the
public clock is turned back, because what E. Antipholus says is
valid only on the assumption that the scene we have just
witnessed (II ii) has not in fact taken place. For E. Antipholus,
his wife is still waiting for him to come home to dinner, as we

see her waiting at the beginning of the second act; for us, she has already gone in to dinner with her husband.

The appearance of congruence between public and private time is appearance only. E. Dromio's insistence on what has been happening to him is alrady threatening his master's 'temporal' stability. If he inquired seriously into the slave's story, the comic world would disintegrate. Fortunately for us, he dismisses it with 'I think thou art an ass' (inevitably recalling his double's earlier comment to his servant) and there follows the debate between E. Antipholus and Balthazar on the comparative merits of good food and a warm welcome. The joke is of course that we have here the ritual without the reality which is to follow it and which is the *raison d'être* of the ritual. After the elaborate discussion as to whether food or welcome is better, 'Here is neither cheer, sir, nor welcome'. When the courtesy debate is reflected later in the distorting mirror of the slanging match between the two Dromios more is involved than the degeneration of ritual into chaos. Time, which had been, in a manner of speaking 'frozen' in the earlier discussion (as it is in much ritual), begins to run again. We are in the flowing present of the play, but it is a muddied and twisting stream.

A collision between the domestic and social worlds of the play appears inevitable at this point. It is averted only by Balthazar's appeal from the baffling disorders of the present to E. Antipholus's 'long experience' of marital harmony. The verse moves from past through present into projected future – 'And about evening come yourself alone' – and once more settles into the smooth rhythms which are its ground bass. But some hint of the way the future itself will begin to twist and turn as it becomes the present is given in E. Antipholus's summing up of his intention: 'And in despite of mirth, mean to be merry'. His last words in this scene – 'this jest shall cost me some expense' has of course two very different meanings for himself and for the audience. Komisarjevsky's production very aptly used it as a kind of Gilbertian refrain repeated in chorus by everyone on stage. . . .

In the scene that now follows (III ii) the tone, the formal rhyming, and the subject matter recall the exchange between

Adriana and her sister which opens the second act. There is
even an explicit reference to the earlier conversation in 'Though
others have the arm, show us the sleeve'. (Compare II ii 173.) It
is, as far as Luciana is concerned, a shunting back in time, an
attempt to get back again through retrospect on to the rails of
normality. She invests Antipholus with a new identity on the
basis of past and future hypocrisy. For his part, S. Antipholus is
entirely willing to accept a new identity, but it is the transformation wrought by love (an absolute, in spite of everything, in
Shakespearian comedy), not by deranged time, which he craves:

> Teach me, dear creature, how to think and speak;
> Lay open to my earthy gross conceit,
> Smother'd in errors, feeble, shallow, weak,
> The folded meaning of your words' deceit.
> Against my soul's pure truth, why labour you
> To make it wander in an unknown field?
> Are you a god? would you create me new?
> Transform me then, and to your power I'll yield.
>
> (III ii 33–40)

The platonic overtones ('my earthy gross conceit', 'my soul's
pure truth', etc.) are entirely appropriate; the affirmation S.
Antipholus wishes to make, though exaggerated in its immediate context, is essentially beyond the vagaries of time. For him
time begins again here, with love:

> Thee will I love, and with thee lead my life;
> Thou hast no husband yet, nor I no wife –
>
> (III ii 67–8)

Though under the influence of S. Dromio's sad tale of pursuit
by Greasy Nell (which is of course a comic parallel of his own
predicament) S. Antipholus decides to flee from the complications of the present ('Tis time I think to trudge, pack and be
gone') we know that in the comic outcome his attempt will
inevitably be thwarted. He accepts 'the offered fallacy' of the
gold chain as he did Adriana's invitation to dinner and this
acceptance once more deflects for him the straight course of
time's arrow.

For a moment, but only for a moment, we are again in the
sphere of public time at the beginning of the fourth act, in the

world of debts due at Pentecost and five o'clock appointments. But with the entry of E. Antipholus and his servant the backward journey on the time machine begins again. 'Neither chain nor goldsmith came to me' – his words take us, with him, to a point before the two scenes we have just witnessed. This is not a world in which past or future have any coherence. Money disappears and so do tangible objects such as gold chains. The difference in the latter case is that more is involved than the trustworthiness or otherwise of a servant. The whole commercial existence of the community depends on the honouring of obligations voluntarily entered into in the past. That existence is now threatened when the immediate past seems to be present in two versions of equal authority but mutually contradictory. Private confusions have now spread into the public domain of Angelo, the Second Merchant and the arresting Officer. The vagaries of the past make future action impossible. Time has twisted itself into an inexplicable knot:

Angelo: Then you will bring the chain to her yourself?
Antipholus E: No, bear it with you, lest I come not time enough.
Angelo: Well sir, I will. Have you the chain about you?
Antipholus E: And if I have not, sir, I hope you have,
                 Or else you may return without your money.
Angelo: Nay, come, I pray you, sir, give me the chain
                                                        (IV i 40–5)

The action literally cannot go forward but for the intervention of the Second Merchant, the only one of the speakers for whom public time still keeps a normal course: 'The hour steals on; I pray you sir, dispatch.' The whole scene of some seventy lines from which I have quoted above is, in terms of the use of performance time, a contrast to the opening scene of the play. There a lengthy tract of the past is encompassed in a few moments of stage-time. Here, several minutes of stage-time are taken up by an action which, save as it keeps turning in on itself, is really no action at all. . . .

When S. Dromio meets his master (IV iii) their two clocks collide, so to speak – 'Why, sir, I brought you word an hour since, that the bark *Expedition* puts forth tonight' – and that way madness lies. The courtesan's speech which ends this scene not only prepares us for the madness to come, but gives us, as it were, a progress report on the action so far, as it is recorded in terms of public duration and behaviour. At the very end of the fourth act, what had before been simple if confusing contradictions in the experiences of different persons become vastly more involved. We see that there is not so much flat contradiction as overlapping combined with divergence in the various accounts of the events of the recent past given by Adriana, E. Antipholus and E. Dromio. Some of what Antipholus says is corroborated by Dromio, some of what Dromio says corroborated by Adriana. Even the presumed madness of Antipholus is insufficient as an explanation of what is going on. In the end, the onlookers are compelled to consider whether it is not they themselves who are mad, when what they have just witnessed (the binding of Antipholus) appears not to have happened: 'God for thy mercy they are loose again!' The audience itself is involved in a sensation of *déjà vu* when the same action (Antipholus with drawn sword) is repeated a few moments later in the encounter with Angelo.

When the last act begins, S. Antipholus is still at the end of Act III (where Angelo had just given him the chain) and Angelo at the beginning of Act IV, where E. Antipholus had denied receiving the chain from him. Our final reminder of public time ('By this I think the dial points at five') comes after Adriana's abortive effort to rescue her husband from the priory (the play is full of such false starts); and it foreshadows the union of the main action of the play, where time has been going crazy, with the over-arching action, where the clock has been ticking steadily away to the hour of doom. The Duke's words to Adriana – 'Long since thy husband served me in my wars' – looks back to a stable past, a centre of normality beyond the confused events of the play. Similarly, Egeon's apostrophe evokes both in its sense and in the measured dignity of its rhythm, the progression of natural time as it is found in ordinary human experience. The imagery of music, light and the seasons evokes a world in which objective time is in harmony with human time, and Egeon's experience, however

severe and testing, is seen as inevitable and therefore natural
and liberating:

> O time's extremity,
> Hast thou so crack'd and splitted my poor tongue
> In seven short years, that here my only son
> Knows not my feeble key of untun'd cares?
> Though now this grained face of mine be hid
> In sap-consuming winter's drizzled snow,
> And all the conduits of my blood froze up,
> Yet hath my night of life some memory;
> My wasting lamps some fading glimmer left;
> My dull deaf ears a little use to hear –
> All these old witnesses, I cannot err,
> Tell me thou art my son Antipholus.

(v i 307–18)

In the Duke's words, 'Why, here begins his morning story
right:' natural time starts flowing again. It is left to the Abbess
to bring the immediate past into alignment with the ordered
perspective of true temporal experience in an image whose
capacity to move is partly due, I think, to the fact that it has,
hovering about it, the resonance of the phrase 'the fullness of
time':

> Thirty three years have I but gone in travail
> Of you, my sons, and till this present hour
> My heavy burden ne'er delivered.

(v i 400–2)

'After so long grief, such felicity.' If the twists and turns of
time in *The Comedy of Errors* do no more than tease us, it is
because we have been put in a position where *our* time-sense is
not threatened. There is no *character* who plays tricks on the
others, so that he knows what they do not know. Only the
outcome of the over-arching action – the real identity of
the Abbess and the family reunion – are withheld from us too
so that at the very end of the play we too begin to feel the
movement of time. For the rest, our superior awareness prevents us from identifying with any of the characters involved,
except indirectly. The play remains a farce where Shakespeare
takes us backstage, as it were, to show us what tricks can be
worked with time without, for the most part, playing such

'tricks' on us, as he does in *The Winter's Tale* and *The Tempest*. For the moment, we are protected from the puzzlements of time dismembered.

SOURCE: ' "Time's deformed hand": Sequence, Consequence, and Inconsequence in *The Comedy of Errors*', *Shakespeare Survey*, 25 (1972), 81–91.

NOTES

1. *University of Toronto Quarterly*, LX (1939), 95–106. Reprinted in *Shakespeare's Comedies, an Anthology of Modern Criticism*, edited by Laurence Lerner (London, 1967).

2. See H. F. Brooks, 'Themes and Structure in *The Comedy of Errors*', in *Early Shakespeare*, edited by J. R. Brown and Bernard Harris, Stratford-upon-Avon Studies 3 (London, 1961). Also Critical Introduction to New Arden edition.

3. Pope's emendation (Folio's 'cooke' to 'clock') is almost certainly correct. See the new Arden editor's note, p. 16.

4. Cf. Sebastian in *TN* IV i 59–62, 'If it be thus to dream, still let me sleep!' Also his later lines at IV ii 9–15: 'For though my soul disputes well with my sense', etc.

Ralph Berry

THE COMEDY OF ERRORS: THE SUBLIMINAL NARRATIVE (1985)

TO see *The Comedy of Errors* as the first of the final romances is no great paradox of vision. It is true that commentators used always to stress the Plautine, and thus the farcical nature of the play. For most of them, *The Comedy of Errors* was in the first instance an adaptation of Plautus's *Menaechmi*, and one took it on from there. But the archaic and primitive elements of the play are now more visible than in the past. Northrop Frye points to its dark underside, 'which brings the feeling of the play closer to the night world of Apuleius than to Plautus'.[1] Such a perception makes the play more of a comedy, less of a farce. Moreover, the romances are now thought of as a vital and ultimately defining area of the canon, to an extent which would not have been conceded a generation ago; so there is a disposition to admit *The Comedy of Errors* as an anticipation, not merely an experiment. Manifestly, the play works towards the experience of reconciliation and discovered identity, anticipating the drift of the romances. That can be taken for granted. I want here to look at some ways in which this curiously layered play organizes our experience. The most helpful commentary on its provenance, for my purposes, is Anne Barton's:

Behind the *Menaechmi*, as behind all the plays of Plautus, lay a Greek original now lost. Mistaken identity and the recovery of lost children seem to have been almost obsessive preoccupations of the New Comedy written by Menander and his contemporaries towards the end of the 4th century B.C. A response, probably, to the political chaos of a Hellenistic world that was filled with displaced persons, where children were often 'lost' by parents too poor or too distracted to cope with them at the time of their birth.[2]

If one substitutes 'under' for 'behind', the metaphor becomes
more pointed. Under the Roman play is a Greek play; under
the Greek play is an action so vaguely apprehensible as to
merit only 'pre-Hellenistic', the archetypal experience of wandering, loss and rediscovery. The lost Greek original silts down
on to a folk memory. This has little to do with 'sources', as
conventionally understood.[3] *The Comedy of Errors* is a palimpsest,
not of composition, but of experience. . . .

I

Roman on Greek: that is our code for the opening. The
allusions, conscious or subliminal, to the *Aeneid* and the *Odyssey*
conduct us into the play world. It is Hellenistic, archaic,
romantic. 'For Shakespeare', says Bullough, 'romance was
mainly of the Mediterranean.'[4] The local associations of Ephesus would also mean something to the Elizabethans. They
thought of it as a great seaport, renowned for its Temple of
Diana. St Paul stayed there for two years.[5] Hence the audience
would connect it with St Paul's *Epistle to the Ephesians*, and its
appeals for domestic unity. They would also remember that
Ephesus was known for sorcerers and exorcists, and for St
Paul's 'curious acts'. The Biblical allusions help to establish the
dark underside of this play. But these cultural referents are
absorbed in the broad symbolism of the action and its background, with the atavistic appeal to collective memories of
wandering and loss. Always at the back of the action is the sea,
as great a presence here as in *The Tempest*. It is the sea that
parts Aegeon and his family, that brings Antipholus of Syracuse
to Ephesus, that calls him throughout. 'For he is bound to sea,
and stays but for it' (IV i 33). 'Both wind and tide stays for this
gentleman' (IV i 46). That sense of the sea – waiting, pulling,
imperious – is strong in *The Comedy of Errors*. Not only is it a
reminder, in its ebb and flow, of the mysterious forces that
govern the individual, it is the image through which the
individual defines himself:

> *Antipholus S*: I to the world am like a drop of water
> That in the ocean seeks another drop,
> Who, falling there to find his fellow forth,
> Unseen, inquisitive, confounds himself;
> So I, to find a mother and a brother,
> In quest of them, unhappy, lose myself.
>
> (I ii 35–40)

> *Adriana*: For know, my love, as easy may'st thou fall
> A drop of water in the breaking gulf
> And take unmingled thence that drop again,
> Without addition or diminishing,
> As take from me thyself and not me too.
>
> (II ii 124–8)

Both Antipholus and Adriana find in the sea the deepest formulas for human identity. It is a symbol that transcends cultural allusion.

In fact, this play constantly reaches towards the universal. If *Measure for Measure* is the most Freudian play in the canon, *The Comedy of Errors* is the most Jungian. It is rooted in the collective subconscious, and archetypes of enduring power are presented. The plot itself is a playful rendering of the hostile brother motif, a theme which as Aronson points out recurs often in Shakespeare.[6] Here, the brothers are unwitting not hostile; it is only through ignorance that Antipholus of Syracuse intrudes upon his brother's domain. The Syracusan appears, archetypally, to be the 'younger' brother; he is defensive, apprehensive, easily daunted (but luckier, for all that). His enduring impulse, when confronted with difficulties, is to take to the boats ('I long that we were safe and sound aboard', IV iv 150), while the 'elder' brother is passionaté, overbearing, a fighter. This mutuality of temperament is a part of the psychic integration of the play. Then again, Luciana provides perhaps the clearest statement in Shakespeare of the anima archetype.

> *Antopholus S*: It is thyself, mine own self's better part,
> Mine eye's clear eye, my dear heart's dearer heart,
> My food, my fortune, and my sweet hope's aim,
> My sole earth's heaven, and my heaven's claim.
>
> (III ii 61–4)

She, for Antipholus, is 'the embodiment of this omnipresent and ageless image [of woman] which corresponds to the deepest reality in man'.[7] The final transformation of the anima is the Abbess, who also combines the functions of Great Mother and Wise Old Man. In the end, the Syracuse merchant attains his 'heaven's claim', too. The archetypes, to which I shall return later, are the inner substance of this drama. The archaic is simply the period costume of the universal.

II

Let us turn to the general experience of the opening scene. Its narrative is, as Northrop Frye says, 'a sophisticated, if sympathetic treatment of a structural cliché'.[8] The hieratic solemnity of the opening has the decorum of tragedy:

> *Aegeon*: Proceed, Solinus, to procure my fall,
>   And by the doom of death end woes and all.
>
>   (I i 1–2)

The speaker – and thus, at this moment of supreme weight, the play – invites the Duke to define the experience as tragic. He, for 23 lines, appears to pronounce the verdict of tragedy. Yet there are hints of unwillingness to complete the definition. 'I am not partial to infringe our laws' begins to sketch an apology; he explains at length that the Syracusans and Ephesans have similar edicts; he indicates that a.heavy fine would suffice, but that Aegeon's property is only a tenth part. He draws the only available conclusion, '*Therefore by law* thou art condemn'd to die.' The Law says, in effect, 'what else can we do?' It is not the brutal imposition of iron statute that the more literal-minded commentators imagine. So, when Aegeon hopelessly acquiesces,

> Yet this my comfort; when your words are done,
> My woes end likewise with the evening sun.
>
>   (26–7)

the Duke, somewhat uneasily, invites Aegeon to keep the
conversation going; something might turn up.

> Well, Syracusan, say in brief the cause
> Why thou departed'st from thy native home,
> And for what cause thou cam'st to Ephesus.
>
> (28–30)

The play now changes, for all its dramatic energies are
concentrated upon Aegeon. The prisoner transforms the court.
As narrator, he takes over; he holds the audience in a spell. It
is a display of magic, the power of the story-teller. In performance it is not to be sabotaged by the director.[9] Length here is
not tedium, but the evocation of a primitive experience, the
submission of an audience to the teller's capacity to create a
world (cf. Sheherezade). Its immediate consequence is a shift
in roles for Aegeon and the Duke. Prisoner and judge become
story-teller and audience; hence Solinus becomes a suppliant:

> *Do me the favour* to dilate at full
> What have befall'n of them and thee till now.
>
> (122–3)

His next speech is openly apologetic, 'Now trust me, were it
not against our laws . . . My soul should sue as advocate for
thee' (142, 145). The power of the teller has already wrought
against the framing definition, tragedy. There are hints in the
main narrative, too: 'happy but for me, / And by me, had not
our hap been bad . . . Was carried towards Corinth, as we
thought . . . By fishermen of Corinth, as we thought' (37–8, 87,
111). The actor is entitled to glean some laughs from the
repeated 'as we thought': he is obeying the larger instructions
of the script, and 'as we thought' is a pointer towards the
whole.[10] Having proposed itself as tragedy, the play converts
into an intimation and promise of comedy. The narrator,
defying the logic of *therefore by law*, wills the marvellous, the
death-suspended, the comic, and the audience assents to the
logic. The 'law' will yield to a yet stronger force.

This force manifests itself through fantasy. *The Comedy of
Errors* is organized along two lines of psychic advance. One is
that of erotic promise, unbelievable good fortune, discovered

identity, the fulfilment of all one's desires. The other is that of
loss, shattered identity, pain. The first line is stronger, and its
triumph never really in doubt. The second is always present,
often uppermost, at all times shadowing the experience of cast
and audience. Threat and promise make up the fantasies of this
play, and we ought to catch at their blurred shapes.

III

Antipholus of Syracuse has the largest speaking part, and
channels much of the play's experience. His character-note is
longing, a yearning for fulfilment in relationship; and the
refused dinner-invitation leads to

> Farewell till then. I will go lose myself,
> And wander up and down to view the city.
>
> (I ii 30–1)

For him the action is compounded of vague threats:

> They say this town is full of cozenage,
> As, nimble jugglers that deceive the eye,
> Dark-working sorcerers that change the mind,
> Soul-killing witches that deform the body,
> Disguised cheaters, prating mountebanks,
> And many such-like liberties of sin.
>
> (I ii 97–102)

and allure:

> To me she speaks; she moves me for her theme.
> What, was I married to her in my dream?
> Or sleep I now and think I hear all this?
> What error drives our eyes and ears amiss?
> Until I know this sure uncertainty,
> I'll entertain the offer'd fallacy.
>
> (II ii 180–5)

The fear, be it noted, is of *foreigners*. The archetypal challenge
to self comes from strangers. Equally, the invitation comes
from the exotic, the alluringly strange. So, through the curtain
of doubts:

> *Dromio S*: This is the fairy land. O spite of spites!
> We talk with goblins, owls, and sprites:
>> (II ii 188–9)

and his own confusions:

> *Antipholus S*: Am I in earth, in heaven, or in hell?
> Sleeping or waking, mad or well-advis'd?
>> (II ii 211–12)

Antipholus goes into the house:

> I'll say as they say, and persever so,
> And in this mist at all adventures go.
>> (II ii 214–15)

The echoes are of a fairy world. There is the house, there is the fair witch, offering whatever inducement of gingerbread or blandishment that can tempt the hero – or victim. Antipholus, a little o'erparted with the hero-role, quakes: but enters.

The play now enters (III i) upon its most intense and symbolically resonant phase, for it becomes the experience of Antipholus of Ephesus, shut out from his own home. The situation is enduringly fascinating: modern folklore abounds with tales of people who slip out of their apartment for a moment, usually in *déshabillé*, and find themselves locked out with alarming consequences. No doubt some of the anecdotes are true, but the market is larger than the instances. Antipholus of Ephesus, rooted in the reality of his calling and on his home territory, sees the world transformed. The familiar marks crumble. Moreover, behind the obvious shock of exclusion, there is a profoundly disturbing sexual threat, one which commentators habitually ignore.

Act III, scene i, as all agree, is based on Plautus's *Amphitruo*. It was a popular grammar school text, and Baldwin thinks that Shakespeare read the Latin original in the fourth form.[11] In the Plautine original, Amphitrion is shut out of his house, while Jupiter makes love to his wife Alcmena. Plautus dramatizes a primal fear. And a section of Shakespeare's audience would recognize the Plautine source. But the remainder of the audience would in any case receive the impression of sexual congress

behind locked doors, which the play creates in its own right.
The previous scene has ended on a note most favourable for
Antipholus of Syracuse: Adriana is clearly in a mood to charm
her husband, and is insistent that they are *not* to be disturbed:

> Come, sir, to dinner. Dromio, keep the gate.
> Husband, I'll dine above with you today
> And shrive you of a thousand idle pranks.
> Sirrah, if any ask you for your master,
> Say he dines forth and let no creature enter.
> Come, sister. Dromio, play the porter well.
>
> (II ii 205–10)

The audience is now to be teased with a sexual fantasy.

It is confirmed in the heavy verbal underlining of III i.
There's an easy bawdry in

> *Dromio E*: Let my master in, Luce.
> *Luce*:   Faith, no; he comes too late . . .
> *Dromio E*: Have at you with a proverb: Shall I set in my staff?
>
> (49, 51)[12]

If Antipholus of Ephesus does not realize the appalling implications of his 'Are you there, wife? You might have come
before' (63), the Elizabethan audience will help him out.
Dromio adds to the effect with 'Your cake here is warm within'
(71), 'cake' being 'woman',[13] and his next line, 'It would make
a man mad as a buck to be so bought and sold' presents his
master as a male deer in rutting season, and a cuckold. The
worst, so the audience is led to suppose, has happened.
Antipholus thinks it too, and evidently plans a sexual revenge
with the co-operation of the Courtesan:

> I know a wench of excellent discourse,
> Pretty and witty, wild, and yet, too, gentle,
> There will we dine. This woman that I mean,
> My wife – but, I protest, without desert –
> Hath oftentimes upbraided me withal.
> To her will we for dinner . . .
> Since mine own doors refuse to entertain me,
> I'll knock elsewhere, to see if they'll disdain me.
>
> (109–14, 120–1)

'Knocking' is standard slang for sexual entry.[14] But above all, the double-entendres and bawdry of the text stem from the stage symbolism itself: the house, perceived from earliest times as the coding for woman, and the knocking at the gates, the male attempts at entry. The symbolism is the more charged if the nature of the inner action is considered. What is held before the audience as a *theatrical* possibility is incest.

Incest takes up some space in the canon. The remarriage of Gertrude to Claudius is held to be incestuous, and the charge is repeated in Hamlet's final words to Claudius ('thou incestuous, damnèd Dane'). Father–daughter incest appears in *Pericles*. Though not named by Henry, the 'incest' of his marriage to his brother's widow is the core of the discussion in *Henry VIII*, II iv. The word is a metaphor for the relations of Isabella and Claudio ('Is't not a kind of incest, to take life / From thine own sister's shame', *Measure for Measure*, III i 138–9), and a type of hypocrisy for Lear: 'thou simular of virtue / That art incestuous' (*King Lear*, III ii 54–5). Lucrece has 'Guilty of incest, that abomination' (*The Rape of Lucrece*, 921). Richard III plans to marry his niece. If one takes the canon as a giant exploration of human consciousness, incest, in several of its variant forms, is more than a marginal presence in that consciousness. Here in III i, at the midpoint of *The Comedy of Errors*,[15] incest is the compelling fantasy which is held before the audience as a likely reality. It is the dark centre of a play shot with fitful visions. Has it happened?

No, it has not. Act III, scene ii, takes the audience away from the vertiginous edge, and conducts it towards sanity and order. It rapidly becomes clear that the encounter between Adriana and Antipholus of Syracuse has been a fiasco. Luciana's first line tells all: 'And may it be that you have quite forgot / A husband's office?' which is plain enough speaking. Luciana upbraids Antipholus for the disastrous dinner-party – here as earlier the play anticipates *Macbeth* – and Antipholus confirms matters with 'Your weeping sister is no wife of mine' (42), by which time, if not earlier, the audience must be aware that Shakespeare has been trifling shamelessly with its sensibilities. The play now modulates into mere comic dalliance with incest,

for Luciana believes herself to be courted by her brother-in-law
(which we know not to be true). A final tease is to come, for
the actress is entitled to garner all she can from Adriana's
'Which of you two did dine with me today?' (v i 369). But that
is Shakespeare the professional milking a situation dry. The
real message, which is one of reassurance, has come earlier
through numerous channels. . . .

IV

The later phases of *The Comedy of Errors* handle archetypes of
serious and compelling authority. Much of Act IV is spun out
of purgatory, or hell.

> *Dromio S*: No, he's in Tartar limbo, worse than hell,
> A devil in an everlasting garment hath him . . .
> One that before the judgment carries poor souls to hell.
>
> (IV ii 32–3, 40)

Antipholus's 'chain' (51) is in the logic of association the bondage
of hell. There are hints of 'redemption' (IV ii 46), and 'Paradise'
(IV iii 16), but the prevailing state is captivity, with 'prison',
'sergeant' and 'durance' the guiding terms. Deliverance is the
ship, 'the bark Expedition put forth tonight' (IV iii 37), which
Antipholus of Syracuse, as in a dream, is unable to reach. Instead
comes the Courtesan, 'Mistress Satan . . . the devil's dam' (IV iii
48–50), to frighten Dromio of Syracuse. Hell, however comically
rendered, is the motif of Act IV. It is a nightmare, a bondage from
which the captive actors struggle to be free.

Hence, in the symbolic logic of the drama, *hell* modulates
into *devil* and then into *possession*, which in turn yields to a ritual
of exorcisement:

> *Dr Pinch*: I charge thee, Satan, hous'd within this man,
> To yield possession to my holy prayers
> And to thy state of darkness hie thee straight!
> I conjure thee by all the saints in heaven!
>
> (IV iv 54–7)

Hell having been redefined as *possession*, the way is open for Act
v's line of strategic advance. Exorcisement gives way to conva-
lescence. Adriana sees the process purely as recovery, 'And
bear him home for his recovery' (v i 41), but the Abbess invests
it with religious associations:

> How long hath this possession held the man?
> . . . he took this place for sanctuary,
> And it shall privilege him from your hands
> Till I have brought him to his wits again,
> Or lose my labour in assaying it . . .
> . . . I will not let him stir,
> Till I have us'd the approved means I have,
> With wholesome syrups, drugs, and holy prayers,
> To make of him a formal man again.
>
> (v i 44, 94–7, 102–5)

A ritual of healing is envisaged. The Priory, before whose gates
the final action takes place, is the *sanctuary* of body and mind,
the guarantor of the values of the close.

But these values are not achieved without an episode of
significant turbulence. The cruel and anarchic spirit of comedy, now operating through Antipholus of Ephesus, breaks out
of bondage and expresses a myth of liberation. It comes in two
versions, the servant-messenger's:

> My master and his man are both broke loose,
> Beaten the maids a-row, and bound the doctor,
> Whose beard they have sing'd off with brands of fire;
> And ever, as it blaz'd, they threw on him
> Great pails of puddled mire to quench the hair.
> My master preaches patience to him, and the while
> His man with scissors nicks him like a fool.
>
> (v i 169–77)

and Antipholus's:

> Along with them
> They brought one Pinch, a hungry lean-fac'd villain,
> A mere anatomy, a mountebank,
> A threadbare juggler and a fortune-teller,
> A needy, hollow-ey'd, sharp looking wretch,
> A living dead man. This pernicious slave,
> Forsooth, took on him as a conjurer,
> And gazing in mine eyes, feeling my pulse,

> And with no face, as 'twere, outfacing me,
> Cries out, I was possess'd. Then all together
> They fell upon me, bound me, bore me thence
> And in a dark and dankish vault at home
> There left me and my man, both bound together,
> Till, gnawing with my teeth my bonds in sunder,
> I gain'd my freedom, and immediately
> Ran hither to your Grace:
>
> (v i 237–52)

The violence of this episode is evidently designed to release the
emotional tensions created by the action. Liberation, we note,
is accompanied by revenge: Antipholus of Ephesus goes in for
outright torture of Dr Pinch, a feature he naturally omits from
his report. That is why Shakespeare needs to plant two
versions. In this most binary of plays, there are always two sides
to events: what it looks like, and what it feels like. The
messenger reports two dangerous lunatics on the rampage;
Antipholus of Ephesus gives us the other side, the experience
of hellish incarceration (in the 'vault at home') with the 'living
dead man', a kind of zombie,[16] as the guardian of the under-
world. *Freedom* becomes a plea to (and for) *Grace*. And, in the
play's terms, grace is bestowed.

It takes on the form of a rebirth:

> Thirty-three years have I but gone in travail
> Of you, my sons, and till this present hour
> My heavy burden ne'er delivered.
>
> (v i 400–2)

says the Abbess, making the entire action the convulsions of
delivery. The symbolism is confirmed in the lines which follow:

> The Duke, my husband, and my children both,
> And you the calendars of their nativity,
> Go to a gossips' feast, and go with me;
> After so long grief, such nativity!
>
> (403–6)

As Alexander Leggatt notes, 'the final image of security is not
a wedding dance but a christening feast, a *family* celebration'.[17]
With the *naming* of characters comes the affirmation of identity,
family, society (for the Duke presides, as he should). The dark

coupling at the centre of the play has led to a rebirth of the family, a restatement of relationship. And in keeping with the standard Shakespearean technique, the frankest statement of the implications is given to a clown:

> *Dromio S*: She now shall be my sister, not my wife.
>
> (416)

The prohibition on incest is the foundation of the family. That, and the graceful settlement of the primogeniture issue, marks the decorous conclusion to the play. What the Dromios exit into, what the audience is left with, is *home*.[18]

SOURCE: '*The Comedy of Errors*: the Subliminal Narrative', *Shakespeare and the Awareness of the Audience* (London, 1985), pp. 30–45.

NOTES

1. Northrop Frye, *A Natural Perspective: The Development of Shakespearean Comedy and Romance* (New York 1965), p. 77.
2. *The Riverside Shakespeare*, ed. G. Blakemore Evans (Boston, Mass., 1974), p. 81.
3. Geoffrey Bullough reprints three works as sources for *The Comedy of Errors*: the *Menaechmi* of Plautus; the *Amphitruo* of Plautus; and a portion of Gower's *Confessio Amantis*, that relating to the story of Apollonius of Tyre. See *Narrative and Dramatic Sources of Shakespeare*, ed. Geoffrey Bullough, 8 vols (London, 1957–75), I, 12–54.
4. Bullough (ed.), *Narrative and Dramatic Sources of Shakespeare*, VIII, 245.
5. For the 'Christianizing' idea of Ephesus, see ibid., I, 10; Foakes (ed.), *Comedy of Errors*, pp. xxix, 113–15.
6. Alex Aronson reviews the 'hostile brother' motif (though without reference to *The Comedy of Errors*) in *Psyche and Symbol in Shakespeare* (Bloomington, Ind., 1972), pp. 113–25.
7. C. G. Jung, *Aion: Researches into the Phenomenology of Self*, 2nd edn (Princeton, NJ, 1968), p. 13.
8. Frye, *A Natural Perspective*, p. 57.
9. J. C. Trewin bears down hard on such directors, in *Going to Shakespeare* (London, 1978), pp. 47–8: 'it was not hard for a director to find appropriate emphases for a yawning Duke: "Well, Syracusian, say *in brief* the cause" '.

10. One would naturally add the information given in the playbill, but there are always some members of the audience who do not take it in. Every box-office manager can tell strange tales of disappointed ticket-holders.

11. Baldwin, *William Shakspere's Small Latine and Lesse Greeke*, 2 vols (Urbana, Ill., 1944), I, 326.

12. The Riverside edition, like Bevington, accepts 'staff' as bawdy.

13. R. A. Foakes (ed.), New Arden edition *Comedy of Errors* (London, 1962), p. 46; and E. A. M. Colman, *The Dramatic Use of Bawdy in Shakespeare* (London, 1974), p. 187.

14. See the entries on *knock* in J. S. Farmer and W. E. Henley, *Slang and its Analogues: Past and Present* (reprt. in 3 vols, New York, 1965); and Eric Partridge, *A Dictionary of Slang and Unconventional English*, 2 vols, 5th edn (London, 1961).

15. It is perhaps worth noting that this play's structure depends on a 'split' centre. Act III has two scenes, and not, as so often in Shakespeare, three.

16. For *zombie*, *Webster's Third New International Dictionary* has (1b) 'the supernatural power or essence that according to voodoo belief may enter into and reanimate a dead body'.

17. Alexander Leggatt, *Shakespeare's Comedy of Love* (London, 1974) p. 17.

18. There are 41 references to 'home' in *The Comedy of Errors*, more than for any other play in the canon.

RECENT PRODUCTIONS OF
THE COMEDY OF ERRORS

THE stage history of *The Comedy of Errors* in many ways reflects its critical fortunes, in that there has been a general reluctance to take it seriously. During this century there have not been many major productions (only eight in Stratford-upon-Avon) though in performance it has often surprised critics with its vitality and excitement. It has both suffered from and triumphed over an irreverent approach to its text since the most widely held view has been that as 'apprentice Shakespeare' a flexible approach to the text is perfectly in order. Most often it has been played fast and furious as frenetic farce, though a more thoughtful approach has sometimes revealed unexpected depths.

After three fairly unremarkable productions at Stratford (the most recent 22 years earlier) audiences were unprepared for the impact of Komisarjevsky's 1938 production. Before it opened there was considerable press speculation about the use and value of coloured bowler hats which accurately predicted the director's sense of fun and anarchic humour. He made extensive use of song and dance, with music by Handel and Antony Bernard, and although there was a general acceptance that he burlesqued the play, there were few regrets. The set featured doll's house buildings (an image of Toy Town) presided over by a large town clock which kept time in unconventional fashion (see Salgādo above). Characters spilled on stage dressed in a mad mixture of costumes; the women, for example, wore semi-Elizabethan dresses but carried modern handbags. The production was an amalgam of ballet, operetta and farce – 'mime, music and madness' (*News Chronicle*, 13/4/38) in a celebration of urban folly. Audiences clearly loved it and the critics were seduced, not only by the Courtesan, an

81

'eye-rolling, hip-swaying Queen of the Flicks' (*Stratford-upon-Avon Herald*, 15/4/38) but also by the transformation of what was generally considered pure nonsense and the most tedious of Shakespeare's plays into such a splendid theatrical occasion. There were very few murmurs of disagreement. The production was a huge box-office success and was revived the following year.

The play's potential for adaptation had been discovered and 1938 also saw the birth of a musical based on the play, *The Boys from Syracuse* at the Alvin Theatre, New York. The strength of the music and lyrics (by Richard Rodgers and Lorenz Hart) rather than the book (by George Abbott) has guaranteed it periodic revivals. In 1940 a production entitled *A New Comedy of Errors or, Too Many Twins*, a combination of Plautus, Shakespeare and Molière (in modern dress with music by Julian Slade) was staged at the Mercury Theatre, London. In 1957 at the Old Vic *The Comedy of Errors* was shortened to one hour in a double bill with an abbreviated *Titus Andronicus*. Robert Helpmann as Pinch stole the show as he exhibited the role's inherent possibilities for tour de force. John Hale staged a rock *Errors* at the Theatre Royal, Drury Lane, in 1960, with Leonard Rossiter as a maniacally funny Dromio and Cy Grant as a singing narrator.

However, for the Royal Shakespeare Company in 1962, Clifford Williams restored the integrity of the text and released the play from the legacy of Komisarjevsky's frenetic humour. What was mounted at short notice as a stop-gap production was simply staged with clarity and conviction. The whole cast, dressed identically in grey, prefaced the performance with a series of patterned movements establishing a strong sense of company both in terms of the actors and the community of Ephesus. They added and exchanged gaudy costume pieces in a preface to the action that anticipated the intricate interplay of meetings and relationships, making a strong statement of equality and shared humanity. The set was just a steeply raked and stepped wooden platform and the style of the comedy was informed by the *commedia dell'arte* tradition, embracing door-knocking and key-turning in mime and Dromios in false noses.

There was real sadness at Aegeon's situation and the bewilderment of Diana Rigg's Adriana was comic yet touching. The production lived for several years. It transferred to the West End, toured to Moscow and Washington DC and was filmed by the BBC. Ten years after it had first opened in Stratford the production returned there. To many it was definitive: Clifford Williams had recognised that farce is 'rooted in human character' and that 'behind the mistaken identities and manic confusions of farce there are often genuinely dark and disquieting forces at work' (Michael Billington, *Guardian*, 21/6/72).

The play's rich potential for adaptation was exploited yet again in 1971 by Frank Dunlop (with Peter James) in a Young Vic production staged in a circus tent erected inside the Haymarket Ice Rink in Edinburgh. A public address system announced that relations between Scotland and England had been broken. Henceforth any Englishman found on Scottish territory would be apprehended. It was played fast (in one-and-three-quarter hours with no interval) with bagpipes, kilts and a car. The text was revised so that, for example, 'Come, sir, to dinner' became 'Come in and get yer mince'. The director was judged to have 'dipped the plot like a toffee apple into a rich coating of timeless Scotch comedy and it works'. Denise Coffey's plump and bossy little Adriana was especially praised, 'her machine gun, but absent-minded delivery of the longer, duller speeches is an inspiration' (*Plays and Players*, October 1971). It played at the Edinburgh Festival in 1971 and 1972, then ran in London. J.C. Trewin praised it as 'the most wholesale burlesque since Komisarjevsky' (*Birmingham Post*, 11/10/72).

When the play next appeared on the Stratford stage it was in a similarly elaborate production. Trevor Nunn's concept was informed by music and dance, with a vigorously contemporary score by Guy Woolfenden. It embraced both romantic ballad and a microphone-hugging Dromio. The production received widespread praise (and audience adulation) for its comic invention and it was informed by an astute response to the text. In an interview Nunn argued that what was 'vital to farce was a collision between what was impossible and what was ordinary;

the society created had to be a real one that the audience could recognise . . . bartering, buying and selling was at the heart of these people's lives. And the money disease intensified the confusion of identities . . . the characters became greater people because of their nightmare experiences; they saw more clearly and they rediscovered their generosity and kindness' (*Mid-Sussex Times*, 30/9/76). John Woodvine's Dr Pinch was 'a combination of con-man, an unsuccessful prestidigitator and an escaped lunatic who believes himself to be Henry Irving' and Judi Dench was an Adriana 'sweeping the plot before her like a tempest on skate-boards, knocking back the Campari with a repeated squeal of combined rage and dismay' (Bernard Levin, *Sunday Times*, 20/11/77). It was certainly fast-moving and very funny, yet Nunn did more than simply 'add songs'. Whilst the music was certainly used to express the excitement of a vital energy, it was also used to heighten and develop an emotional subtext. Irving Wardle identified it as a 'lucky play' for the RSC, feeling that Nunn had moved from the 'balletic economy' of Clifford Williams' version to the 'opposite extreme of lavish ornamentation' (*The Times*, 30/9/76). It was revived the following year and was filmed for television by ATV. It has subsequently been released on video.

In 1983 Adrian Noble's production for the RSC exploited elements of circus, silent film, music hall, *commedia dell'arte* and roaring rag-time music. The Antipholuses had blue faces, the Dromios red noses. This 'compendium of 20th-century comic acting' was felt to have 'more verve than wit' (Eric Shorter, *Daily Telegraph*, 10/8/83). J. C. Trewin regretted that the play had become little more than a punch ball for directors and he remembered 'wistfully what Clifford Williams did 20 years ago' (*Birmingham Post*, 10/8/83).

In the same year Manchester Contact Theatre set the play in the Wild West, with the Duke as the town sheriff and the whole production was laced with country and western music. The Dromios were played as mastizo women who had 'to adopt broken English on top of their sex change' (*Stage*, 19/5/83). Also in 1983 James Cellan-Jones directed the play as part of the BBC television Shakespeare. He chose to exploit the opportunities the medium offers for trickery and cast Michael Kitchen as both Antipholuses and Roger Daltry as both Dromios. He justified this decision by arguing that Shakespeare intended the two Antipholuses and the two Dromios in each case to be played by the same actor, glossing over the obvious difficulties posed by the end of the play. It may only be for three minutes that they are on stage together but in terms of the emotional fabric of the play it is a crucial period. This device cuts short an audience's cathartic experience, offering instead sleight of hand. This was even more apparent when Ian Judge employed the same device in his 1990 production for the RSC. Not only did trickery take precedence over characterisation but a fundamental dimension of the play's effectiveness in terms both of comedy and seriousness was lost. The play depends in some crucial ways upon the audience distinguishing clearly between brother and brother, servant and servant. The most successful productions (like the best criticism) appreciate that beyond the surface gloss there is a rich and moving emotional subtext.

PART TWO

The Taming of the Shrew

CRITICAL COMMENT BEFORE 1950

Samuel Pepys (1667)

9 April 1667 – To the King's house [. . .] and there we saw *The Taming of a Shrew* [*Sawney the Scot or The Taming of a Shrew*, John Lacy's adaptation of Shakespeare's play] which hath some very good pieces in it, but generally is but a mean play; and the best part, Sawny, done by Lacy; and hath not half its life, by reason of the words, I suppose, not being understood, at least by me. *2 Nov. 1667* – To the King's playhouse, and there saw a silly play and an old one, 'The Tameing of a Shrew'.

SOURCE: *The Diary of Samuel Pepys*, edited by Robert Latham and William Matthews (1970).

Charles Gildon (1710)

Catherine's harangue to her Sister and the Widow on the Duty of Wives to their Husbands, if the Ladies would read it with a little Regard, would be of mighty Use in this Age.

SOURCE: Charles Gildon, *Notes on Shakespeare's Plays* (1710).

Samuel Johnson (1765)

Of this play the two plots are so well united that they can hardly be called two without injury to the art with which they

89

are interwoven. The attention is entertained with all the variety of a double plot, yet is not distracted by unconnected incidents.

The part between Katherina and Petruchio is eminently sprightly and diverting. At the marriage of Bianca the arrival of the real father [Vincentio] perhaps produces more perplexity than pleasure. The whole play is very popular and diverting.

SOURCE: Samuel Johnson, *Notes on the Plays* in his edition of 1765.

William Hazlitt   (1817)

The Taming of the Shrew is almost the only one of Shakespeare's comedies that has a regular plot, and downright moral. It is full of bustle, animation, and rapidity of action. It shows admirably how self-will is only to be got the better of stronger will, and how one degree of ridiculous perversity is only to be driven out by another still greater. Petruchio is a madman in his senses; a very honest fellow, who hardly speaks a word of truth, and succeeds in all his tricks and impostures. He acts his assumed character to the life, with the most fantastical extravagance, with complete presence of mind, with untired animal spirits, and without a particle of ill humour from beginning to end.

SOURCE: William Hazlitt, *Characters of Shakespeare's Plays* (1817).

Henry Morley   (1856)

The 'Induction' to the *Taming of the Shrew* enables Mr Phelps to represent, in Christopher Sly, Shakespeare's sketch of a man purely sensual and animal, brutish in appetite, and with a mind unleavened by fancy. Such a presentment would not suit the uses of the poet; it could excite only disgust; if it were not throughout as humorous as faithful. Mr Phelps knows this; and perhaps the most interesting point to be noted in his Christopher Sly is that the uncompromising truth of his portraiture of the man buried and lost in his animal nature is throughout, by subtle touches easy to appreciate but hard to follow, made subservient to the laws of art, and the sketch, too, is clearly the more accurate for being humorous: throughout we laugh and understand.

Hamlet and Christopher Sly are at the two ends of Shakespeare's list of characters, and, with a singular skill, Mr Phelps, who is the best Hamlet now upon the stage, banishes from his face every spark of intelligence while representing Sly. Partly he effects this by keeping the eyes out of court as witnesses of intelligence. The lids are dropped in the heavy slumberousness of a stupid nature; there is no such thing as a glance of intelligence allowed to escape from under them; the eyes are hidden almost entirely when they are not widely exposed in a stupid stare. The acting of this little sketch is, indeed, throughout most careful and elaborate. There is, as we have said, no flinching from the perfect and emphatical expression of the broader lights and shadows of the character. Christopher is, at first, sensually drunk; and when, after his awakening in the lord's house, the page is introduced to him as his lady-wife, another chord of sensuality is touched, the brute hugs, and becomes amorous. Of the imagination that, even when there are offered to the sensual body new delights of the appetite, is yet able to soar beyond the reach already attained, Mr Phelps, in the details of his acting, gives a variety of well-conceived suggestions. Thus, to the invitation, 'Will't please your mightiness to wash your hands?' Christopher, when he has grasped the fact that a basin is being held before him in which he must wash, enters upon such a wash as sooty hands of tinkers only can require, and, having made an end of washing and bespattering, lifts up instinctively the corner of his velvet robe to dry his hands upon.

The stupidity of Sly causes his disappearance from the stage in the most natural way after the play has warmed into full action. He has, of course, no fancy for it, is unable to follow it, stares at it, and falls asleep over it. The sport of imagination acts upon him like a sleeping-draught, and at the end of the first act he is so fast asleep that it becomes matter of course to carry him away. The *Induction* thus insensibly fades into the play, and all trace of it is lost by the time that a lively interest in the comedy itself has been excited.

SOURCE: Henry Morley, *Journal of a London Playgoer*, 6 December 1856.

George Bernard Shaw   (1897)

The Taming of the Shrew is a remarkable example of Shakespear's repeated attempts to make the public accept realistic comedy. Petruchio is worth fifty Orlandos as a human study. The preliminary scenes in which he shews his character by pricking up his ears at the news that there is a fortune to be got by any man who will take an ugly and ill-tempered woman off her father's hands, and hurrying off to strike the bargain before somebody else picks it up, are not romantic; but they give an honest and masterly picture of a real man, whose like we have all met. The actual taming of the woman by the methods used in taming wild beasts belongs to his determination to make himself rich and comfortable, and his perfect freedom from all delicacy in using his strength and opportunities for that purpose. The process is quite bearable, because the selfishness of the man is healthily goodhumored and untainted by wanton cruelty, and it is good for the shrew to encounter a force like that and be brought to her senses. Unfortunately, Shakespear's own immaturity, as well as the immaturity of the art he was experimenting in, made it impossible for him to keep the play on the realistic plane to the end; and the last scene is altogether disgusting to modern sensibility. No man with any decency of feeling can sit it out in the company of a woman without being extremely ashamed of the lord-of-creation moral implied in the wager and the speech put into the woman's own mouth. Therefore the play, though still worthy of a complete and efficient representation, would need, even at that, some apology.

SOURCE: George Bernard Shaw, *Saturday Review*, 6 November 1897.

R. Warwick Bond   (1904)

Putting aside the exaggerated language, e.g. 'She is my goods, my chattels,' etc., as merely proper to the part [Petruchio] is playing, the single point which jars upon me is the order in the last scene to throw off her cap and tread on it. Though not intended to humiliate her, but rather to convince his sceptical friends, it always strikes me as a needless affront to her feelings, not excusable like former freaks as part of a wise purpose, but offered at the very moment when she is exhibiting a voluntary obedience. I suppose this retention from the old play would, like her oration, be defended on the ground of the required dramatic demonstration; but I feel it as a case where the poet has failed to reconcile the dramatic with the psychic requirements.

SOURCE: R. Warwick Bond, Introduction to Arden edition of *The Taming of the Shrew* (1904, revised 1929).

John Masefield   (1911)

[Shakespeare] indicates the tragedy that occurs when a manly spirit is born into a woman's body. Katharina is vexed and plagued by forced submission to a father who cannot see her merit, and by jealousy of a gentle, useless sister. She, who is entirely honest, sees the brainless Bianca, whom no amount of schooling will even make passably honest, preferred before. Lastly, she is humbled into the state of submissive wifely falsehood by a boor who cares only for his own will, her flesh, and her money. In a page and a half of melancholy claptrap broken Katharina endeavours to persuade us that:

> Such duty as the subject owes the prince,
> Even such a woman oweth to her husband.

Perhaps it is the way of the world. Women betray womanhood as much by mildness as by wiles. Meanwhile, what duty does a man owe to a fine, free, fearless spirit dragged down to his by commercial bargain with a father who is also a fool?

SOURCE: John Masefield, *Shakespeare* (1911).

Margaret Webster   (1942)

The 'brutality' and 'coarseness' of the main plot have been much criticised. Audiences do not seem to be so squeamish. Nevertheless, Katharine and Petruchio should not be played simply as an 'irksome, brawling scold' and a 'mad-brained rudesby, full of spleen', nor the progress of their relation interpreted solely as the taming of intolerable bad temper by equally intolerable physical violence. There is more wit inherent in it than that, and much more humanity.

Suppose that the two of them do actually fall headlong in love at their very first encounter; in his heart, each knows it of himself, but not of the other. This will take a little more ingenuity in the handling of the wooing scene than the set of variations on kicking, scuffling, raging, ramping, and all-in wrestling with which it is usually provided. But a few pauses, a few inflections will do it; the very moments of physical contact between the two of them, when Katharine is in Petruchio's arms, can be made to help.

If this is established, the whole play takes on a different tone. The contest will be one which we shall wish resolved. We shall know that Katharine, in her heart, wishes it just as deeply. It will be her pride that is broken, not her spirit. We shall enjoy watching the antagonists dealing blow and counterblow, not without zest, matching each other in a duel which is not based on a thorough mutual dislike, as it has sometimes appeared, but increasingly informed with love and finally overwhelmed in laughter.

Katharine has the harder task, for Petruchio scarcely lets her get a word in edgewise; but she is amply rewarded in the ironic wit of her final surrender. Agreeing, with deceptive docility, to call Vincentio 'fair, lovely maid', and to accept the sun and the moon as interchangeable planets, she contrives triumphantly to better Petruchio's instruction. Here at last is a 'marriage of true minds'. It is not the destruction of one by the brutality of the other. Petruchio could never have endured a tame wife.

Katharine has not become a cipher; she has merged her brilliance and masked her strength. This is not the woman to deliver the final speech as a groveling creature, fatuously exalting the male sex in general. Her lines are filled with a delicious irony, by no means lost on Petruchio, in their delicate overpraising of a husband's virtues. Katharine has changed her technique.

> I am ashamed that women are so simple,
> [*a wealth of meaning in this 'simple'*]
> To offer war where they should kneel for peace;
> And seek for rule supremacy and sway
> Where they are bound to –
> [*'quote' says Katharine for Petruchio's ears and ours*]
> – serve, love and obey. [*'unquote'*]

And a few lines further on:

> But now I see our lances are but straws,
> Our strength as weak, our weakness – [*with a beatific smile*]
> – past compare,
> That seeming to be most which we indeed least are.

At the finish the two come together in a beautifully negotiated, not an imposed peace.

SOURCE: Margaret Webster, *Shakespeare without Tears* (1942).

MODERN STUDIES

Muriel Bradbrook

DRAMATIC ROLE AS SOCIAL IMAGE: A STUDY OF *THE TAMING OF THE SHREW* (1958)

I

SINCE the approach to Shakespeare's plays through poetic imagery rather than character was first propounded, about thirty years ago, the unwary have seen it as an alternative method to the approach through character and story. The antithesis is, of course mistaken, since dramatic characters are only another, though the most complex, form of image, projections of the poet's inner vision, interpreted by the actors and re-formed within the minds of spectators, in accordance with those inward images which shape and dominate the deeper levels of thought and feeling in every one.[1]

This 'internal society' is made up of images first imprinted in early childhood, which though differently charged with love or hate, and differently arranged, are basically the same in all men. The more truly representative an artist's work the more completely can it offer to the artist and the spectator an opportunity to harmonize the conflicts of their 'inner society' by projection upon the persons imaged. Art thus becomes a species of abreaction, with a directly therapeutic function. No one need resort to those fanciful clinical reductions with which certain psychiatrists have attempted to explain the tragic characters of Shakespeare,[2] since this is a process which applies equally to the 'normal' and healthy; indeed the production and appreciation of art may be taken in itself as a sign of health.

It has always proved difficult to extract from the comedies any structure of images other than images of man; and some of these are well-known stage types, which might seem at first sight to be too stiff and rigid to supply the delicate and complicated adjustment required for individuals, each differing from the other. In real life, to see persons as merely fulfilling one or two roles, as merely a lawyer, a priest, a mother, a Jew, even as merely a man or a woman is to see them as something less than images of God; for practical purposes this may be necessary. The distinction between acquaintances and friends may be measured by the greater variety and flexibility of roles in which we meet our friends. Assigning and taking of roles is in fact the basis of social as distinct from inward life; in comedy, characters tend to be presented socially, in terms of roles, which, as in the case of classical comedy or the *commedia dell'arte*, are fairly stereotyped. Recipes for depicting clowns, young lovers, pantaloons, boastful cowards are necessary as the social basis for drama; the images must be current coin, negotiable in the common market, but the artist will always select, recombine, and break up the ingredients of the familiar roles.[3] He may in addition, by means of those subsidiary images through which one character in a play describes another (imagery that is, of the kind usually opposed to character-drawing) suggest attitudes and approaches for the audience which may run contrary to or modify the main presentation of the role; such images indeed constitute minor alternative roles for the character in question. Other images may not be verbalized but presented only in mime. Thus the constant grouping and regrouping of roles for any dramatic figure may be varied by different spectators or actors (who will notice those which suit themselves and ignore those which do not). So many men, so many Shylocks, Falstaffs, Rosalinds, Katharines.

To accept liberty of interpretation yet accept also community of experience is perhaps an act of faith, yet of rational faith. In looking at the role as image, it is necessary to remember always the nature of Shakespeare's theatre and audience, as providing not the last word in interpretation, but the first. He was addressing a crowd socially heterogeneous, mostly masculine, who required a delicate adjustment of native popular traditional art with the socially more esteemed classical and foreign models.

In his earlier plays these different needs are met by different groups, serious lovers, comic clowns; as his art developed, he succeeded in blending the roles more subtly and freshly.

II

The Taming of The Shrew repays examination from this point of view. It is an early comedy (before 1594),[4] with a main plot based on the popular dramatic role of the Shrew, but highly original in treatment, and a subplot drawn from an Italian model, Ariosto, as adapted in Gascoigne's *Supposes*; both deftly worked together and strengthened by an Induction organically related to the main theme. In *The Taming of A Shrew* mediocrity shows what could be done to destroy the inner fabric of the vision while preserving the outlines of the story.

The wooing of Katherine takes up rather less than half the play, and her part is quite surprisingly short; although she is on the stage a good deal, she spends most of the time listening to Petruchio. The play is his; this is its novelty. Traditionally the shrew triumphed; hers was the oldest and indeed the only native comic role for women. If overcome, she submitted either to high theological argument or to a taste of the stick. Here, by the wooing in Act II, the wedding in Act III and the 'taming school' in Act IV, each of which has its own style, Petruchio overpowers his shrew with her own weapons – imperiousness, wildness, inconsistency and the withholding of the necessities of life – combined with strong demonstrations of his natural authority. Petruchio does not use the stick, and Katherine in her final speech does not console herself with theology. To understand Shakespeare's skill in adaptation, the traditional image of the shrew, as she had developed from Chaucer's time, must be recalled.

Shrews might be expected to be especially common in England, that 'Hell of horses, purgatory of servants and paradise of women', but stories of shrews belong to the general medieval tradition of bourgeois satire, as well as to folk tales. Jean de Meung's portrait of 'La Veille', Eustace Deschamps' *Miroir de Mariage, Les Quinze Joyes de Mariage* and the *Sottie* have their English equivalents in Chaucer, the Miracles and the interlude. The Wyf of Bath is the great example of the shrew triumphant; in the Miracle plays Noah's wife evolves from simple boozing and brawling to a notable housewife, from a formula to a simple dramatic role. The gossips' league which appears in the plays is given a courtly setting in Dunbar's poem, 'Twa Mariit Wemen and the Wedo'.

Two short plays on shrews from the early Tudor stage are *Johan Johan* (1533/4) and *Tom Tyler and his Wife* (c. 1561). In both these plays, the pusillanimous husband is the centre of the picture. Tib, wife of Johan Johan, deceives her husband with the parish priest; his tremendous opening speech, in which he proclaims his intention of beating her, and beating her horribly, directs the audience's attention firmly to his abject but boastful state. Only at the end does a three-cornered fight develop. The remarkable miracles with which Sir Jhan the priest edifies the supper party, his smooth graciousness give him an odious mastery over poor Johan Johan who, deprived of his eagerly expected pie (like Katherine of the beef) and sent away from table is so poor-spirited a wretch that his sudden onslaught most unexpectedly relieves all the pent-up hatred of priestly hypocrisy which is the serious, though covert, intention of Heywood's farce.

Tom Tyler is another such meek-hearted husband; misled by Desire, the Vice, he has married with Strife. She, with her gossips Sturdy and Tipple, forms a drinking party, but chases Tom back to his work when he ventures to seek a pot of beer. His valiant friend Tom Taylor puts on the Tyler's coat, and undertakes the correction of Strife; but after he has beaten her

into submission, Tom Tyler foolishly confesses the trick and
gets a worse drubbing than ever. Two sage parsons, Destiny
and Patience, introduce and wind up the gay little frolic, in
which the rival conspiracy of men to combat the gossips'
league, though at first unsuccessful, is able with the church's
help finally to tame a shrew. Flat morality is in sharp contrast
to lively fun; the two artisans alone are characterized as people,
and this helps to concentrate the sympathy on them. They are
wage earners, whose wives do not share their work as country
wives must do, but are free to gad about with no supervision
and to spend their husband's earnings. The valiant Taylor is
contrasted with the hulking inoffensiveness of the Tyler, and
both with Strife, who is much less of a morality figure than the
rest, being one of those 'sklendre wyves' 'egre as a tygre yond
in Inde' whom Chaucer had celebrated, a true daughter of the
Vice. She exploits her husband as drudge and provider:

> What a husband have I, as light as a flye?
> I leap and I skip, I carry the whip,
> And I bear the bell; If he please me not well,
> I will take him by the pole, by cocks precious soul.
> I will make him to toil, while I laugh and smile,
> I will fare of the best, I will sit and take rest . . .
> I will teach him to know the way to Dunmoe.
> At board and at bed I will crack the knave's head,
> If he look but awry, or cast a sheep's eye;
> So shall I be sure to keep him in ure,
> To serve like a knave and live like a slave.[5]

All the moralizing is subject to parody, including that of
Patience, who leads the final song and dance, and, after the
fighting, justifies submission all round, with a perhaps unin-
tended hit at a very exalted personage:

> Which God preserve our noble queen.
> From perilous chance that has been seen,
> And send her subjects grace, say I,
> To serve her highness patiently.

Tom Tyler is close in spirit to the ballad and the jig; in 'The
Wife Wrapt in a Wether's Skin' (Child, 277) a timid husband
finds a surer method of punishment by proxy; his wife is too

highborn to spin, wash, or work, so Robin wraps her in a
wether's skin, and since he may not beat her because of her
great kindred, he beats the wether's skin till he has tamed his
wife. In a longer, more savage version, the wife is beaten till
she swoons and then wrapped in the salted hide of Morell, an
old horse. This seems to be a magic charm: she is to stay in the
salt hide for ever if she does not submit. The jest ends with a
party at which the wife shows her obedience, and the conclusion reads:

> Finis quoth Mayster Charm her
> He that can charme a shrewde wyfe,
>   Better than this
> Let him come to me and fetch ten pound
>   And a golden purse.
>
> (Hazlitt, *Early Popular Poetry*, iv, 179)

Tom Taylor and Tom Tyler, at the height of their triumph,
likewise rejoice in a song which puts a wife among the higher
domestic animals:

> Blame not Thomas if Tom be sick,
> His mare doth prance, his mare doth kick,
> She snorts and holds her head so high,
> Go tie the Mare, Tomboy, tie the Mare, tie.

The two plays differ in their appeal, though they are alike in
theme. *Johan Johan* has shown anticlerical colouring; *Tom Tyler*
in spite of its moral framework is the more frivolous. They are
alike in stressing the husband's part, and in the similarity of
name that links him with the tamer, who seems therefore like
another self. Johan Johan has been server to Sir Jhan the priest
and Tipple observes of Tom Tyler 'Belike he hath learned in
a new school'.

III

The theme of the School for Henpecked Husbands was one of
those taken up by Shakespeare. Although he used many
features of the older tradition, his play has the advantages both

of novelty and familiarity. It is unnecessary to postulate a lost
source play unless Shakespeare is held to be constitutionally
incapable of inventing a plot; for there is no sound external
evidence for it.

Petruchio, keeper of the taming school in which the 'tutors'
Hortensio and Lucentio are his immediate pupils (IV ii 54–8)
and Christopher Sly a more remote one, owes his victory to his
eloquence and his natural vigour. He enters full of enthusiasm
to see the world and enjoy his inheritance, blown by

> Such wind as scatters young men through the world
> To seek their fortunes farther than at home,
> Where small experience grows.
>
> (I ii 48–50)

and the first two dozen lines show his readiness to let his fists
walk about a man's ears. Shrews commonly marry old men, or
their social inferiors; Petruchio undertakes his 'labour of Hercules' in the spirit of an explorer, and the challenge of his
America, his Newfoundland, exhilarates him. When she breaks
his friend's head, he asserts with a significant oath:

> Now, by the world, it is a lusty wench,
> I love her ten times more than e'er I did.
> O, how I long to have some chat with her!
>
> (II i 159–61)

His demonstrations of physical exuberance, wit and bawdry
are provocative courting plumage, of Mercutio's style in wooing rather than Romeo's. The wedding night has as climax his
sudden bout of unclerkly asceticism. 'Come, I will bring thee
to thy bridal chamber' he exclaims, and the servants, stealing
back, observe:

> He kills her in her own humour.
> Where is he?
> In her chamber. Making a sermon of continency to her,
> And rails, and swears, and rates, that she, poor soul,
> Knows not which way to stand, to look, to speak.
>
> (IV i 164–9)

For contrast, there are no less than four old men. Katherine
is the first shrew to be given a father, the first to be shewn as

maid and bride; she is not seen merely in relation to a husband. The savage and hysterical attack on her sister is counterbalanced by the comic description of her bash at her tutor. She is unteachable; the point is explosively made.

At the beginning both characters are shewn at their least attractive. Kate's first speech is vulgar, thick-sown with proverbs; she threatens to 'comb' her suitors' 'noddles' with a three-legged stool and they in turn defie her roundly:

> From all such devils, Good Lord deliver us.
>
> (I i 66)

'This fiend of hell', 'the devil's dam', 'Is any man so very a fool as to be married to hell?' The image persists through the first scene, with the charitable alternatives that she is 'stark mad' or that she should be 'carted' like a whore. It is all very violent and in a 'low' style. Petruchio is introduced in a low comedy turn with his servant, and with a great flourish proclaims his intention to marry for money – a wife as hideous and old as the hag of the Wife of Bath's Tale if need be (I ii 69). Money is always to the fore in tales about shrews, and Katherine's father, by offering his younger daughter to the highest bidder, effectively shews that he prizes it; Petruchio after all takes little trouble to secure the best offer, but takes the first good one that comes. When at the end, he bets on Katherine's duty – a very safe bet, and a large one –

> I'll venture so much of my hawk or hound,
> But twenty times so much upon my wife.
>
> (V ii 71–2)

Baptista backs Bianca, but at the end sportingly comes forward with a second dowry for Katherine 'for she is changed as she had never been'. The 'old Italian fox' lives like a lord; but money helps to set the shrew where she belongs, within the merchant class. When Henry V woos another Kate, he thinks in terms of fair French towns, though he too finds that the role of a bumpkin has its value in a whirlwind courtship.

Petruchio gets a plain description of Katherine's accepted role; she is 'renowned in Padua for her scolding tongue'; but

his tongue is equally renowned among his own servants (I ii
106–15). Natural exuberance is matched in him by variety and
colour of speech; he has every rhetorical weapon at command,
from the high-flown terms of his address to Vincentio to the
fluent cursing which he bestows upon servants and trades-
people. The basis is bluntness, 'russet yeas and honest kersey
noes', and when he uses the high style it is a spirit of mockery,
in contrast with the learned eloquence, in the opening scene,
of Lucentio, the student.

The short scene between his resolution to woo, and the
wooing scene itself shows Katherine beating Bianca and Bianca
subtly retaliating under the guise of sweet compliance:

> If you affect him, sister, here I swear
> I'll plead for you myself, but you shall have him.
>
> (II i 14–15)

Katherine frankly wants a husband, and abuses her father for
preferring Bianca.

She is met by her wooer with a teasing shower of contradictory epithets: 'plain ... bonny ... sometimes curst ... prettiest
Kate in Christendom ...' that ends according to a plan already
confided to the audience by Petruchio:

> Hearing thy mildness praised in every town ...
> Myself am mov'd to woo thee for my wife.
>
> (II i 190, 193)

Kate's wits are waked, and a quick crossfire of repartee leads to
the traditional slap. If however the audience expect a fight they
do not get it; Petruchio, in his role of Hercules, simply holds his
Protean enemy fast, and indulges his humour of finding everything agreeable, provoking her with oratorical flourishes to
another wit combat and then issuing his absolute fiat.

> For by this light, whereby I see thy beauty,
> Thy beauty that doth make me like thee well,
> Thou must be married to no man but me;
> For I am he am born to tame you, Kate.
>
> (II i 265–8)

Katherine furiously tells her father that he has offered to wed
her to a lunatic. She repeats it, as later she stands waiting for

her bridegroom; he is a 'frantic fool' maliciously jesting with
'poor Katherine' as she tearfully calls herself, so that she may
be mocked by the world:

> 'Lo there is mad Petruchio's wife,
> If it would please him come and marry her'.
>
> (III ii 19–20)

It is in fact as a madman that Petruchio appears in the end.
He has assumed the part she assigned him, the traditional fate
of a shrew's husband, as the Abbess had lengthily explained to
Adriana in the *Comedy of Errors* (v i 68–86). The most important
passages about the wedding are given in description; the
broken-down horse, who is anatomized at much greater length
than his rider, with Petruchio's wild attire, prepare the listener
for the church scene in which the bridegroom swears, hits out
and plays the part of a madman who is also possessed. The
likeness of the pair only brings out Petruchio's pre-eminence.

> He's a devil, a devil, a very fiend
> – Why, she's a devil, a devil, the devil's dam.
> – Tut, she's a lamb, a dove, a fool to him . . .
> Such a mad marriage never was before.
>
> (III ii 151–3, 178)

Though at one point it is suggested that 'he hath some meaning
in his mad attire', no one seems to disagree when Bianca sums
up at the exit of the pair, 'Being mad herself, she's madly
mated'. The central point, the knot of the play, is here.

Petruchio has already invited the audience to stand with him;
he confides his plan just before the wooing starts (II i 167–79).
He will ignore Kate's forward behaviour and describe it instead
as if it were what it ideally should be. He will assume a virtue
for her if she has it not; maintain before her the image of
perfection which he is trying to create; or (if the audience are
prepared to be so subtle) will pierce below the surface of Kate's
angry, thwarted, provocative abuse to the desire to be mastered
and cherished which her conduct unconsciously betrays.

This mastery he asserts immediately after the wedding, with
an unequivocal statement of his legal rights, and a mimic
marriage by capture.

> I will be master of what is mine own –
> She is my goods, my chattels, she is my house,
> My household stuff, my field, my barn,
> My horse, my ox, my ass, my anything . . .
>
> (III ii 225–8)

In the next scene, after the full horrors of the journey – again given to one of the clowns for embellished description – Kate does not fail to address him respectfully as 'husband'.

Having drawn his ideal in wooing, he now holds up a mirror to her worser self, and gives her a travesty-performance of her own behaviour. She had beaten Hortensio; he beats his men. She had tied up Bianca; he hurries her breathlessly about. All is done, as he explains to the audience in the central soliloquy which is the grand exposition of his strategy, to 'curb her mad and headstrong humour'.

He is not preparing the audience for what is to happen, but directing them how to take it. The image he uses is that of manning a falcon.[6]

> My falcon now is sharp and passing empty,
> And till she stoop, she must not be full-gorg'd,
> For then she never looks upon her lure.
> Another way I have to man my haggard,
> To make her come, and know her keeper's call:
> That is, to watch her, as we watch these kites,
> That bate and beat, and will not be obedient . . .
>
> (IV i 174–80)

Kate is not to be wrapt in a wether's skin; a more subtle form of the animal tamer's art is called for, but it is animal-taming none the less. Only it allows Petruchio to maintain a pretence which may be taken as rather more than a subterfuge:

> Ay, and amid this hurly I intend
> That all is done in reverend care of her . . .
> This is the way to kill a wife with kindness.
>
> (IV i 183–4, 192)

He concludes with a triumphant and direct appeal to the audience (both Sly and the Globe spectators) to identify themselves with him:

He that knows better how to tame a shrew,
Now let him speak; 'tis charity to shew.

(IV i 194–5)

The full torrent of his eloquence is finally loosed in the tailor's scene, not without some occasional plain hints to Kate ('When you are gentle, you shall have one too', if she wants a gentle-woman's cap). All the usual desires of the shrew, clothes, feasts, company, lovemaking, are dangled before her only to be snatched away. She is shewn what it means to be Petruchio's household stuff; finally she capitulates and enters his private universe, in which 'it shall be what o'clock I say it is', in which Petruchio decides whether the sun or the moon is shining in the sky.

But this universe turns into the public one without warning; at the end of the act it is Kate whom he accuses of madness, when, obediently following his eloquent lead, she greets Vincentio in high style as

Young budding virgin, fair and fresh and sweet.

(IV v 36)

She meekly apologizes for 'my mad mistaking'.

Petruchio's last demand is a mere flouting of decorum; he wants a kiss in the public street. He gets it, with one un-called-for endearment that shows how far Hortensio's

Petruchio, go thy ways, the field is won

(IV v 23)

falls short of the fullness of victory. The shrew's role is transformed, and the charming young woman whom Petruchio imagined, he has now, like Pygmalion, obtained in the flesh.

Katherine has never been in league with society, like older shrews, but always at odds with it. Henceforth her relations to others, as she shows in Act V, are to be through Petruchio. Very early in the play he had based his confidence of taming her on his knowledge of a man's world:

Think you a little din can daunt mine ears?
Have I not in my time heard lions roar?
Have I not heard the sea, puff'd up with winds?

(I ii 196–8)

Have I not above all, he concludes, been in battle!

On the same ground Katherine bases her final plea for obedience. Her grand oration does not invoke the rather muddled theology which winds up *The Taming of A Shrew*, but recalls man's social claims as breadwinner, protector and temporal lord (those claims which Tom Tyler's wife so shamelessly ignored). A man

> commits his body
> To painful labour, both by sea and land,
> To watch the night in storms, the day in cold,
> While thou liest warm at home, secure and safe.
>
> (v ii 148–51)

Women are incapable of man's work; their minds should be as soft as their bodies. Kate's plea is in the high style, directly opposed to the 'low' style of her first speeches; but it has little more weight than the sermon of Patience in *Tom Tyler*. It is the lovers' battle that the audience is really invited to enjoy – the raillery which conceals attraction, the 'war' of wits which allows love and hate open play, in the fashion of Berowne and Rosaline, Benedick and Beatrice. Kate, though overmatched, remains the lusty wench Petruchio had sought; even at the end, she demonstrates her powers by haling the other recalcitrant wives before their husbands. She is not simply transformed into the image of Bianca, who at the opening had displayed such readiness to strip off her finery at Kate's bidding, as Kate now does at Petruchio's. Bianca takes Kate's likeness more completely; for with her violent retort to the bridegroom's plaint, 'The more fool you, for laying on my duty', the younger sister clearly assumes the scold. The third bride, being a widow already, has a tone of easy practised insolence; it is she who flings back the old taunt of shrewishness, Kate's original role, of which in the last couplet she is divested for ever.

> – Now go thy ways; thou hast tam'd a curst shrew.
> – Tis a wonder, by your leave she will be tam'd so.
>
> (v ii 188–9)

SOURCE: Extract from 'Dramatic Role as Social Image: A Study of *The Taming of the Shrew*', *Shakespeare Jahrbuch*, XCIV (1958): reprinted in *Muriel Bradbook on Shakespeare* (Sussex, 1984), pp. 57–71).

NOTES

1. For a brief and lucid discussion, see John Rickman, *Selected Contributions to Psychoanalysis* (London, 1957), p. 159.

2. See Kenneth Muir, 'Some Freudian Interpretations of Shakespeare', *Proceedings of the Leeds Philosophical Society*, VII, part I (July 1952), 43–52.

3. See Bernard Hart, *The Psychology of Insanity*, 5th edn (Cambridge, 1957), pp. 115–16.

4. The date of publication of *The Taming of A Shrew*, which I take to be derivative from Shakespeare.

5. This does not prevent her complaining of his unmanliness in striking a woman.

6. Taming a falcon by keeping it without food or sleep brings about a strong sense of conflict described by the modern falconer T. H. White.

Cecil C. Seronsy

'SUPPOSES' AS THE UNIFYING THEME IN *THE TAMING OF THE SHREW* (1963)

AGREEMENT among Shakespearian editors and critics is well-nigh universal that in *The Taming of the Shrew* the three plot strands of shrew-taming, love intrigue or 'supposes', and induction are interwoven with great skill and that Shakespeare, as presumable author, has brought them into a unity far superior to that achieved in the anonymous contemporary play *The Taming of a Shrew*. There is fairly general concurrence too, with some differences in emphasis, in what this unity consists of.[1] The accepted view appears to be that Shakespeare's art lies in the manipulation of the various strands of plot, with the shrew theme at its centre. It has often been held that the subplot of *The Shrew*, along with its language, is tamer than the shrew plot – a debatable matter – but that the two plots are nevertheless well-woven. Opinion among those who have considered the problem carefully seems agreed that Shakespeare's play is well unified and that the shrew plot is the force that draws a less vital subplot into this unity.

However, I believe that the unity of Shakespeare's comedy goes much deeper than the mere fitting and joining of the various plots, and I question whether the shrew theme is the principal instrument of this organization of parts. Instead, the subplot, with its theme of 'supposes' which enters substantially into both the shrew action and the induction, appears to offer a better explanation – one which will account in large measure for Shakespeare's superior handling of all three elements of the plot. If one is to judge by the way the subplot has

111

in most discussions been somewhat lightly dismissed or at least has been given relatively little emphasis, the likelihood appears that the full significance of the idea behind 'supposes', with its possibilities for dramatic enlargement, has been overlooked. There is no reason to assume that the word 'supposes' itself must be limited now or in sixteenth-century usage to mean only 'substitutions' of characters for one another in a mere mechanical routine of outward disguise.[2] For Elizabethans it had substantially the same values in meaning as it has for us: 'supposition', 'expectation', 'to believe', 'to imagine', 'to guess', 'to assume'.[3] If we keep before us this wider sense of the word, it is not difficult to see how it becomes a guiding principle of Petruchio's strategy in winning and taming the shrew, and it may well be the key to what Mark Van Doren notes as our secret occupation in observing the stages by which Petruchio and Katharina 'surrender to the fact of their affection.'[4] . . .

Both Petruchio and Katharina in the process of learning from each other make subtle adjustments in attitude. His motive for marriage is at first wealth, yet, while that remains an important consideration, he comes to see that she possesses other qualities which make her worth the trouble of winning over. These evidences of Katharina's real nature as against her supposed temperament, are present in the first scene with her father. Petruchio sees these traits and hits upon a novel method of bringing them into realization. One of Shakespeare's happiest strokes (as distinguished from *A Shrew*) is to exhibit Petruchio's own system of tutoring and thus closely relate the themes of shrew-taming and supposes. Petruchio's method is to suppose (and he is correct) or assume qualities in Katharina that no one else, possibly even the shrew herself, ever suspects. What he assumes as apparently false turns out to be startlingly true. His 'treatment' is a steady unfolding of her really fine qualities: patience, practical good sense, a capacity for humour, and finally obedience, all of which she comes gradually to manifest in a spirit chastened but not subdued. There can be no question about the justice of his tactics, if measured by the end product, for he enables her first to see herself as others see her, and then, her potentiality for humour and self-criticism having been brought out, she is able to discover in herself those qualities he is so sure she possesses. He is a superb teacher whose method is not unknown to many another teacher. And, since his system of make-believe is a profounder one than that effected in the more conventional, superficial, and mechanical disguises of the inherited subplot, there emerges a lively and pointed contrast between the two sets of complications. For, whereas in the subplot, although the theme of supposes is to some extent already enriched and deepened in Shakespeare's play, supposition is still based for the most part upon intrigue and the purely physical circumstances of name, situation, and the like, here in the shrew plot the supposition represents a deeper, more conscious effort, the will to believe and make real and establish beyond cavil what everyone else fails to see. The distinction is one between outer circumstance and inner conviction, a kind of triumph of mind or personality over a world of stubborn outward 'fact' not quite so real as had been supposed.

How all this is specifically realized in the play can be made clear by a detailed examination of Shakespeare's handling of the shrew plot; and reference to corresponding situations in *A Shrew*, which follows a more or less parallel line of incidents, will reveal how substantially *The Shrew* is rendered superior through the functioning of the 'supposes' motif.

At her very first appearance (I i) Katharina makes it clear that she will resist all attempts to make her anything other than what she thinks she is. Assumed to be a shrew, she will not change; so great is the power of suggestion upon her. She will not be made a 'stale amongst these mates', though Hortensio punningly tells her that no mates are possible unless she becomes gentler and milder. She bitterly resents being 'appointed hours' on what proves, however, to be a false supposition about her powers: 'as though, belike, I knew not what to take, and what to leave, ha?' (I i 103–4). All this whets our interest in Petruchio's forthcoming tactics of transforming her. In the following scene Baptista has almost given up hope that Katharina will ever marry, 'Supposing it a thing impossible' (I ii 123), as Hortensio says, but this turns out to be a false 'suppose'. On the other hand, Petruchio at that moment is just as confident that he can woo and tame her, and thereby accomplish the supposedly impossible. He who has heard the stormy sea raging like a lion and the thunder of artillery on the field of battle is not to be daunted by 'a little din' coming from a woman's tongue. His method begins to take shape even before he meets her: he will suppose the shrew's raging as neglible or non-existent simply by refusing to hear it. Soon he will meet her and then proceed from this negative mode of not positing (or supposing) *bad* traits in her to the positive supposing of such *good* traits in her as gentleness, good humour, patience, and obedience, which have not yet come to the surface. Already he seems to have an insight, lacking in her father, her sister, and others, into the potential existence of these finer qualities in Katharina.

This sharper insight emerges in (1) his first visit to Baptista and (2) his first interview alone with Katharina, both in Act II. For in his opening speech to the father, still having not yet seen the daughter (note how skilfully suspense is accumulated by allowing the audience to watch the building up of Petruchio's design), he asks (II i 42–3), 'Pray, have you not a daughter/Call'd Katharina, fair and virtuous?' He goes on to extol the young woman for her reported beauty, wit, affability, bashful modesty, and mildness – purely fictionalized qualities as yet, so far as anyone knows. His humour is to proceed with her *as if* these *were* existent traits in her, as indeed in the testing they later prove to be. He jauntily assures Baptista that the obtaining of his daughter's love will be no task at all, and when he hears Hortensio's account of Katharina's striking him with the lute, he interprets even this action favourably, as a sign of her being 'a lusty wench' and he longs 'to have some chat with her'. All her actions, whether or not objectionable, are to be assimilated into the image he wills and imposes. And, when alone, waiting for her to appear, he announces in soliloquy his plan of winning her by contraries, by playing a calculated game of supposes:

> Say that she rail; why then I'll tell her plain
> She sings as sweetly as a nightingale;
> Say that she frown; I'll say she looks as clear

As morning roses newly wash'd with dew:
Say she be mute and will not speak a word;
Then I'll commend her volubility,
And say she uttereth piercing eloquence:
If she do bid me pack, I'll give her thanks,
As though she bid me stay by her a week:
If she deny to wed, I'll crave the day
When I shall ask the banns and when be married.

(II i 171–81)

Then immediately upon her coming to him, he puts his system of make-believe to work. He assumes familiarity by addressing her as 'Kate' and smothers her angry remonstrances by adding that his 'Kate' is 'plain', 'bonny', 'sometimes Kate the curst', but 'pretty' withal, 'super-dainty', and possessed of mildness. Then follows the punning wit-combat, from which it is clear that he has taken her measure, most certainly as she has not his. In this exchange the many mutual animal epithets that fly between them are a key to the extent of this understanding of one another. Her attributions are most often wrong, his are right. Thus, her 'asses are made to bear, and so are you' is an inappropriate judgement proved wrong in the sequel; his 'women are made to bear, and so are you' is gentler, more playful, and more nearly valid, to say the least. He is far from being the 'jade' she calls him; and it can be held that more truly she buzzes like a bee, as he says, than that he acts like the buzzard (a useless hawk or stupid person), as she supposes. For him, Katharina is a 'slow-wing'd turtle' and a 'wasp'. For her, Petruchio is a 'coxcomb' and a 'craven'. The point here is not that Katharina comes off the worse in this wit-combat; indeed she carries on the battle on pretty equal terms with him. It is simply that in the choice and manipulation of epithets Shakespeare subtly suggests two sets of suppositions: Petruchio's, whose distortions and exaggerations are deliberate and cannily near the truth; and Katharina's, which are tinged with anger and show wrong judgement.

Petruchio next boldly exhibits to her his strategy of 'supposes', which she has not yet grasped. This he does by presenting a fine series of contrasts between unflattering reports he has *heard* of her, though for the most part deliberately 'supposed' (she is rough, sullen, frowning, limping), and what he has supposedly *found* in her (she is pleasant, gamesome, courteous, soft, affable, straight as the hazel-twig – indeed all the things he wants her to be, and which she is, in fact, capable of becoming). And after commending her as a very Diana, he announces that it is his destiny to tame her. By thus making veritable destiny out of his expectations, his 'supposes', he is asserting the triumph of mind and character. This is reflected in his reply to the returning Baptista's asking him how successful he has been in his suit (II i 284–5): 'How but well, sir? how but well? / It were impossible I should speed amiss.' He has, he says, found the daughter modest, contrary to all reports, and he has concluded in agreement with her, though that agreement is wholly his own 'suppose', that Sunday will be their wedding-day. When at this point others in the company intervene on behalf of the now faintly protesting shrew, who is by this time clearly losing the fight, Petruchio 'supposes' himself her defending champion against interlopers. Meanwhile, the game of supposes goes on merrily in the other plot, where, at the end of the act, Tranio, disguised as Lucentio, has apparently won the field in behalf of his master, and now, being required to produce a father and prove his claim of supposedly great possessions, wittily says (II i 409–10), 'I see no reason but supposed Lucentio / Must get a father, call'd "supposed Vincentio".' The motif of 'supposes' in both plots has thus been firmly established by the end of Act II.

When Katharina next appears (III ii) she still fails to see Petruchio's game as she waits for him to arrive at the wedding, falsely supposing him to be fickle, a mere jester, and a bitter one at that. When he does come late before the assembled wedding party dressed in the most outlandish way, he acts *as if* he cannot understand why they frown at him, *as if* they saw (III ii 98) 'some comet or unusual prodigy'. But we see something real behind all this strange pretence in his declaration (III ii 119): 'To me she's married, not unto my clothes.' It is as though the 'suppose' he adopts serves to point up the reality that lies behind appearance and as though he here is whimsically rebuking them all for mistaking the shadow for the substance. Then, despite his unaccountably rude behaviour in church, particularly his conduct towards the priest, and possibly on account of it, Katharina remains quiet throughout, and we see that his 'suppose' is gradually becoming reality, as evidenced in his reference to her (III ii 197) as 'this most patient, sweet, and virtuous wife'.

Although by her compliance she has borne out his hard-worked hypothesis at this point, she makes, shortly after this, a last serious attempt at a showdown, when her temper flares up at his insistence, against her inclination, upon not staying for the wedding feast. For a moment he relaxes the reins by letting her think she is gaining the ascendance, and then in mocking yet basically sound supposal of her independence of others, he orders her to command that the feast is to proceed. But the bride-who-is-to-be-obeyed has falsely supposed that she is not to be commanded by her husband, and Petruchio pulls in the reins, asserting his prerogative as master and ordering her to accompany him. Finally, at the close of the scene, he once again becomes her supposed champion, this time as her rescuer from supposed 'thieves', and encourages her against a supposed fear of them. It is all a masterpiece of imposed superior will.

The game goes on in Act IV with the arrival of the newly-wedded couple at the country house. Petruchio's good-humouredly bidding Katharina to be merry at a moment when she is tired and oppressed by the cold, uncomfortable journey thither, his rejection of the meat brought in to the hungry wife on the ground that he acts thus only out of solicitude for her against 'choler', his reported sermon to her on continency in the bedchamber, as if she needs to be guarded against the supposed raging passions of a body already worn out with hunger and fatigue – these are all pieces of the same device he continues to employ, all supposedly 'done in reverend care of her' (IV i 207), as he himself puts it, and all comprising, as he later confides in soliloquy (IV i 211), 'a way to kill a wife with kindness.' Even though the shrew has not yet been wholly tamed, his supposal of patience in her has led her a little earlier (IV i 159) to counsel this very virtue in him when he strikes the servant. She has already learned enough of that virtue which he so ardently and uncompromisingly supposes in her to begin teaching it to him.

With Tranio's announcement to Bianca in the following scene that Hortensio, heretofore supposed Licio the music teacher, having removed himself as a rival, is now intent upon winning and mastering a wealthy widow, and for that purpose has gone to Petruchio's country house, to his 'taming school', the two plots are neatly brought together again. Even the servant Grumio has learned something of his master's technique, as we see (IV iii) when he alternately offers, then withdraws her food, as if acting out of regard for her good. Petruchio, with his newly-arrived 'pupil' looking on, further displays his technique in the scene with the haberdasher and tailor, when he denies Katharina the cap and gown on a trumped-up supposal that these items are unbecoming to her.

Petruchio's triumphant strategy reaches its climax on their return trip to Padua. Here his unyielding supposal converts the sun to the moon and then reverses itself, to all of which Katharina dutifully assents, while he protests that it is *he* (IV v 10) who is 'evermore cross'd and cross'd'. Next, on meeting Lucentio's real father, who is soon to encounter an impostor disguised as himself, Petruchio 'disguises' the old man by sheer supposal as a young girl, then returns him to his identity as an old man. To all of this the erstwhile shrew assents, being now completely converted to her husband's supposal of things, no matter whither it leads. She now sees as he sees, and in a triumph of comic reversal she responds with a humour that redeems her from the hint, danger-ously close, of abject submission. This comes first in her well-known speech of acquiescence:

> But sun it is not, when you say it is not;
> And the moon changes even as your mind.
> What you will have it named, even that it is;
> And so it shall be so for Katharine.
>
> (IV v 19–22)

But her master-stroke comes when, in addressing the old man 'restored' to his true identity by Petruchio's whim, with still finer humour she neatly ties together *both* of her husband's two

feats of make-believe in a delightful, less commonly noticed
pun (italics mine). Petruchio had told her earlier in the scene,
during the sun episode,

> Now, by my mother's *son*, and that's myself,
> It shall be moon, or star, or what I list.
>
> (ll. 6–7)

Now she brilliantly concurs in his reversal of the old man's
identity with

> Pardon, old father, my mistaking eyes,
> That have been so bedazzled with the *sun*
> That everything I look on seemeth green:
> Now I perceive thou art a reverend father;
> Pardon, I pray thee, for my mad mistaking.
>
> (ll. 45–9)

The field is now won for Petruchio, as Hortensio has already
perceived. It may not be altogether fanciful to see an allusion
to Katharina's gradually-won perception of things, her buoyant
self-discovery, in the line 'That everything I look on seemeth
green'. In this final encounter, she enjoys more than a half-
share of the honours as the two of them enter into full
partnership.

The final scene of the play presents a shrew not only tamed
but enthusiastically joining her husband in the game of showing the others a profitable example of what wifely obedience
can be. Victory has crowned a method in which nearly all
expectations, or suppositions, have been reversed except Petruchio's. Hortensio and Lucentio, supposed masters of their
wives, are not masters after all. Apparently Hortensio's apprenticeship in Petruchio's taming school did not last sufficiently
long, nor was it thoroughgoing enough. Bianca and the
Widow, supposedly sweet and accommodating, offer more than
a trace of shrewishness themselves, whereas Katherine, the
supposed shrew, is really the obedient and understanding wife.
Petruchio has made of his supposal, originally fictive but later
supported by an insight into the real truth of his wife's nature,
a triumphant fact. The other husbands, acting on probability,
on the apparently predictable outcome, find their suppositions

faulty. Petruchio's is a triumph of the imagination, of a well-worked-out hypothesis, and Theseus' comment on the artisans' play in *A Midsummer Night's Dream* (v i 213–14) applies with equal truth to the psychological facts here: 'The best in this kind are but shadows; and the worst are no worse, if imagination amend them.'

SOURCE: Extract from ' "Supposes" as the Unifying Theme in *The Taming of the Shrew'*, *Shakespeare Quarterly*, 14 (1963), 15–30.

NOTES

1. Thus E. P. Kuhl, in 'The Authorship of *The Taming of the Shrew'*, *PMLA*, XL (1925), 551–618, demonstrates this unity on the basis of the style, vocabulary, and characterization, and further shows how Shakespeare has rendered Petruchio and Katharina into far more sympathetic characters than their counterparts in *A Shrew*, although with no mention of the influences of the subplot itself upon this transformation – a probability advanced in the present article. H. B. Charlton (*Shakespearian Comedy*, London, 1938), p. 77, comments upon the three English dramatic handlings of the Shakespearian subplot in this wise: in Gascoigne's *Supposes* it is the main and only plot; in *A Shrew* it is substantially the main plot; and in *The Shrew* it is a subplot, 'markedly subdued to the temper of the main taming plot'.

2. 'Substitutions' is the explanation provided by Hardin Craig to 'counterfeit supposes' (V i 120) in his edition of *The Complete Works of Shakespeare* (Chicago, 1951). This explanation may apply reasonably well to the context here, but it is wrong to accept it as Gascoigne's understanding of the term as he used it in his comedy *The Supposes*.

3. See, for example, the glossaries of Kittredge and Sisson in their editions of Shakespeare.

4. *Shakespeare* (New York, 1939), p. 49.

David Daniell

THE GOOD MARRIAGE OF KATHERINE AND PETRUCHIO (1984)

NOWADAYS, *The Taming of the Shrew* is taken in its entirety, without mutilation, crude business with whips (imported by Kemble) or announcements of the embarrassing incompetence of the prentice Shakespeare. It is winning increasing praise, for the structure of its interlocking parts among other things, and is becoming understood as a fast-moving play about various kinds of romance and fulfilment in marriage.[1]

Problems remain, of course, particularly with Katherine's final speech: modern solutions making it a statement of contemporary doctrine, or of male fantasy, or of almost unbelievably sustained irony, do not any of them seem to suggest that there is much for Katherine and Petruchio to look forward to in marriage. The speech is a disappointment after the tender moment of 'Nay, I will give thee a kiss' (v i 133) which suggested that something was coming with a lot of good feeling in it, an impression later supported by her having the wit to win Petruchio's wager for him. Moreover, submission, as it is first, and strongly, presented in the play, in the Induction, scene i, is denigration, a game played by pretended attendants; and *wifely* submission, shown even more strongly in the following scene, is sport by a page dressed as the sham wife of a ridiculously deceived 'husband'. It is all a pastime, and false.

Sly, however, disappears for good, and this is surely right in view of the serious point about marriage which can be seen to be made at the end of the play by Katherine. I want to suggest that it is a truly Shakespearian marriage-play, and as such takes

121

marriage seriously and makes as high a claim for the state of
matrimony as, from experience of him elsewhere, we should
expect Shakespeare to do. The way into this, I suggest, is
through the play's special sense of theatricality, linked with an
understanding that it is wrong to think of such a marriage-play
having a firmly closed ending.

That *The Taming of the Shrew* is imbued with a fresh excitement
about the potentials of theatre now needs little elaboration.
The most modern commentators take that as understood, and
indeed enlarge on the matter with some precision. G. R.
Hibbard in the New Penguin edition refers to

> bravura pieces, conscious displays of the rhetorical arts of grotesque
> description, farcical narrative, and inventive vituperation. Language
> is being deliberately exploited for effect; and what, in another context,
> might well appear cruel, outrageous, or offensive is transformed into
> comic exuberance by a linguistic virtuosity that delights in the exercise
> of its own powers.

Brian Morris in his Arden edition notes among much else a
contrast of 'physical violence with the eloquence of persuasions
and the rituals of debate'. H. J. Oliver sums up a major part
of the introduction to his Oxford Shakespeare edition with the
words 'Shakespeare certainly plays with the subject of theatrical illusion, and through the Induction and elsewhere seems
to warn his audience of the ambiguity of "belief".'[2] Theatricality is everywhere. The Bianca plot works because people
dress up as other people and assume roles. Petruchio, as is now
frequently said, plays a part like an actor until he has subdued
Katherine. It is universally agreed that the Induction spells out
clearly that theatrical illusion can have powerful effect, and
that this is important for the rest of the play. In the Lord's two
long speeches which so dominate the play's first 136 lines he
shows himself to be obsessed with the notion of acting, particularly with the careful creation of an illusion of a rich world for
Sly to come to life in. This is even more developed in the
following scene as his servants get the hang of the idea and
fantasize freely about what sensual delights are in their power

to offer. By the time Lucentio and Tranio enter to start the specially mounted play some quite large areas of the capability of theatre to create illusion have been coloured in.

Two things should reinforce the importance of this stress on theatricality itself for the rest of the play. The first is that the opening two scenes are not, in Folio, quite as detached as they are often assumed to be. The labels 'Induction, scene i' and 'Induction, scene ii' used in virtually all modern editions, though in some senses technically correct (if un-Shakespearian) only go back as far as Pope.[3] The Folio text begins firmly '*Actus primus. Scoena Prima.*' (and then forgets all about divisions until '*Actus Tertia*'). Though the non-appearance of Sly in the Folio after the end of the first scene of the Bianca plot causes worry to some critics, the Folio arrangement of the scenes might prevent a general tendency to detach him too far. As I shall show, it is not true to say that Sly's concerns are later absorbed into the main action – that Katherine's arrival in a new world created for her has, as it were, consummated Sly's action. But the relentless insistence on the creation of controlled illusion from '*Actus primus. Scoena Prima.*' does, as we shall see, have an important effect on the main actions, and particularly on the relation between Petruchio and Kate.

Secondly, it is difficult to miss the point about theatrical illusion when two early moments of transition in the first scene are so odd. It is peculiar that the hunting Lord's first thought on seeing the 'monstrous beast' (having apostrophized death in one line) should be to play such an elaborate trick. That is hardly an expected response. Then, to cap that, he hears a trumpet, and confidently expects 'some noble gentleman that means, / Travelling some journey, to repose him here'. But it is no such thing. It is 'players / That offer service to your lordship'. Their arrival, in view of the game of 'supposes' that he has in hand, is altogether too apt.

The two opening scenes bring together three of the play's chief concerns: hunting, acting, and the creation of an illusion of a powerfully rich world. As the second play-within-the-play begins (the first is 'Sly as lord') Lucentio and Tranio are caught up in a business which carries all three things forward. Lucentio has no doubt of the richness of Bianca: '. . . I saw sweet beauty in her face . . . I saw her coral lips to move, / And with her breath she did perfume the air' (ɪ i 162, 169–70). With Tranio, he is going to hunt her down: 'I burn, I pine, I perish, Tranio, / If I achieve not this young modest girl' (ll. 150–1). And he is soon involved in a situation which makes play-acting both essential and exciting. The direct wooing of Bianca is forbidden by her father, and there are rivals. Indeed, disguise and part-playing are positively invited, as Baptista encourages the rivals to produce 'schoolmasters' who will be kept 'within my house'. The theatrical game spins merrily, with Tranio playing Lucentio, Lucentio playing 'Cambio', Hortensio playing 'Licio' – and Bianca playing the adorable young girl. Presently a Pedant plays Vincentio. At the end of the play all the disguises have come off. Lucentio is himself and successfully wedded to Bianca who, married, is not quite as she appeared to be when wooed. Tranio is himself, and seems to have been forgiven, as he comports himself boldly. The Pedant and the real Vincentio have, in a good deal of wonderfully rapid business, faced each other out and the truth has triumphed.

All this, however, is more a matter of simple change of name. The Pedant does not even need a disguise. Lucentio is disguised, and Tranio puts on Lucentio's finery ('*Enter Tranio brave*', ɪ ii 214). Hortensio dresses up. But the deceptions that are practised lack depth, and belong to the very fast-moving world of amorous intrigue. Everyone receives the appropriate reward, and the two who are married at the end of this plot, Lucentio and Hortensio, have wives who, as G. R. Hibbard says of Bianca, have realized that 'deception is a woman's most effective weapon'.[4]

Inside this action is the other, that of Katherine and Petruchio. This can also be seen in the primary colours of hunting, acting and a special richness. It is so clearly set inside, like a jewel in a mounting, that the resulting extension of the significances comes to be unmistakable. By this device, the action is moved on to another plane, as it were: almost on to another dimension. If *The Taming of the Shrew* is seen as a set of Chinese boxes, then the opening of the last one has some magic qualities. Katherine is most firmly inset. Consider: the audience is in a theatre watching a play about a Lord who makes a play for a tinker who watches a play about two young Italians who watch 'some show to welcome us to town' (I i 47) inside which is a play about the surreptitious wooing of an *amorosa* by a love-sick hero and his rivals. Inside that is set another play about, by contrast, the very blatant wooing of her sister. Katherine does not say very much; compared with Rosalind, or even Beatrice, she is positively silent; but she is undoubtedly the heart of the play. She is introduced at five removes, it might be said, from street-level. At each remove the illusion increases. (We might note that Petruchio's very late entry into the action could well be said to make a sixth remove; the play has run for 524 lines at his entry, before which he is not even mentioned.)

On this interior plane, displacements are not of name or clothes, but of two entire personalities, a very different thing altogether. Indeed, Petruchio has announced himself vigorously from his first entry into the action, and he bombards Katherine, in the very first seconds of their first meeting, with her own name – eleven times in seven lines. He forbids his wife the new cap and gown the Tailor has provided, and his change of clothes for the wedding makes a mockery of dressing-up.

Nor are the displacements, like the others, temporary. Katherine, her 'lesson' learned, will not revert to being a shrew. Petruchio, having tamed her, will not revert to bullying. Except that I do not believe that Shakespeare's play says anything quite so obvious, or so final. If, rather than dramatic life on a different plane, there were a straight parallel here with the Bianca plot, it would have to be argued that Petruchio was 'really' a gentle person who put on roughness only while he was wooing Kate. To say so is to forget that he enters the play knocking his servant about and his servant calls him, twice, quarrelsome and mad (I ii 13–32). It is to argue too that Kate is 'really' an emotionally mature young woman ready for marriage thrown temporarily into desperation by her impossible father and sister. But within thirty-five lines of meeting someone who has come to woo her, who announces 'Good Kate; I am a gentleman' she is crying 'That I'll try' and '*She strikes him*' (II i 216). Both have strong violent streaks. Katherine says she will not be made a puppet (IV iii 103) to be knocked about, or not, for ever after. Rather, as the further inside, the more the increase of illusion, so the illusion now is of a greater 'reality', not less. Unlike 'Cambio' and 'Licio', Katherine and Petruchio are 'real' people. *Their* theatrical dimension allows them to do something quite different, and much more interesting. Katherine and Petruchio can be seen to grow to share an ability to use theatrical situations to express new and broadening perspectives in a world as unlimited as art itself. . . .

The Taming of the Shrew is a play unusually about marriages as well as courtships, and the quality of the marriage of Katherine and Petruchio might be expected to depend, as I said at the beginning of this essay, on more than a wink and a tone of irony, or a well-delivered paper on the necessity of order in the State. I am suggesting that a special quality of mutuality grew between Katherine and Petruchio as the play progressed, something invisible to all the others in the play and sealed for them both by Kate's last speech. It is surely unsatisfactory for Kate simply to flip over from one state into its opposite, or for Petruchio to have 'really' been gentle all along. I suggest that they have found, led by Petruchio, a way of being richly together with all their contradictions – and energies – very much alive and kicking. Beatrice and Benedick go into their marriage at the end of *Much Ado About Nothing* as witty and spirited as ever, but together and not apart. I believe that Katherine and Petruchio do the same, and do it through an understanding of the power of acting, of being actors.

That Petruchio sets out to play a part is now commonly understood. Theatricality, however, attaches to him rather more than has been seen. He is an actor – a man who loves acting with a full-spirited craftsmanship far ahead of the Lord's thin-blooded connoisseurship. He has a violent streak, and is impetuous: but he has an actor's power of control, as well as an actor's apparent sudden switch of mood. He arrives quarrelling with his servant and is still smouldering when Hortensio has parted them (I ii 1–45). But presented instantly with Hortensio's offer of a 'shrewd ill-favour'd wife' (which is only Hortensio's thirteenth line) Petruchio shows excellent manners, saying like any easy guest 'Sure I'll go along with it'. More, he says it as if he were Pistol, in high style full of classical tags:

> Be she as foul as was Florentius' love,
> As old as Sibyl, and as curst and shrewd
> As Socrates' Xanthippe or a worse.
>
> (ll. 67–9)

We then watch him move, step by step, towards Katherine. He learns that their fathers knew each other, so he is on visiting terms. He discovers that she has a wider reputation as 'an irksome brawling scold' (l. 184) but is loud in his claim not to be put off: indeed, he speaks like a mini-Othello:

> Think you a little din can daunt mine ears?
> Have I not in my time heard lions roar?
> Have I not heard the sea, puff'd up with winds,
> Rage like an angry boar chafed with sweat?
> Have I not heard great ordnance in the field,
> And heaven's artillery thunder in the skies?
> Have I not in a pitched battle heard
> Loud 'larums, neighing steeds, and trumpets' clang?
>
> (I ii 196–203)

Of course he hasn't: or at least, some of it is unlikely. He has only just left home by his own confession, apparently setting off for the first time (ll. 48–56). He is using one of his voices. We soon hear another one, in the one delicious sentence from the sideline with which he sums up Tranio's posturing (as opposed to acting) – 'Hortensio, to what end are all these words?' (l. 246). He visits Baptista to present 'Licio' (Hortensio) and sees for himself the peculiarities of the household. He understands the 'little wind' with which the father and sister increase Katherine's fire, and offers himself, in another voice, as a 'raging fire'.

He quickly takes two big steps towards her, first when Hortensio enters '*with his head broke*' (II i 140) and then when he hears as it were a tape-recording of her voice in Hortensio's report (' "Frets, call you these?" quoth she "I'll fume with them" ') and finds that she can make a theatrically appropriate strong action while saying a witty line, and that she has a liberated tongue ('with twenty such vile terms') – in other words, she could well turn out to have the stuff of actors too. He is eager to see her, and sets up in soliloquy a programme not based on violence ('raging fires') but on his actor's ability to present her with a new world for her to live in ('I'll tell her plain / She sings as sweetly . . .').

They meet, and fall in love. Both are taken aback. Petruchio is surprised to lose some rounds of the wit-contest on points. But he holds to his purpose, though she has struck him and made him forget the part he is acting ('I swear I'll cuff you, if you strike again', II i 217).

Thereafter it is possible to watch him acting his way through his relationship with her, and with everyone else. From the moment of meeting, he is hunting, and in deadly earnest. He uses all his skills to make worlds for her to try to live in, as he does, as an actor, even in what appears to be bullying.[5] (She seems, pretty well from the start, to understand him as an actor. 'Where did you study all this goodly speech?' she asks [II i 255].) In all his dealings with her, he acts out a character, and a set of situations, which present her with a mirror of herself, and in particular her high-spirited violence and her sense of being out in the cold and deprived. She who had tied up her sister's hands – apparently because she was dressed up (II i 3–5) – finds her own hands tied, as it were, in the scene with the Tailor, where she can't actually get her hands on the finery that was ordered. The speed of all this action in the central scenes, in the third and fourth acts, helps by presenting not so much development of 'character' as a set of projected slides, almost cartoons, of the wedding, the journey, the honeymoon, and so on. Katherine is not alone in finding it all 'unreal': it is part of a play.

But the play has a clear direction. It is always worth asking what Shakespeare does *not* do. Brian Morris points out what can be learned by seeing what appealed to the young playwright looking for ideas in the old Italian comedy. Shakespeare's Lucentio is not desperate for money, and has not seduced Bianca and got her pregnant, as Erostrato, his equivalent in *Supposes*, has done. Instead, he is seen 'to fall instantly, rapturously, romantically in love with her at first sight . . . It is this potential for romance, for love leading to marriage, which Shakespeare detected and exploited in Gascoigne's work.'[6] Indeed, no one in *Shrew* is desperate for money. There is no seduction or rape. The horrifying violence of such folk-tales of shrews tamed as have been sometimes produced as 'sources', or even analogues, is removed far away, mercifully, as is any tone of cynicism.

The direction of the play, for Katherine and Petruchio, is towards marriage as a rich, shared sanity. That means asserting and sharing *all* the facts about one's own identity, not suppressing large areas. Sly, floundering in the Lord's trickery, tried to assert himself like that (Induction ii 17–23). But then he sinks into illusion and is never undeceived. That is important. He 'does *not* become what others pretend him to be'.[7] Nor does Katherine. If she is a true Shakespearian heroine, in marriage she becomes herself only more so: in her case, almost as capable of future strong, witty, over-verbalized action as Beatrice. Marriage is addition, not subtraction: it is a sad let-down if the dazzling action of the play produces only a female wimp. But at the end of the play she shows that she shares with Petruchio an understood frame for both their lives. Whatever Petruchio has done, he has given her his full attention in action; she has learned to act too, in both senses. This, with the special ability of acting to embrace and give form to violence, is the mutuality they share.

Her first clear step was when she learned that simple deception worked (something her sister had, infuriatingly, known by instinct). She privately called the sun the moon, and then publicly greeted Vincentio as a 'Young budding virgin, fair and fresh and sweet' (IV v 36). Soon after this, she and Petruchio are shown not only married, but tenderly in love (the kiss). Her final step is when she shows to Petruchio that she has understood that they, the two of them, can contain violence and rebellion in their own mutual frame.

> Now civil wounds are stopp'd, peace lives again –
> That she may long live here, God say amen!
>
> (*Richard III*, V v 40–1)

are the last lines of the Roses tetralogy. The 'war of white and red' ends in a true union of strong, almost over-strong, dynasties, and not in the impoverishment of one side. (Sly had suggested such a link in the fourth line of the play: 'Look in the chronicles'.)

Muriel Bradbrook made clear what a new thing Shakespeare was making. 'Katherine is the first shrew to be given a father, the first to be shown as maid and bride . . .'

Traditionally the shrew triumphed; hers was the oldest and indeed the only native comic role for women. If overcome, she submitted either to high theological argument or to a taste of the stick . . . Petruchio does not use the stick, and Katherine in her final speech does not console herself with theology.[8]

Instead of the stick, or theology (which is certainly present at that point in *A Shrew*) Shakespeare makes Kate move herself further into, rather than out of, a play-world. Her final deed is to act a big theatrical set-piece, speaking the longest speech in the play, its length totally disrupting the rhythms presented by the other plot. 'Women', she says – that is, the conventionally married in front of her – are to be submissive. But she has been hunting with Petruchio as a couple for some time now, and she sends him, inside the speech, a message about themselves, Katherine and Petruchio, in the language of dramatized civil war. The play would founder – which it doesn't – if Katherine had merely surrendered to a generalization about 'women', and said nothing intensely personal about herself and Petruchio.[9]

She concludes, and starts the final run of couplets, by admitting that women are weak in such wars, and must accept it, and indeed, with a startling theatrical gesture she demonstrates it ('place your hands below your husband's foot'). She has successfully acted a long speech with interior reference to an imaginary history play, though only Petruchio can appreciate that. Partly she is telling him that the civil war in her is over, and she will not fight her rescuer. Partly she is rejoicing in their new world.

Brian Vickers demonstrates 'the speed and fluidity with which Shakespeare can modulate from one medium to the other as his dramatic intention requires'. He comments on the last lines of *Shrew* Act v, scene i ('kiss me, Kate'). He also analyses the verse and prose of the Sly scenes, making an excellent point about the 'new' Sly's blank verse, 'a step up to an assumed dignity and style', which is then exploited 'by inserting into this new frame fragments of the old Sly that we used to know ... The incongruity between style and subject-matter is now so marked that it re-creates on the plane of language the visual effect of Sly sitting up in bed, newly washed and nobly attired.'[10] I see a much developed and mature incongruity in the violence with which Katherine uses, in a speech about the experience of marriage, the vocabulary and rhythms of a contentious claimant to a throne from a history play. It is right that it is incongruous. The married state of Katherine and Petruchio has, from the end of the play, no connection with the married state of Lucentio and Bianca or Hortensio and his Widow. ('If she and I be pleas'd, what's that to you?' [II i 295].) For them, as Lucentio fatuously said, the war was over. For Katherine and Petruchio, it has barely started. This is the play which is beginning. *The Taming of the Shrew* has shown us ('So workmanly the blood and tears are drawn' [Induction ii 58]) a conflict of very close relationship – in play terms. Petruchio, having met her, 'thought it good' that she should 'hear a play' (Induction ii 131). Now she shows that she has understood. They go back to the beginning, as it were, to watch a play that they are creating. That is the true Shakespearian touch, going back at the end of a comedy, in a spiral movement, to the same point only higher. Thus Portia and Bassanio *begin*, at the end of *Merchant*, in a Belmont modified by the play-scene of the trial in Venice. Thus Beatrice and Benedick, at the end of *Much Ado*, start again ('Then you do not love me? ... No, truly, but in friendly recompense'), but now together and changed by the play-scene at the church.

Together, Katherine and Petruchio have filled-in many more areas of the capability of theatre than seemed possible at the beginning. In particular they have, like Beatrice and Benedick after them, created an open world for each other; they are themselves, only more so being now together. Their mutuality is based on the power of acting. Kate's speech is rivalled in length only by those of the Lord in the Induction when he is setting up a play-world. This shared power can encompass continual challenges for sovereignty, and even violence, together. Far from such things splitting their marriage apart, they will bring them into closer union. 'We three are married, but you two are sped.'

SOURCE: Extracts from 'The Good Marriage of Katherine and Petruchio', *Shakespeare Survey*, 37 (1984), 23–31.

NOTES

1. Brian Morris concludes the Introduction to his Arden edition (1981) with a long section 'Love and marriage', pp. 136–49.

2. G. R. Hibbard, *The Taming of the Shrew* (Harmondsworth, 1968), p. 8; Brian Morris, p. 105; H. J. Oliver, *The Taming of the Shrew* (Oxford, 1982), p. 57.

3. 'His contemporaries found the implied play metaphor of the induction device extremely attractive; Shakespeare himself seems to have preferred the less artificial form of the play within the play.' Anne Righter, *Shakespeare and the Idea of the Play* (1962), p. 104.

4. Hibbard, p. 8.

5. John Russell Brown, in *Shakespeare and his Comedies* (1957), p. 98, comes near to making this point, but then veers off to something else.

6. Morris, pp. 82, 83.

7. Oliver, p. 38.

8. M. C. Bradbrook, 'Dramatic Role as Social Image: A study of *The Taming of the Shrew*,' *Shakespeare Jahrbuch*, 94 (1958), 139, 134–5.

9. The play would go down even faster if she were using the forty-four lines to declaim a thesis about 'order', as maintained by G. I. Duthie, *Shakespeare* (1951), p. 58, and Derek Traversi, *An Approach to Shakespeare I: Henry VI to Twelfth Night* (1968), p. 89.

10. Brian Vickers, *The Artistry of Shakespeare's Prose* (London and New York, 1968), pp. 13, 14.

RECENT PRODUCTIONS OF
THE TAMING OF THE SHREW

The Taming of the Shrew is by far the most frequently performed of the plays considered here. There have been performances of the play in 42 of the first 94 years of this century at Stratford-upon-Avon compared with 9 (*The Two Gentlemen of Verona*), 13 (*Love's Labour's Lost*) and 14 (*The Comedy of Errors*). Limitations of space make it impossible to map out the stage history production by production. The detailed survey given by Tori Haring-Smith's book is recommended. The sheer number of performances reflects the theatrical vitality of the play and is evidence that it has box office appeal. Nowadays there is understandable resistance to the notion of the play as knock-about farce but it is clear that energetic, frenzied playing of the text supported by slick comic business often contributes to enjoyable theatre. Custard pies and strings of sausages featured in Tyrone Guthrie's 1939 Old Vic production. The Christopher Sly frame is usually included, often supplemented with lines from *A Shrew*. A wildly comic Sly unable to sit still (Stratford, 1939) or a cherubic Bernard Miles presiding over events from above (New Theatre, 1947) can make a significant difference to the relationship between the audience and the play. If Sly occupies the real world and ends the play, he displaces the audience's focus from Katherina and Petruchio. The idea of Sly returning home to 'tame' his wife is more likely to amuse than disturb. Highly stylised settings from *commedia dell'arte* to the Wild West have also served to locate the play in fictional realms sufficiently remote from the audience's world to avoid disturbing parallels.

Despite (or perhaps because of) the controversy surrounding the play it is still regularly performed. Three recent RSC productions contrast starkly. In 1978 Michael Bogdanov gave

133

the play a contemporary setting. He included the Induction not in order to set the action at a remove but on the contrary to break down any dislocating frames. Indeed the demolition was a literal one. As the audience took their seats a bearded, drunken young man in the stalls roughly resisted attempts by an usherette to eject him. No woman was going to push him around, he announced. He then climbed onto the stage and proceeded to wreck the picturesquely period set before falling asleep. Having thus sought to establish Christopher Sly as part of the same insistent reality as the audience, that drunken young man became Petruchio and the usherette Katherina. Through this reshaped opening Bogdanov was seeking to remove the historical and theatrical wrapping in which the play had become cocooned in order to shock a modern audience into experiencing the depressing and disturbing immediacy of a play written 400 years ago. Modern dress here was designed to make the audience uncomfortably aware of the parallels. The wager was set up by lounging men with loosened ties and eye shields grouped around a baize-covered table. Although Katherina's last speech was thought by some to be played ironically, others saw it delivered 'in a spiritless, unreal voice and received without much appreciation by the men, and with smouldering resentment by the women' (*Times Literary Supplement*, 19/5/78). Michael Billington commended Bogdanov's honesty in exposing the 'ugliness' of this 'barbaric and disgusting play' (*Guardian*, 5/5/78) but restated his antipathy to the play and argued it should not be performed.

Barry Kyle's 1982 production sought to suggest that Petruchio was helping Kate on the road to self-knowledge but that interpretation was more fully developed by Jonathan Miller, first in the BBC version he directed in 1980 (with John Cleese and Sarah Badel) and then even more starkly for the RSC in 1987. In both productions he cut the Induction and Christopher Sly, substituting at Stratford a Renaissance wind band to establish very firmly for the audience the historical frame within which he insists the play needs to be viewed. The design even incorporated a front curtain to reaffirm the proscenium arch. The director argues that 'The past is a foreign country with different customs and values from our own' and through the play it is possible 'to try to understand what is now the radically unvisitable past' (*Subsequent Performances*, p. 119). He believes that the play is about the need for order.

Brian Cox's Petruchio appeared stocky and tough but his knockabout with Grumio was playful. Hortensio came upon them rolling around like puppies. In soliloquy Petruchio allowed the audience to see his uncertainty: suggesting that his swaggering persona was self-protective role play. In the wooing-scene he fixed his eyes forward, not looking at Kate until 'thy beauty sounded' when he revealed powerfully how moved and taken aback he was by her appearance. His next line: 'Yet not so deeply as to thee belongs' (II i 193) was invested with sincere commitment.

Fiona Shaw was a disturbed Katherina. She wielded vicious-looking scissors on her first entrance, driving the points into the wooden wall and stabbing at the floor. Her instinct was aggressively defensive but Petruchio was not what she was expecting. When she slapped him, he paused before issuing a low-toned warning that she respected. Petruchio was never brash, never confident of his course of action and he emphasised his '*hope* to end successfully' (IV i 175). In her turn Fiona Shaw emphasised Kate's resistance to what she did not understand and her self-protective reluctance to give very much of herself. Their relationship was founded on a love that grew in tandem with a mutual respect. Scales of mistrust fell from Katherina's 'mistaking eyes' and there was a relaxed good humour in their banter with Vincentio. Kate now could share a perspective with her husband, a joke and even his hat. Her sister Bianca was played throughout (by Felicity Dean) as flirtatious and duplicitous. Her final words to Lucentio were sharply pointed and as Petruchio and Katherina left the stage Bianca defiantly tossed back a glass of wine. The action sought to cover a gnawing jealousy as she suppressed the painful realisation of the emptiness of her own relationship in comparison with that of her sister.

Bill Alexander's production began life on a small-scale tour. Its freshness and success with a younger, new audience led to

it being restaged at Stratford to open the 1992 season. The
Induction was included but in a re-worked, modernised text.
The opening scene showed the outside of a public house
(perhaps unsubtly named The Ugly Duckling). The Lord and
his men were yuppies whose fascination with the sleeping Sly
was snobbish and patronising. They viewed him as a specimen
of the working class and they thought it would be fun to 'mess
around with his mind' for a while.

The actors were a modern group hired to put on a play for
Lord Simon and his friends to celebrate Valentine's Day.
When Lord Simon met the actor in charge of the group (who
would play Petruchio) the social tension was evident. Tranio's
relationship with Lucentio took this issue further. His willingness to change places with his master was pragmatic self-inter-
est rather than servile willingness and Biondello's 'would I were
too' was discontentedly jealous. Tranio's forward planning; 'to
have the next wish after/That Lucentio indeed had Baptista's
youngest daughter' (I i 236–7) prepared the way for wooing
more for himself than his master. He was aided by a Bianca
who revelled in male attention. His desperate attempt to cling
on to his disguise when faced by Vincentio showed a man
fighting against the odds to cling to a status infinitely preferable
to his own.

The interpretation of Petruchio (Anton Lesser) and Katherina
(Amanda Harris) was in the Brian Cox–Fiona Shaw tradition with more emphasis upon drama as therapy but still
grounded in an emotional bonding initiated in the wooing
scene. Genuinely inventive was the device of casting the
watchers to play the members of Petruchio's household. Each
of them had a name and identity and their prominent position
upstage throughout provided a detailed on-stage audience
which functioned as both touchstone and provocation for the
reactions of the theatre audience. They were conscripted by
Petruchio, the group's actor-manager, and were initially embarrassed, awkward and amused. Clutching their scripts they
remained firmly themselves so a class-based resentment was
tangible as they were ordered to fetch and carry. Their
treatment of Sly was being meted out to them and they did not

like it. On cue Petruchio hit one of the girls and it provoked a complex reaction from both stage and theatre audience. Lines from *A Shrew* were included and so Sly's belief in the world of the play added further to the exploration of reality and illusion. His interruption to prevent Vincentio being taken to prison was moving, informed as it was by the sense that he alone among the stage audience was impelled to speak up for the innocent Vincentio as earlier he had held out his food to the hungry Kate. Petruchio reassured him kindly: 'It is only a play'.

One of the county girls was cast as the Widow. Putting her script aside she spoke for herself. The Widow's voice was heard then as that of a twentieth-century critic of the Katherina-Petruchio relationship. This emphasised the fact that Kate's last speech is essentially a response to the Widow's ungenerous taunts. In this production, Katherina was provided with a tougher opponent than the play's shadowy, anonymous Widow. In answering her Katherina achieved a double triumph. At the end of the play the girl who had been enlisted to play the Widow chose to leave with the actors. The metatheatrical dimension freed the text from the stultifying straitjacket of being interpreted as a one-issue play.

PART THREE

The Two Gentlemen of Verona

CRITICAL COMMENT BEFORE 1950

Alexander Pope   (1725)

This whole Scene [I ii] like many others in these Plays (some of which I believe were written by *Shakespeare*, and others interpolated by the Players), is compos'd of the lowest and most trifling conceits, to be accounted for only from the gross taste of the age he liv'd in; *Populo ut placerent.* I wish I had authority to have them out, but I have done all I could, set a mark of reprobation upon them; throughout this edition.†††

SOURCE: Alexander Pope, *Preface to Shakespear's Work* (1725).

Benjamin Victor   (1762)

It is the general opinion that this comedy abounds with weeds, and there is no one, I think, will deny, who peruses it with attention, that it is adorned with several poetical flowers such as the hand of a Shakespeare alone could raise. The rankest of those weeds I have endeavoured to remove; but was not a little solicitous lest I should go too far and, while I fancy'd myself grubbing up a weed, should heedlessly cut the threads of a flower.

The other part of my design, which was to give a greater uniformity to the scenery and a connection and consistency to the fable (which in many places is visibly wanted), will be deemed of more importance if it should be found to be executed with success.

141

SOURCE: Benjamin Victor, from his adaptation of *The Two Gentlemen of Verona*, performed at Drury Lane on 22 December 1762. He provided two additional scenes for Launce and Speed in the last act.

Samuel Johnson   (1765)

When I read this play I cannot but think that I discover both in the serious and ludicrous scenes the language and sentiments of Shakespeare. It is not indeed one of his most powerful effusions, it has neither many diversities of character, nor striking delineations of life, but it abounds in γνωμαι [maxims] beyond most of his plays and few have more lines or passages which, singly considered, are eminently beautiful. I am yet inclined to believe that it was not very successful and suspect that it has escaped corruption only because being seldom played it was less exposed to the hazards of transcription.

In this play there is a strange mixture of knowledge and ignorance, of care and negligence. The versification is often excellent, the allusions are learned and just; but the author conveys his heroes by sea from one inland town to another in the same country; he places the Emperor at Milan and sends his young men to attend him, but never mentions him more; he makes Proteus, after an interview with Silvia, say he has only seen her picture and if we may credit the old copies he has by mistaking places left his scenery inextricable. The reason of all this confusion seems to be that he took his story from a novel which he sometimes followed and sometimes forsook, sometimes remembered and sometimes forgot.

SOURCE: Samuel Johnson, *Notes on the Plays* in his edition of 1765.

William Hazlitt (1817)

This is little more than the first outlines of a comedy loosely sketched in. It is the story of a novel dramatised with very little labour or pretension; yet there are passages of high poetical spirit, and of inimitable quaintness of humour, which are undoubtedly Shakespeare's, and there is throughout the conduct of the fable a careless grace and felicity which marks it for his. . . . The style of the familiar parts of this comedy is indeed made up of conceits – low they may be for what we know, but then they are not poor, but rich ones. The scene of Launce with his dog (not that in the second, but that in the fourth act) is a perfect treat in the way of farcical drollery and invention; nor do we think Speed's manner of proving his master to be in love deficient in wit or sense, though the style may be criticised as not simple enough for the modern taste.

SOURCE: William Hazlitt, *Characters of Shakespeare's Plays* (1817).

John Masefield (1911)

Shakespeare's method is simple. He shows us two charming young men becoming morally blind with passion, in a company not so blinded. The only other inconstant person in the play (Sir Thurio) is inconstant from that waterlike quality in the mind that floods with the full moon, and ebbs like a neap soon after. Even the members of the sub-plot, the two servants, are constant, the one to his master, who beats him, the other to the dog that gets him beaten. . . . The two gentlemen are limited by the play's needs. The figure of Valentine is the more

complete of the two. He is an interesting study of one of those
grave young men who, when tested by life, show themselves
wise beyond their years. Among the minor characters, that of
Eglamour, an image of constancy to a dead woman, is the most
beautiful. He is one of the strange, many-sorrowed souls,
vowed to an idea, to whom Shakespeare's characters so often
turn when the world bears hard.

SOURCE: John Masefield, *William Shakespeare* (1911).

A. Quiller-Couch   (1921)

Shakespeare, first and last, was sadly addicted to finishing off a
play in a hurry. But the final scene of the Two Gentlemen is
vitiated (as we hope to show) by a flaw too unnatural to be
charged upon Shakespeare. . . . We come now to the final
scene, and, in particular, to the passage which has offended so
many critics of sensibility: the lines in which Valentine 'emp-
ties' – as the Germans say – 'the baby with the bath,' and after
pardoning his false friend, proceeds to give away (in every
sense) his most loyal lady-love to her would-be ravisher. [cites
v iv 73–85] 'All that was mine in Silvia I give thee' – one's
impulse, upon this declaration, is to remark that there are, by
this time, no gentlemen in Verona.

  We must not, without a second thought, pronounce that this
and the preceding lines are not Shakespeare's – could not have
been written by Shakespeare. They are uncouth: but he wrote,
first and last, many uncouth lines, and his present editors will
not challenge an obvious retort by making affidavit of their
private conviction – firm though it be – that he never wrote
these. They are dramatically inconsistent: they disappoint all
that we suppose ourselves to know of Valentine's character,
and so unexpectedly, that we feel it like a slap in the face. . . .
We believe, at any rate, that no one can re-read this scene

carefully without detecting that pieces of it are Shakespeare's and other pieces have been inserted by a 'faker' who was not only not Shakespeare, but did not possess even a rudimentary ear for blank verse. . . .

And where is Silvia in all this business? She is merely left. She utters not a word after Valentine's pseudo-magnificent, pseudo-romantic, renunciation. 'A curious essay,' says Dowden, 'might be written upon the silences of some of the characters of Shakespeare.' It would be an ingenious one if it could account for Silvia's silence here save by the alternatives, either of her being sick and tired of both her lovers, or of the whole scene's being (as we submit) a piece of theatre botchwork patched upon the original. . . .

We know that when Shakespeare was old enough, and craftsman enough, to devise the 'recognition' in the last scene of Cymbeline, with its

> Why did you throw your wedded lady from you?

he could do better: and we believe that even in The Two Gentlemen he wrote something which, if theatrically ineffective, was better, because more natural, than the text allows us to know.

SOURCE: A. Quiller-Couch, Introduction to New Shakespeare edition of *The Two Gentleman of Verona* (1921).

H. B. Charlton (1938)

Launce is another who insists on remaining in the memory. He has no real right within the play, except that gentlemen must have servants, and Elizabethan audiences must have clowns. But coming in thus by a back-door, he earns an unexpected importance in the play. Seen side by side with Speed, his origin is clear. Whilst Speed belongs to the purely theatrical family of the Dromios, with their punning and logic-chopping asininities, Launce harks back to the native Costard. And as Costard shows his relationship to Bottom by his skill in village theatricals, so Launce reveals by his wooing his family connection with Touchstone, and Touchstone's Audrey, who was a poor thing, but his own. All the kind of the Launces are thus palpably a mighty stock. Their worth, compared with that of the Speeds and the Dromios, is admirably indicated by Launce's consummate use of Speed's curiosity and of his better schooling. Launce gets his letter deciphered; he gets also an opportunity to display his own superior breeding, and to secure condign punishment for the ill-mannered Speed: 'now will he be swinged for reading my letter; an unmannerly slave, that will thrust himself into secrets! I'll after, to rejoice in the boy's correction'.

Launce is happiest with his dog. Clownage can go no farther than the pantomimic representation, with staff and shoe and dog, of the parting from his home-folks. Laughter is hilarious at Launce's bitter grief that his ungrateful cur declined to shed a tear. That Launce should expect it is, of course, the element of preposterous incongruity which makes him a clown. But when he puts his complaint squarely, that his 'dog has no more pity in him than a dog', the thrust pierces more than it was meant to. Romance itself has expected no less largely of Valentine, of Proteus, and of the rest. It has demanded that man shall be more than man, and has laid upon him requisitions passing the ability of man to fulfil. At the bidding of romance, Valentine and Proteus have become what they are in the play, and the one thing they are not is men like other men. A further incident in which Launce is concerned takes on a similarly unexpected significance. He has made as great a sacrifice as did Valentine himself: he has given up his own cur in place of the one which Proteus entrusted him to take to Silvia. But the effect hardly suggests that self-sacrifice is worldly-wise. And so once more, it seems to bring into question the worldly worth of the code which sanctifies such deeds. Unintentionally, Launce has become the means by which the incompatibilities and the unrealities of romantic postulates are laid bare. And Launce is palpably the stuff of comedy: awakening our comic sense, he invariably sharpens our appreciation of the particular range of incongruities which are the province of comedy – the incongruity between what a thing really is and what it is taken to be.

Romance, and not comedy, has called the tune of *The Two Gentlemen of Verona*, and governed the direction of the action of the play. That is why its creatures bear so little resemblance to men of flesh and blood. Lacking this, they are scarcely dramatic figures at all; for every form of drama would appear to seek at least so much of human nature in its characters. But perhaps the characters of the Two Gentlemen are comic in a sense which at first had never entered the mind of their maker. Valentine bids for the sympathy, but not for the laughter of the audience: the ideals by which he lives are assumed to have the world's approbation. But in execution they involve him in most ridiculous plight. He turns the world from its compassionate approval to a mood of sceptical questioning. The hero of romantic comedy appears no better than its clowns. And so topsy-turvy is the world of romance that apparently the one obvious way to be reputed in it for a fool, is to show at least a faint sign of discretion and of common sense. Thurio, for instance, was cast for the dotard of the play, and of course he is not without egregious folly. But what was meant in the end to annihilate him with contempt, turns out quite otherwise. Threatened by Valentine's sword, he resigns all claim to Silvia, on the ground that he holds him but a fool that will endanger his body for a girl that loves him not. The audience is invited to call Thurio a fool for showing himself to be the one person in the play with a modicum of worldly wisdom, a respect for the limitations of human nature, and a recognition of the conditions under which it may survive. Clearly, Shakespeare's first attempt to make romantic comedy had only succeeded so far that it had unexpectedly and inadvertently made romance comic. The real problem was still to be faced.

SOURCE: H. B. Charlton, *Shakespearian Comedy* (1938).

H. T. Price   (1941)

Then Valentine gives Silvia to Proteus. It ought to be clear that by this action Shakespeare is wringing the last drop of silliness out of Valentine's conventions. With the idea of smashing a particularly ridiculous convention, Shakespeare has set out to prove Valentine a fool. Any explanation of this scene that implies that Shakespeare was serious does rather less than justice to Shakespeare's sense of humor.

SOURCE: H. T. Price, 'Shakespeare as a Critic', *Philological Quarterly*, xx, III (July 1941).

MODERN STUDIES

Harold F. Brooks

TWO CLOWNS IN A COMEDY (TO SAY NOTHING OF THE DOG): SPEED, LAUNCE (AND CRAB) IN '*THE TWO GENTLEMEN OF VERONA*' (1963)

DESPITE warm appreciation of Launce as a comic character, it has often been denied that he and Speed have an organic part in the structure of *The Two Gentlemen of Verona*. According to Professor H. B. Charlton, for instance, 'Launce has no real right within the play except that gentlemen must have servants, and Elizabethan audiences must have clowns.'[1] This is to see the dramatic structure too exclusively in terms of plot.[2] There does appear to be only a single place where the behaviour of one of the clowns contributes to the progress of events; the critical moment when Julia, disguised as 'Sebastian', seeks service with her truant Proteus. Here, Proteus is influenced by Launce's recent misconduct: he is the readier to enlist the well-bred Sebastian because Launce has been missing for two days, and by the account he now gives of himself is proved too boorish to be entrusted with further missions to Silvia. Without question, dramatic unity is stronger when, as with Bottom or Dogberry, the clown impinges upon the romantic plot more obviously and decisively than this. There can be unity however, resulting from development of theme as well as from development of plot: when a play has a plot and themes, the *action*

149

(which is what must have unity) may be regarded as comprising the development of both.[3] Side by side with the causal sequence that carries forward his romantic plot, Shakespeare, in the parts he has given to Speed and Launce, is developing his play by means of comic parallels that illustrate and extend its themes. The parallels, as well as the causal sequence, are part of the organic structure.

They have not gone altogether unrecognized. '*Two Gentlemen* is . . . more integrated and patterned than has often been supposed,' writes Professor Danby in the *Critical Quarterly* (Winter, 1960); and although it is not his purpose to demonstrate the particular pattern I am concerned with, he remarks an item of it: 'Even Launce and his dog going through the pantomime of leave-taking translate the central seriousness into a comic mode.' The existence of the pattern, and half a dozen of its leading features, were emphasized by R. W. Bond in the old Arden edition (1906); he was the editor of Lyly, and familiar with the same technique in him. Had Bond's observation been fully accepted, and his fifteen lines on the subject been followed up, there might have been no occasion, by this time, to say more. But in the New Cambridge Shakespeare edition (1921) Quiller-Couch took no notice of them; and Professor T. W. Baldwin's reference, in *William Shakespeare's Five-Act Structure* (1947), is sceptical, perhaps because he is thinking more in terms of characters than of themes: 'Bond, indeed, has suggested,' he writes, 'that each servant is a comic foil to and partial parody of his master, but this appears true to me only in its most general sense.'

The themes in question are those of friendship and love, the first and second subjects of *Two Gentlemen*, which, as in *The Knight's Tale* and some of Shakespeare's own sonnets, are treated in relation to each other. The friendship is that which in Renaissance literature is constantly held up as an exemplar of noble life.[4] The love is courtly.[5] Julia, seeming at first full of 'daunger', soon reveals her 'pité',[6] and later sets out as Love's pilgrim. Valentine, like Troilus in Chaucer, begins as the Love-heretic, but quickly becomes the penitent votary. Proteus, from Love-idolator falls to Love-traitor, until reclaimed and redeemed from his treachery both to love and friendship by the sacrificial fidelity of his lover and the sacrificial magnanimity of his friend. Thurio is Love's Philistine, and the clowns, in this pattern, are Love's plebeians.

From Launce's first entry, each of his scenes refers, by burlesque parallels, to the themes of friendship on the one hand and of love on the other. Speed's scenes earlier, so far as I can see, do not depend on this particular sort of parallelism: Speed is not shown in burlesque roles as lover or friend, except momentarily, when he explains a piece of negligence, comparable to his lovelorn master's, by confessing he was in love with his bed. The scenes for the clowns are mostly built up from comic turns. Together, they play at cross-questions and crooked answers; Launce has his monologue of impersonations with the aid of comic 'props'; and Speed on his first appearance (I i) has his mock-disputation (like Dromio of Syracuse) and his routine of witty begging (like Feste).[7] The episode, all the same, is not irrelevant clownage. It underlines at a single stroke both Proteus' friendship and his love: the friendship with Valentine has allowed him to make Speed, his friend's man not his own, carry his love-letter to Julia. So, at the outset, a clown is linked with both themes. Speed reports Julia 'hard as steel'; thus preparing for the next scene of her metamorphosis to the compassionate lover. Proteus has exclaimed already:

> Thou, Julia, thou hast metamorphis'd me;[8]

the motif is implied in his name, and belongs especially to him: yet Julia and Valentine are each to know metamorphoses, too. In the mock-disputation and its sequel here, this motif (as elsewhere in Shakespeare) is accompanied by imagery of human beings as animals. Speed (or alternatively Valentine) is a 'sheep', and he and Julia are 'muttons'. He is, moreover, a 'lost mutton', and in literal fact is in search of his master: he is in peril of failing to sail with him, a serious defection. The situation, then, and some of the backchat, are in keeping with a drama where defection, near-loss, and seeking are to be important: where Proteus' defection is almost to lose him his true self,[9] and cause him to be lost to Valentine and Julia; where

Valentine is almost to lose Silvia, and the heroines must seek their
lovers. Among the clown-scenes themselves, two others form a
series with this one. Launce at his parting (II iii) is likewise in
danger of missing the ship, and is warned that he would thereby
lose his master and his service. And his ultimate dismissal in
favour of 'Sebastian' (IV iv) echoes not only that warning, but
Proteus' final comment on Speed here, that he is too unprepos-
sessing a love-messenger and another must be found.

Some of these correspondences an audience will never be
consciously aware of, though it will be affected by them. In the
next clown-episode, in II i, everyone sees the relation between
Speed's humour and Valentine's high-flown romance. Speed
comments directly on his master's love-melancholy. In taking
over Valentine's former part as critic of love's absurdities, he
helps to mark the metamorphosis:[10] the critic of Proteus' love
has become vulnerable to similar criticism himself. The parallels are brought out when Speed quotes him on Proteus and
tells him he is blinder now than Proteus was. As critics of love,
Speed and Valentine are not, of course, the same. With the eye
of yet unconverted scepticism, Valentine had seen its irration-
ality and its exactions; with the plebeian eye, permanently
limited though clear, Speed sees its absence of practical common sense. In one respect, his function is that of the Duck and
the Goose in Chaucer's Council of Birds, assembled on St
Valentine's Day. Love in the courtly manner, partly because it
is so stylized, is very liable, once we entertain an inadequate,
everyday view of it, to arouse mere mockery and impatience.
Aware of this, both Chaucer and Shakespeare embody the
dangerous attitude within the poem or play itself, so as to
control and place it; but they place it somewhat differently. In
Chaucer, the plebeian view, whatever sympathy he may have
with it outside the poem, is introduced chiefly to be rejected.
But when Speed protests that while his master may dine on
Silvia's favour, he himself needs meat, this is not 'a parfit
resoun of a goos': it commands sympathy within the ambit of
the play, and partial assent: it is one contribution to the
complex dramatic image of courtly love that Shakespeare is
building up.

In contrast, there is the admired elegance of the device by which Silvia confesses her love for Valentine. The dullness which prevents his understanding it is a perfectly orthodox effect of love-melancholy;[11] besides, as her true 'servant' he has too much humility to be expecting any such confession. That so ultra-courtly a gambit has to be explained to him by the uncourtly Speed is humorous enough. And it is ironical that Speed should do him this office of a good friend in his love, when his courtly friend Proteus is soon to be his false rival. Diffidently blind here in love, Valentine is to be too rashly and confidingly blind in friendship. The theme of blindness and sight, especially love-sight, is one of the most central in the play. It is because Proteus' fancy is bred only in his eyes, which until the dénouement see no further than outward beauty, that he is altogether unstable.[12] The truest praise of Silvia is that

> Love doth to her eyes repair
> To help him of his blindness.[13]

The theme continually recurs; and in the present scene the greater part of Speed's cut-and-thrust with Valentine relates to it: 'Love is blind,' 'if you love her you cannot see her,' and the rest, from Valentine's question, on the marks of the lover, 'Are all these things perceived in me?' to Speed's, on Silvia's 'invisible' stratagem, 'But did you perceive her earnest?'[14]

From Launce's entry, the relation between the clown episodes and the leading themes, of love and friendship, becomes simpler to describe; for it rests quite evidently throughout on the principle of comic parallelism. One has of course to bear in mind that in Elizabethan as in medieval work, burlesque need not mean belittlement of what is burlesqued.

The scene of Launce's parting (II iii) is a counterpoise to the high courtly parting of friends, with which Valentine and Proteus open the play. More directly, it is the humorous sequel to the scene of pathos which it follows, the lovers' parting between Proteus and Julia (II ii). One phrase, on Launce's sister, 'as white as a lily and as small as a wand,' is in the very idiom of love-romance. Proteus has punned emotionally on the

tide or season of his departure, and Julia's 'tide of tears';
Launce puns outrageously on the tide and 'the tied,' namely
Crab. At the end of the lovers' scene, Julia, weeping, has made
her escape in silence: 'Alas!' cries Proteus in his exit-line, 'this
parting strikes poor lovers dumb.' The clown enters in tears,
but voluble, and in his monologue re-enacts the weeping of all
his kin. Crab's silence is taken otherwise than Julia's; unaccom-
panied by tears, it is supposed to betoken hardness of heart,
and gives his master great offence. Attempting to identify the
dramatis personae of the re-enactment with the 'props' available,
Launce confuses himself completely, and in this self-confusion
about identities the comic mode of his monologu e chimes with
what Professor Baldwin[15] has called the inward self-travesty of
Proteus and the outward self-travesty of Julia, soon to be seen,
and indeed with the whole theme of true identity and its
recognition. The final claim Launce makes for his tears and
sighs is likewise in tune with what is to happen. If he did miss
the tide, he declares, they would float him and waft him to
overtake Proteus. To overtake Proteus is just what Julia's
love-sorrow, of which they are the comic counterparts, will
shortly impel her to do.

The reunion of Launce and Speed in Milan (II v) immediately succeeds that of the friends, their masters; and their
dialogue comments on the love-theme. It is certain, Launce
tells his comrade, that it will be a match between Proteus and
Julia. Proteus has just left the stage soliloquizing on his change
of allegiance, and is about to return resolving to court Silvia as
though Julia were dead. Yet in the end, Launce will prove right
after all. Again, he furnishes a comic reminder of the discretion
proper in communicating love-secrets even to the bosom-
friend. His display of caution ('Thou shalt never get such a
secret from me but by parable') contrasts with Valentine's
indiscreet disclosure to Proteus of the plans for his elopement,
a disclosure made in the previous scene (II iv). In the next (II
vi) Proteus determines on betraying his friend's confidence to
the Duke. His entry alone, meditating this treachery, is set
against the amicable exit of Speed and Launce, going off 'in
Christian charity' to drink together.

The episode of Launce and his letter (which ends III i) affords even more striking parallels with both the love and friendship themes. It evokes comparison with the two romantic letter-scenes earlier (I ii, II i): Julia receiving Proteus' love-letter, and Silvia giving Valentine the love-letter she has made him write on her behalf. In burlesque contrast with Julia's emotion and Silvia's graceful device, Launce's letter is a step towards a bargain in the marriage-market. It is a report from a go-between on the merits and demerits of his intended; and on the strength of it he makes up his mind to have her, because though toothless she is well-off. This love-transaction, which is not pursued in the courtly way, by courtship of the lady, and which is clinched by mercenary considerations, clean against the canon of true love, casts a light on the next scene (III ii) and its sequel (IV ii). Here, by the courtliest kind of courtship – a serenade – but no less against the canon of true love, the assault upon Silvia's loyalty to Valentine is planned on behalf of the foolish Thurio, whom her father prefers for his wealth, and is used by the faithless Proteus as cover for his own pursuit of her. Beside the moral deformity of Proteus' conduct in love, the comic deformity of Launce's is as nothing.

When the letter-episode begins, we have just seen Valentine banished, in consequence of having enlisted Proteus' counsel about the elopement. Launce soliloquizes on Proteus' knavery, and his own secrecy: 'I love . . . but what woman I will not tell myself' – burlesquing at once the code and Valentine's breach of it. Then, like Valentine, he enlists a confidant; and like Proteus, betrays his friend. He cajoles Speed into helping him read the letter, and rejoices that Speed will earn a beating by it. Though the roles are switched (since the confidant, not the confider, is betrayed), the parallel is clear.

Launce's last monologue, just before his dismissal by Proteus and from the play (IV iv), is of course his tale of Crab's crimes at court, with his own quixotic devotion and fidelity to the ungrateful, ill-conditioned cur. It comes almost straight after Proteus' nocturnal courtship of Silvia, in triple treachery to Julia, Valentine, and Thurio; and between the arrival of Julia in her devotion and fidelity, only to witness this treachery of

his (IV ii), and her taking service with him (in IV iv), ungrateful
and ill-conducted as she has found him. 'When a man's servant
shall play the cur' – so Launce starts his complaint of Crab,
and so Proteus might complain of Launce himself, 'who still . . .
turns [him] to shame.' But we have heard this word 'servant'
repeated in the sense of 'courtly lover': what when a lady's
'servant' shall play the cur? Yet Julia does not refuse the
quixotic task of bearing Proteus' love-plea to her unwilling
rival.[16]

I am hinting a comparison of Proteus with Crab; and I do
not think it extravagant, provided one is not too serious about
it, to see reflected in Crab, comically and a little pathetically,
the transgressor in Proteus. The want of sensibility to old ties
and to his friend Launce's feelings which Crab is alleged to
show at parting from home, is ominous as a parallel to Proteus'
parting from Julia and impending reunion with Valentine. As
a present for Silvia, Crab resembles the love that Proteus
proffers her. He is a sorry changeling for the true love gift
Proteus meant to bestow. He is unfit for Silvia (persecuting her
with most objectionable attentions!), and offensive where true
courtliness should rule. Like Proteus, he gets his friend into
trouble. And as Crab is only saved by Launce's quixotic,
self-sacrificial affection, so Proteus is only saved by the ex-
tremes to which Valentine is ready to carry his friendship and
Julia her love. From them Proteus learns his lesson. As in *Love's
Labour's Lost*, an opening debate in which love and education
were pitted against each other has led into a drama of
education in and through love. The theme of education is
touched occasionally in the earlier clown-scenes (Speed has
been corrected for inordinate love – of his bed), but it appears
more plainly when Launce reproaches Crab: 'did I not bid thee
still mark me, and do as I do?' Crab cannot learn; but Proteus
learns the value of constancy from the example and reproaches
of Julia, Valentine, and Silvia.[17] Whether Crab says ay or no,
and whatever the antics of Proteus the transgressor,[18] it is a
match between the regenerate Proteus and his Julia. Yet with
all this, Crab is the clown's dog, not a symbol or a piece of
allegory: I mean simply to suggest that the impression the dog

makes on an audience has this various aptness to the main action and its themes.

The structural use of parallels between main and subsidiary actions, in conjunction with plot or otherwise, is not infrequent in our drama. In subsequent plays of Shakespeare's there are many examples. Hal's interview with his father is rehearsed beforehand in Eastcheap, and Malvolio, no less than Orsino and Olivia, cherishes an illusory ideal of love. The underplot of *The Changeling* owes its relevance to the same technique. But while Bond was right to discern it in *Two Gentlemen*, he was in error when he traced it solely to Lyly. It was not initiated, as he seems to have thought, by *Endimion*: it unites the comic and serious actions in the *Secunda Pastorum* (*c.* mid-fifteenth century) and in *Fulgens and Lucres* (*c.* 1500). It is not confined to plays 'in two tones'; the most famous instance of all is the double plot of *King Lear*. It is something to look for before assessing a dramatist's construction. Congreve's intrigue-plots are not among the finest features of his art, but he is a master of construction in parallel, witness the successive quarrel-scenes in the second Acts of *Love for Love* and *The Way of the World*; and the fourth Act of the latter, made up of contrasted wooings. In Shaw's *Major Barbara*, the organic contribution of the first episode is better appreciated when we recognize the parallelism of theme: the play is about different kinds of power, and the opening shows the sort of power Lady Britomart wields in her household. Similarly, to look at the use of parallels in *The Two Gentlemen of Verona* alters our estimate of its construction.

SOURCE: 'Two Clowns in a Comedy (to say nothing of the dog): Speed, Launce (and Crab) in *The Two Gentleman of Verona*', *Essays and Studies*, XVI (1963), 91–100.

NOTES

1. *Shakespearian Comedy* (1938).
2. I am confining 'plot' to the causal sequence; not extending it, with Una Ellis-Fermor in her fine chapter 'The Nature of Plot in

Drama' (*Shakespeare the Dramatist*, 1961), to cover what she and Professor Wilson Knight call the 'spatial' pattern of a play.

3. By 'action' I intend the total movement of the play, the enacted development of everything the play is vitally concerned with (story, situation, character, mood, theme, whatever that concern may comprehend), which conducts to the conclusion. So developed, and so concluded (even if sometimes the conclusion is deliberately inconclusive), these concerns, in good drama, are formed into an artistic whole, a whole greater than the unity of plot alone. The test of dramatic relevance is the contribution made to this larger whole, and the contribution may well be, not to the causal sequence, but to some other element in the developing pattern. 'Action' is perhaps the most variously used term in dramatic criticism. According to context, it can mean, for example: (1) 'business'; physical action as opposed to speech; (2) that part of the story which is enacted on the stage, in contrast with that part which is 'reported' or implied; (3) the events, especially the decisive events, of the drama, whether physical or mental, and whether occurring on stage or off; and perhaps (4) the designed sequence of those events, preferably, I think, called 'plot'.

4. Cp. J. W. Lever, *The Elizabethan Love Sonnet* (1956), p. 164.

5. Cp. M. C. Bradbrook, *Shakespeare and Elizabethan Poetry* (1951).

6. For 'daunger' and 'pité', see C. S. Lewis, *The Allegory of Love*, on the *Roman de la Rose*.

7. Cp. L. Borinski, 'Shakespeare's Comic Prose', *Shakespeare Survey*, 8 (1955); and (on Launce and Will Kempe's slippers) J. Isaacs, 'Shakespeare as Man of the Theatre,' *Shakespeare Criticism 1919–35*, ed. Anne Bradby (1936).

8. Quotations and references are from *William Shakespeare: The Complete Works*, ed. Peter Alexander (1951).

9. Well indicated by his sophistical argument to the contrary, II vi 19–22.

10. 'And now you are metamorphis'd with a mistress' (II i 26).

11. Cp., e.g. the Dreamer in Chaucer's *Boke of the Duchesse*.

12. Bradbrook, *Shakespeare and Elizabethan Poetry*; and J. R. Brown, *Shakespeare and his Comedies* (1957), q.v. for the whole topic of the lover's ability or failure to see beyond appearance.

13. Richmond Noble overlooks this (in *Shakespeare's Use of Song*) when he finds the lyric comparatively lacking in dramatic relevance.

14. See the passages in full: II i 29–71, 124–45.

15. Baldwin, *William Shakespeare's Five-Act Structure* (1947).

16. Though it must be admitted that, unlike Viola, she doesn't propose to put her heart into it.

17. Cp. Harold Jenkins, 'Shakespeare's *Twelfth Night*', *The Rice Institute Pamphlet* , XLV 4 (Jan. 1959).

18. 'If he say ay, it will; if he say no, it will; if he shake his tail and say nothing, it will.' (II v 31).

Stanley Wells

THE FAILURE OF *THE TWO GENTLEMEN OF VERONA* (1963)

The Two Gentlemen of Verona has not been a favourite of the critics. Not all have been as damning as that uninhibited lady, Mrs Charlotte Lennox: 'This Play every where abounds with the most ridiculous Absurdities in the Plot and Conduct of the Incidents, as well as with the greatest Improprieties in the Manners and Sentiments of the Persons'.[1] But Coleridge, in making a chronological table of Shakespeare's plays, dismissed it as a 'sketch'; Hazlitt, who was not altogether unappreciative, used similar terms: 'This is little more than the first outlines of a comedy lightly sketched in'; E. K. Chambers considered that no other play of Shakespeare's 'bears upon it such obvious marks of immaturity'[2] and T. M. Parrott found it 'full of faults'.[3] Sketchy though it may be, its inclusion in Francis Meres's list suggests, perhaps that it was acted, and at least that it was regarded as a completed piece of work; so it may fairly come up for critical examination. On the other hand, it is not amenable to those techniques of modern interpretative criticism which are applied to fully developed and highly organised works. There is, perhaps, some danger of under-rating it simply because it is not as good as other plays in which Shakespeare used similar materials. It contains, as has often been remarked, many anticipations of later plays, such as *The Merchant of Venice* and *Twelfth Night*; but to consider this too deeply has its dangers. It may lead to a too easy dismissal on the grounds, not that the play is unsuccessful in itself, but that it does not provide the critic with what he wants, and finds elsewhere. It may on the other hand lead to over-interpretation, such as

John Vyvyan's theory[4] that the outlaw scenes represent in parable-form Valentine's need to learn control of his baser instincts.

A more helpful approach is probably that through earlier literature, such as H. B. Charlton adopts in a chapter of *Shakespearian Comedy* (1938) which remains perhaps the most extended critical discussion of this play. Charlton clearly demonstrates Shakespeare's dependence, in the play's more serious aspects, upon the conventions of romantic love as derived from the mediaeval tradition and its modifications by Petrarch and the neo-Platonists; and he adduces some close parallels of idea. In discussing the use Shakespeare made of these conventions, Charlton comes to the conclusion that something went wrong. His thesis is perhaps fairly summed up in his penultimate sentence: 'Clearly, Shakespeare's first attempt to make romantic comedy had only succeeded so far that it had unexpectedly and inadvertently made romance comic.' In order to test the truth of this, it is necessary to look at the methods used by Shakespeare to project and organise his raw material.

The plot – I use the word in a fairly wide sense, to refer both to the actions and to the methods of narrative presentation – seems to me to exhibit a number of peculiarities, limitations and plain faults, which for convenience I divide into the superficial, the technical and the organic. The superficial ones can be passed over with little comment. Dr Johnson drew attention to the play's peculiar geography, and to the fact that it is not even self-consistent; but this might almost be regarded as a normal feature of romance. Johnson's further complaint that, at the end of II iv, Shakespeare 'makes Protheus, after an interview with Silvia, say he has only seen her picture' is probably answered by the fact that 'picture' could mean 'appearance' (cf. *Hamlet*, IV v 86 and *Merchant*, I ii 78) and here implies only superficial acquaintance. In any case, these peculiarities are neither more numerous nor more striking than those to be found in many other, greater plays.

The technical limitations of the plot are, I find, more interesting and revealing. It is a curious fact that Shakespeare's technique in this play is limited almost exclusively to three devices: soliloquy, duologue, and the aside as comment. Thirteen of the twenty scenes go no further than this: they are I i, ii and iii; II i, ii, iii, v, vi and vii; IV ii, iii and iv; and V i. Moreover, several other scenes, including three of the play's longest (II iv; III i; V iv), escape inclusion in this list only by virtue of a few lines of more complicated dialogue. The climax of this structural method is reached in IV ii, in many ways the best scene. It begins with a soliloquy from Proteus, followed by a dialogue between him and Thurio, with the musicians in the background; then the Host and Julia enter and speak together unheard by the others; their conversation is broken by the song; it is followed by a brief passage between Proteus and Thurio, after which Sylvia makes her appearance; her conversation with Proteus is commented on in asides by Julia, and the scene ends after Proteus's exit with a few lines between Julia and the Host. The patterning is simple but effective. The silences of the Host and Julia are, of course, explained by their situation; those of Proteus and Thurio offer some difficulty to the producer, but can be partially covered by the preparations for the serenade and by the continuance of instrumental music after it. There is no reason to wish that Shakespeare had attempted anything more complex: the limited technique justifies itself; it could be entirely deliberate.

However, what happens when Shakespeare steps outside these limits may well suggest that they are the consequence of an underdeveloped technique rather than a deliberately restricted one. Several times a character is left in unnatural silence when the dialogue switches from him to someone else. I iii, for instance, begins with a duologue between Antonio and Panthino. When they have come to a decision, Proteus enters 'in good time' and Panthino stands silently by during the conversation between Antonio and his son until he is haled off by Antonio. In III i, a feeble effort is made to keep Launce in the picture after he enters with Proteus at 1.188, but he soon drops out and says nothing for 40 lines. In the next scene, where a truly three-cornered dialogue might well have been expected, Thurio speaks only two of the twenty-eight speeches uttered when he is on stage with the Duke and Proteus.

II iv gives a notable illustration of the author's failure to think in terms of a number of characters at once. Valentine, Sylvia, Speed and Thurio are on stage. Sylvia addresses Valentine, but they are interrupted by Speed who has a very brief conversation with Valentine. This ends at 1.7, and Speed is heard no more for the rest of the scene – editors give him an (unmotivated) exit. After this Sylvia tries again to talk to Valentine, but again there is an interruption, this time from Thurio, and again Valentine is diverted into two-handed back-chat. Sylvia makes a few interjections, replied to by Valentine. On the Duke's entrance, attention is switched entirely to him and Valentine; the others are silent while we hear of Proteus's arrival at Court. Having given his news, the Duke departs. There follows a short duologue between Sylvia and Valentine, with one twitter from Thurio. On Proteus's entrance we have a brief passage of three-cornered dialogue, which does not extend beyond presentations and compliments. Thurio poses problems here; either he is silent on-stage during this passage, in which case his next line, 'Madam, my lord your father would speak with you', is apt to sound like clairvoyance; or else he must slip off during the presentations, to return a few lines later with his message. Sylvia takes him off with her, and the rest of the scene passes easily in duologue and soliloquy. A crowning insult is offered Thurio in III i, where he is dismissed speechless in the first line. The failure of the outlaw scenes, where the ability to deal with a group of characters is of prime importance, is too obvious to require further notice.

Of the entire play, no scene has given rise to more unfavourable comment than the last; it has been emended, rewritten, reviled and rejected. The difficulties here are complex: both technical and organic. On the latter I reserve comment until later; for the present, it may be worth noticing the inflexibility of technique displayed. Though six important characters as well as a band of outlaws are on-stage, the scene ends with a long duologue between the Duke and Valentine. Thurio has two speeches in the entire scene (admittedly, he enters late),

and Sylvia says nothing at all while she is first donated by
Valentine to Proteus, then rejected by him in favour of Julia,
then claimed by Thurio, only in his next breath to be re-
nounced by him, and finally handed back to Valentine by her
father. Was ever woman in this humour won?

The basic technical failure of the play, I suggest, arises from
the fact that Shakespeare is still a tyro in dramatic craftman-
ship: he has not yet learned how to manipulate more than a
few characters at once. This explains the complete failure of
that chaste wraith, Sir Eglamour, and of Thurio, since the
dramatist did not consider them important enough to be given
soliloquies or a foil; and it also goes a long way towards
explaining the failure in the last scene to develop a tricky
situation in a way that would have achieved a fully articulate
emotional resolution. And it is this more than anything else
that gives the impression of sketchiness. It does not ruin the
play: along with, and partly because of, the sketchiness, there
is a wholly charming simplicity and directness: what Hazlitt
called 'a careless grace and felicity' 'throughout the conduct of
the fable'; but there is not that density and harmonic richness
which come where the characters of a play have a subtle
complexity of cross-relationships such as we find in *Twelfth
Night* and would, to some degree, have been desirable here.

Before going on to discuss the more 'organic' deficiencies of
the play, I may be permitted a few more general considerations
arising from this discussion of a technical aspect which has not,
so far as I know, been previously remarked.[5] First, the particular technical limitations of which I have been speaking are
characteristic, not only of many Tudor interludes, but also, and
to a marked degree, of a play Shakespeare knew very well:
Gascoigne's *Supposes*. Secondly, I find it difficult to imagine how
a dramatist with a technique of character-manipulation as
limited as this play reveals, not only in scenes, such as the last,
where he had to wrestle with thematic complexities, but also in
straightforward scenes of exposition, could, unaided, have
plotted, for instance, the last scenes of *The Comedy of Errors* and
The Taming of the Shrew, and much of *Richard III*: plays often
thought of as earlier than *The Two Gentlemen of Verona*. The

problem of chronology is of course exceedingly complicated, and cannot be solved simply by considering the flexibility of character-manipulation; but it is a consideration that seems to have been neglected. Thirdly, I suggest a possible fallacy implicit in many discussions of the chronology of Shakespeare's early plays: the idea stated (though not necessarily endorsed) by Geoffrey Bullough: 'Since it [*The Two Gentlemen of Verona*] replaces the dry hardness of *A Comedy of Errors* and *The Shrew* with some of the warmth and eloquence, the surplusage of word-play, found in *A Midsummer Night's Dream* and *Love's Labour's Lost*, the play probably belongs to the same group, though it may be earlier than these, for it treats its romantic theme with a somewhat jejune absence of self-criticism hardly possible after their delighted mockery of Love'.[6] It seems to me equally possible that a young writer should begin with 'warmth and eloquence' and only then, discovering in himself technical deficiencies, restrain these qualities at the risk of 'dry hardness' in order to acquire greater formal discipline.

The organic deficiencies of the play are the result of Shakespeare's failure to devise a plot which will enable characters conceived within the conventions of romantic love to behave in a manner compatible with these conventions. We are, for instance, invited to sympathise with Valentine; he is the attractive, intelligent young courtier whose love for Sylvia is seriously and forcefully presented; the man who at the end is capable of the grand romantic gesture of offering to sacrifice love to friendship. But the exigencies of the plot require this intelligent young man to behave in a manner not merely unrealistic, but downright stupid. Realism, of course, we have no right to expect; the trouble is that Shakespeare cuts across the convention by using his romantic hero as a vehicle for a type of comedy which deprives him of his whole basis of existence. The scene in which Valentine fails to realise that the letter he is writing on Sylvia's behalf is addressed to himself might perhaps have been acceptable as a tenderly absurd illustration of the lover's traditional blindness: the wit made weak with musing; but when the humour of the situation is explicitly pointed for us by Speed, who here shows much more intelligence than his master, the tenderness is in great danger of being lost in the absurdity. A later scene that quite deflates our confidence in the young man is that in which he ingenuously reveals to the Duke his plan for eloping with the Duke's daughter. If the person concerned had been Thurio, all would have been well; but as it is, the situation is at variance with the character.

A somewhat similar difficulty arises with Proteus. Again our first impressions are sympathetic. Before long, not merely is he behaving in the most caddish manner imaginable, but he is inviting our sympathy in what he takes to be a moral dilemma. It must be admitted, I think, that his soliloquy at the beginning of IV ii comes near to redeeming him as a dramatic character, for he shows quite powerfully his awareness of his falseness to Valentine, his injustice towards Thurio and his worthlessness in comparison with Sylvia; he grows in depth when he tells how, 'spaniel-like, the more she spurns my love, The more it grows and fawneth on her still'. The mature Shakespeare could have done much with this obsessed lover (witness Angelo); but at this stage he has not yet learned to maintain this depth of characterisation, and in a few seconds Proteus goes on to perform with no apparent difficulty the treacheries he has just been deploring. The result is a loss of moral coherence; it is paradoxical that this would have been less evident if Proteus had been more shallowly presented throughout.

In these characters we see the strain imposed by a discrepancy between plot and convention. This aspect of the play has been brilliantly handled by G. K. Hunter, who finds that its 'Lylian kind of structure will, however, only work when the characters are as simple as are Lyly's.' As he says, in Valentine we see the matter at merely intellectual focus, whereas in Proteus 'we have a psychological dimension as well'.[7] A further strain is imposed by the juxtaposition of these figures with the much more realistically conceived Julia. Her letter scene (I ii) is true comedy infused with genuine feeling; in technique it might fairly be considered an anticipation of Shakespeare's use of blank verse to show us the thought-processes of the Nurse in *Romeo and Juliet*; and throughout, the character is consistently, economically and touchingly presented. The misfortune is that this exposes the hollowness of Valentine and Proteus. As Madeline Doran says, 'too much "character" in Julia has fouled up the conventional lines of Shakespeare's story'.[8]

These difficulties reach their climax in the passage of the last scene which has become the most notorious literary and dramatic crux of the play: when Valentine, impressed by Proteus's repentance, says:

> And, that my love may appear plain and free,
> All that was mine in Silvia I give thee.
>
> (V iv 82–3)

This has provoked many different reactions. In J. P. Kemble's acting edition,[9] it is materially altered. After Proteus's molestation of Sylvia (toned down from the original), she and Valentine are given a brief conversation (italicised below):

Val.: Thou friend of an ill fashion!
Pro.: Valentine!
Val.: Comrades, lay hold on him. –
         [The Outlaws seize Proteus, – Julia runs to him.
    My dearest Silvia!
    Indulgent Heaven at length has heard my prayer,
    And brought again my Silvia to my arms;
    No power on earth shall ever part us more.
Sil. *It is delusion all, – Alas, we dream,*
    And must awake to wretchedness again.
    O, Valentine, we are beset with dangers.
Val. *Dismiss those fears, my love; here I command:*
    Thou common friend . . .

Valentine's forgiveness of Proteus is postponed till after the recognition of Julia, Proteus's penitence is expanded, and Valentine's gift to him of Sylvia is omitted. Other alterations include the provision of extra speeches for Sylvia and Thurio, and of a final speech for Proteus:

> *Thanks, generous Valentine: – and I myself*
> *Will be the trumpet of my Julia's worth,*
> *Her steadfast faith, her still-enduring love,*
> *And of my own misdoings. – Pardon me,*
> *Ye who have ever known what 'tis to err! –*

And be this truth by all the world confess'd!
That lovers must be faithful to be bless'd!

These are a theatre-man's attempts to make the scene work-
able in his own terms. It has given equal trouble in the study,
where doubts have been cast upon both its authenticity and its
textual integrity. Dowden, rejecting arguments for 'duplicity of
authorship', yet believed that 'If the fifth act came from
Shakespeare's pen as it now stands, we must believe that he
handed over his play to the actors while a portion of it still
remained only a hasty sketch, the *denouement* being left for
future working out'.[10] Dover Wilson and Quiller-Couch could
not stomach it at all, and propounded an elaborate theory of
play-house interference, tentatively adopted and modified by
Parrott.

On the other hand, attempts to justify the scene as it stands
have been made, for instance, by drawing parallels with the
Sonnets, and even (by Masefield)[11] with a real-life situation
between Shelley and Thomas Jefferson Hogg; and Allardyce
Nicoll calls the renunciation 'a testimony to love's perplexing
and unassailable power'.[12] There can be no doubt, I think, that,
whatever our opinion of the rest of the scene, its climactic
situation in itself would have been perfectly acceptable to an
Elizabethan audience. As M. C. Bradbrook has written: 'The
school-boy cries of "cad" and "scoundrel" with which Valentine is pelted by critics, the epigrams of Q ("By now there are
no gentlemen in Verona") would have struck Shakespeare's
audience as simply a failure in understanding'.[13] And John
Munro very pertinently observes that 'in the "Brotherhood"
stories (on which the Valentine – Silvia – Proteus romance is
based), of which . . . [M.] Leach examined some eighty-six
closely related versions, one of two men woos and wins, or is
won by, or even weds, a woman, only to transfer her to his
beloved companion in the all-dominating urge of sworn friendship. Shakespeare should perhaps have disembarrassed himself
of this incident in the plot; but he let it stand, bent at this stage
on adhering to the tale. At a later stage, interested much more
in character, as against plot, he would, no doubt have acted

differently'.[14] My only objection to this is the implication that Shakespeare was here more 'interested' in plot than in character. The trouble is two-fold: partly that he had not *enough* interest in the plot to see how it should have been moulded to synthesise with the other elements of the play; and partly sheer inadequacy in the mechanics of his craft, which rendered him incapable of manipulating his characters in a convincing way.

The comic characters, as I have suggested, at times impinge inappropriately upon the serious ones; but they are more often used to provide a wholly successful comic implied commentary on the romantic agonies of the lovers. When Speed comments on the letter scene between Valentine and Sylvia, he makes Valentine look an ass; he does not simply comment on the romance: he (at least momentarily) destroys it. On the other hand, when he and Launce discuss Launce's requirements of his girl-friend, they provide an attitude that can co-exist with the other: they are not mutually incompatible, but mutually illuminating. The first does, as Charlton says, inadvertently make romance comic; the second provides a perfectly legitimate comic counterpoint to the romance.

In its overall organisation, then, I see this play as a failure. It shows Shakespeare accepting dramatic conventions with one hand and throwing them overboard with the other. He fails, partly because he puts more into the framework than it can hold, and partly because he still has much to learn about the mechanics of his craft. But the play is very far indeed from being a total failure. There are partial successes even in its attempts to be an integrated poetic comedy. Already Shakespeare is making some use of recurrent and significantly placed imagery to prepare us for the turns of the story; we may notice for instance the emphasis on the blindness of love, on the way it 'metamorphoses' a man, so that he wars with good counsel, and his wit is made weak with musing; and the two developed images of the transitoriness of love (II iv, 200–2; III ii 6–10). These go some way towards preparing us for Valentine's partial blindness and for the shift in Proteus's affections: though they do not make them completely successful, they erode the frontiers of our disbelief. Even the word-play, mechanical as it often is, sometimes takes on anticipatory depths, as in the passage between Julia and the Host:

> *Host*: How now! are you sadder than you were before?
>   How do you, man? the music likes you not.
> *Jul.*: You mistake; the musician likes me not.
> *Host*: Why, my pretty youth?
> *Jul.*: He plays false, father.
> *Host.* How? out of tune on the strings?
> *Jul.*: Not so; but yet so false that he grieves my very heart-strings.
> *Host*: You have a quick ear.
> *Jul.*: Ay, I would I were deaf; it makes me have a slow heart.
> *Host*: I perceive you delight not in music.
> *Jul.*: Not a whit, when it jars so.
> *Host*: Ay, that change is the spite.
> *Jul.*: Hark, what fine change is in the music!
> *Host*: You would have them always play but one thing?
> *Jul.*: I would always have one play but one thing.
>
> (IV ii 54–72)

Julia's answers are misunderstandings, but being functional, they are not comic: they stress her isolation and loneliness. There is wit here, but its effect is not one of hilarity; it serves rather to sharpen the poignancy of Julia's situation.

The very tenuousness of the plot, and the shadowiness of some of its characters, help us to accept the situations as it were on a hypothetical basis, and to follow with interest the ways in which they are developed. In this the play resembles the prose romances of the period, in many of which the story exists merely as a machinery to place the characters in interesting situations; then rhetoric takes over, and the emotional ramifications are developed at great length. The parallel does not hold entirely, for there are clear signs that Shakespeare was trying to do more than this; but at least it may help us to see where to look for the play's virtues. And the looseness of action does above all allow Shakespeare to bring in the estimable figure of Launce and the silent Crab, who are much more relevant thematically than structurally, and who show how marvellously creative Shakespeare's imagination already was when given a free rein. Again, though I have stressed the limitations of dramatic technique in this play, it must be repeated that Shakespeare is often wholly successful within the limits of a single scene. And the most important reason for the play's successes is that, however immature he may be in other ways, he is already completely assured as a writer of comic prose, of lyrical verse, and even sometimes of genuine dramatic verse. When we try to get below the surface of the play, we find that it rests on shaky foundations. In these circumstances the best thing to do seems to be to come up to the surface again and examine that; then we may return to Johnson: 'It is not indeed one of his most powerful effusions, it has neither many diversities of character, nor striking delineations of life, but it abounds in γνῶμαι beyond most of his plays, and few have more lines or passages which, singly considered, are eminently beautiful.'[15]

SOURCE: 'The Failure of *The Two Gentlemen of Verona*,' *Shakespeare Jahrbuch* XCIX (1963), 161–73.

NOTES

1. *Shakespear Illustrated* (London, 1753–54), III, p. 44.
2. *Shakespeare: A Survey* (London, 1925), p. 49.
3. *Shakespearean Comedy* (New York, 1949), p. 108.
4. *Shakespeare and the Rose of Love* (London, 1960), pp. 107–11.
5. E. K. Chambers perhaps came closest when he remarked on 'the lack of adroitness which allows the characters, as in *The Comedy of Errors*, and even, a little later, in *A Midsummer Night's Dream*, to fall into pairs'.
6. *Narrative and Dramatic Sources of Shakespeare*, I (London, 1957), p. 203.
7. *John Lyly* (London, 1962), p. 324.
8. *Endeavors of Art* (Madison, Wis., 1954), p. 325.
9. Cumberland's British Theatre (London, n. d. [?1830]). Based on Ben Victor's adaptation (1763).
10. *Shakespeare: His Mind and Art* (London, 1875), pp. 57–8.
11. *Shakespeare* (London, 1911), p. 41.
12. *Shakespeare* (London, 1952), p. 95.
13. *Shakespeare and Elizabethan Poetry* (London, 1951), p. 150.
14. *The London Shakespeare* (London, 1958), I, p. 266.
15. *Johnson on Shakespeare*, ed. Walter Raleigh (London, 1908), p. 74.

Inga-Stina Ewbank

'WERE MAN BUT CONSTANT, HE WERE PERFECT': CONSTANCY AND CONSISTENCY IN '*THE TWO GENTLEMEN OF VERONA*' (1972)

I

IN the early spring of 1855 George Eliot (still Marian Evans) read *The Two Gentlemen of Verona* and found that the play

disgusted me more than ever in the final scene where Valentine, on Proteus's mere begging pardon when he has no longer any hope of gaining his ends, says: 'All that was mine in Silvia I give thee'! – Silvia standing by.[1]

In itself there is nothing unusual about George Eliot's reaction. Most critics of the play have felt that in this, his first, dramatization of romance narrative Shakespeare was tied and partly defeated by the conventions he was attempting to use. Such 'disgust' as has been expressed has often focused on the last scene as typifying the play's problems: in the unbelievable magnanimity of Valentine (at two girls' expense), thematic considerations appear to override any thought of character development or psychological motivation. As an affirmation of male constancy it may have satisfied an Elizabethan audience; for, insofar as they believed with Geron, in Lyly's *Endimion*, that friendship is 'the image of eternitie, in which there is nothing moveable, nothing mischeevous' and that there is as much difference between love and friendship as between 'Beautie and Vertue, bodies and shadowes, colours and life', they would have seen Valentine's lines as a noble and universally valid climax to the action of the play.[2] But this moment in the play has troubled audiences and readers ever since.

172

It may have been particularly troubling to George Eliot, who, like Julia, had defied the notions of 'modesty' held by her society, and who may have given special assent to Julia's couplet against a double standard:

> It is the lesser blot, modesty finds,
> Women to change their shapes than men their minds.
>
> (v iv 108–9)

If so, her objection would again have been part of a more general one, for Valentine's grand gesture is all the more inconsistent in that, up to the final scene where Sylvia is mutely handed around from one man to another and Julia's chief contribution is a swoon, the women in the play have been the active ones, going forth to seek their lovers, making decisions on a basis of profound love *and* commonsense, while the men talk or write letters and poems about their love. Like Shakespeare's more mature comedies but unlike the traditional friendship story, where the woman tends to be merely an object or a touchstone in the testing of friends,[3] the play has shown us some of the most important parts of the action from a woman's viewpoint. Though it is in Valentine's idealistic words that Proteus' betrayal is forgiven, it is through Julia's eyes and mind that we have seen what that betrayal really means. Valentine's attitude resolves a theme, but it is Julia's heartbreak which, if anything, has proved the human content of that theme on our pulses. Valentine's constancy appears to be built on a dramatic inconsistency; and one wonders how far Proteus' reply to Julia,

> Than men their minds! 'tis true. O heaven, were man
> But constant, he were perfect!
>
> (v iv 110–11)

is, wittingly or unwittingly, a self-reproach on the part of the dramatist.

But there is also a background to George Eliot's reaction to *The Two Gentlemen of Verona* which makes it more remarkable and more interesting as a departure point for an exploration of the play's inconsistencies – which indeed makes those inconsistencies more worth exploring – than other similar reactions.[4] She was reading, or rather re-reading, the play during some lonely weeks at Dover, while George Henry Lewes was in London arranging his affairs and hers, as well as those of his legal wife and children. The two of them had just returned to England, after eight months in voluntary exile, to face the music of outraged Victorian morality and to try to build a life together. She trusted the man in whom she had 'garner'd up her heart', but she must also have known how precarious their liaison looked to outsiders, and how even her best friends were praying 'against hope' that the protean Lewes would prove constant. So when, in the evenings, she turned from translating Spinoza's *Ethics* to reading *The Two Gentlemen of Verona* – and it may speak more of her emotional state than of a scholarly desire to be chronologically thorough that she was also reading *Venus and Adonis, The Passionate Pilgrim* and some of the sonnets – it was with a peculiar personal involvement. Between the lines of her journal entry we may sense that the play, in provoking disgust, had activated a deep fear at the centre of her life. 'Could men really bandy a noble woman's love about like that?' is how her biographer puts into words what she dared not express, even to herself.[5] Out of the allegedly 'romantic and dehumanized atmosphere' of this play, something must have spoken to her about what it feels like to be alive and loving – and therefore vulnerable.

Now, *The Two Gentlemen of Verona* is not a play usually discussed in those terms. Shakespeare seems not yet to have developed the uncanny way he later has of engaging with our own lives so that our own experiences modify our reactions to his lines, and *vice versa*: so that we read *King Lear* differently once we have an aged parent in the household, or reject Lady Macbeth each time we nurse our babies, or even feel able to 'identify' with the anguish and confusion of the puppet-like movements of the lovers in *A Midsummer Night's Dream*. The sphere of human experience in *The Two Gentlemen of Verona* is not only narrow – excluding alike birth, copulation and death – but it is so restricted by remote codes and patterned by an artificial language that we tend to feel it represents a world to which Shakespeare was not much committed. Perhaps we feel that, if our feelings go out to anyone in the play, it is to Launce with his dog Crab. A great deal has recently been written on the dramatic technique of the play, and in particular on the way in which Shakespeare has managed to make the parodic scenes of Speed and Launce (and Crab) into organic parts of the structure;[6] but no one has felt like saying, borrowing T. S. Eliot's words about Tennyson, that the poet's technical accomplishments were intimate with his depths. Most discussions conclude either that Shakespeare was preoccupied with form at the expense of truth to human feeling, or that he was laughing at the feelings embodied in courtly convention, or both – that is, that he criticized the convention most of the time but, with an inconsistency worthy of Proteus, found it dramatically expedient to embrace it at the end. Either way – whether we nod an Elizabethan assent to the friendship code or laugh at 'Shakespeare wringing the last drop of silliness out of Valentine's conventions'[7] – we have an explanation for Valentine's gesture and words which does not involve us, or Shakespeare, very deeply. But George Eliot's reaction, from a disturbed and divided consciousness, prompts one to consider the possibility that Shakespeare is here at least trying, if with very partial success, to be as truthful to troubled, complex human relationships as he was in the sonnet celebrating an apparently similar plot situation, 'Take all my loves' (40). Possibly he is saying about the moment of Valentine's magnanimity *not* 'this is what life should ideally be', nor 'this is not life', but 'this is, and is not, life'.

II

Clearly it will not do to pretend that *The Two Gentlemen of Verona* is really a *Troilus and Cressida*. Clearly this very early play[8] is in many ways a piece of apprenticeship (so that one natural reason for anyone's 'disgust' with it is that it is not as good as the rest of Shakespeare) and a seed-bed for themes, characters and situations which are to be developed in later plays. But it can be unhelpful to pre-judge the play according to notions of development: to assume that the reason why *The Two Gentlemen of Verona* troubles us is that Julia is not as 'rounded' as Viola, that the Proteus–Valentine relationship is not as fully realized as the friendship of Bassanio and Antonio, or that the outlaw scenes do not have the thematic importance of their counterparts in *As You Like It*. What is more helpful, if we want to see what impulses produce the particular inconsistencies of *The Two Gentlemen of Verona*, is to relate the play to the sonnets. Whatever the exact chronology of either play or sonnets, a kinship between them has long been a recognized fact. It consists both of verbal echoes – similar, often Petrarchan, topics and conceits being developed through similar vocabulary – and of a kind of plot similarity.[9] Whatever the true story behind either play or sonnets, in both cases Shakespeare is creating a fiction to explore the joys and agonies, the betrayals and fulfilments, of interconnecting love relationships. Proteus, the betrayer of both love and friendship, is most like the Youth of the sonnets, with an element of the Dark Lady; Valentine and the two girls all share features of the sonnets' 'I': adoration of the beloved, faithfulness, constancy; and Valentine in the end takes up the all-forgiving and renouncing position of, for example, Sonnet 40. Obviously I am not concerned here with 'plot' similarities as indicating any autobiographical truths behind these works: the 'truth' of the sonnets lies in Shakespeare's dramatic ability – unique among Elizabethan sonneteers[10] – to create a sense of 'what it feels like' in a given human situation. Paradoxically, that dramatic ability is less evident in the combinations and permutations of love and friendship (with, it should be noted, the friendship theme being given much less scope than the love theme) which make up the pattern of the play. Nor am I suggesting that a single sonnet, like 40, *justifies* the final scene of the play, but that it may help to illuminate its dramatic inconsistencies.

For, in the end, the really important relationship between *The Two Gentlemen of Verona* and the sonnets seems to me to have to do with Shakespeare's attitude to his own poetry and to the traditions of love poetry in which he finds himself writing. More important than any local similarities is the fact that the sonnets, like the play, show us Shakespeare working within a well-established convention, both using it and criticizing it – writing, as it were, through and around it. Apart from a handful of simply conventional Petrarchan exercises, his aim (explicit and implicit) in the sonnets is to subordinate his style to his subject matter, to use the convention only insofar as it helps him to render the true image of the person he is writing to and of.[11] Thus, to take an extreme example, what he wants to say about the Dark Lady in Sonnet 130 only makes sense through an evaluation of the Petrarchan convention; yet the real point of the poem remains the 'rareness' of the Lady, not the dig at the convention. Related to this feature of the sonnets is Shakespeare's attitude to language: an apparently paradoxical combination of a tremendous belief in the powers of his own poetry (again both implicit in the writing itself and explicitly stated) with an equally insistent sense that language is inadequate to express the beloved's identity – the quintessential statement being 'that you alone are you' (84). It is in the sonnets that Shakespeare most clearly faces the problem which, of course, he shares with any love poet: that he needs language to define the uniqueness of the beloved and his feelings about him or her, but that, at the same time, language itself is conventional and conventionalizes experience.

When love poetry is transferred to the stage, when the inner drama of a sonnet's 'I' and 'thou' has to be translated into the flesh-and-blood interaction of two lovers and probably also their conflicts with several other 'I's and 'thou's, then the problem is further confounded. In *Romeo and Juliet* Shakespeare partly solved it by contrasting the empty attitudinizing of Romeo's love for Rosaline with the beauty of the formality which surrounds and expresses his love for Juliet, from their first meeting on a shared sonnet.[12] Present-day playwrights, handling a tired and cliché-ridden language, have to face the problem in one extreme form – as Arnold Wesker discovered when he wanted a lover to tell his lady that she had 'autumn soft skin' and found that this would put audiences in mind of TV advertisements for Camay soap[13] – and generally find it easier to let their characters make love in the flesh than in words. The playwrights of the 1590s were not afraid of verbal cliché in the same way; and the lovers in *The Two Gentlemen of Verona* can liken each other to the sun, or the moon, or the stars, can be blinded by love or weep floods of tears, or generally draw on the stock-in-trade of Petrarchan love poetry. But, as in the sonnets, Shakespeare in this play also shows an awareness that conventionalized language, like conventionalized behaviour, may be false. In this self-consciousness about conventional language and situations lie many of the play's inconsistencies, but also much of its sense of life.

We do not have to read or listen to *The Two Gentlemen of Verona* for very long before we discover a tendency in its main characters to be self-conscious about the language they use, to veer between exuberance and deflation, indulgence in Lyly-like wit games and sudden dismissals of them. In I i Valentine deflates Proteus' love rhetoric even before he has had time to utter any of it; in II iv the positions are reversed, as Valentine takes up exactly the role he ascribed to Proteus in the first scene and, in his turn, has his hyperboles punctured:

> *Pro.*: Why, Valentine, what braggardism is this?
> *Val.*: Pardon me, Proteus; all I can is nothing
>   To her, whose worth makes other worthies nothing;
>   She is alone.
> *Pro.*:   Then let her alone.
>
> (II iv 160–3)

Proteus shifts the sense of Valentine's 'alone' – reminiscent of the sonnets' 'that you alone are you' – with a brusqueness which anticipates Timon's dismissal of the Poet:

> *Poet*:   I am rapt, and cannot cover
>   The monstrous bulk of this ingratitude
>   With any size of words.
> *Tim.*: Let it go naked: men may see't the better.
>
> (*Timon of Athens*, V i 62–5)

This effect of contrast and deflation does not seem to be tied to character as much as to the needs of the situation or scene. In II iv Silvia initially has something of the same function of commonsense critic as, at other times, is given to Speed or Launce. She undercuts the sparring between Valentine and

Thurio, and she exposes the absurdity of Valentine's conceits to the cold light of reason:

> *Val.*: This is the gentleman I told your ladyship
>   Had come along with me but that his mistress
>   Did hold his eyes lock'd in her crystal looks . . .
> *Sil.*: Nay, then, he should be blind; and, being blind,
>   How could he see his way to seek out you?
>
> (II iv 82–9)

Not that this stops Valentine's flow of images; on the contrary, Silvia has supplied him with the perfect cue for a further conceit,

> Why, lady, Love hath twenty pair of eyes,

and this gives Thurio, too, a chance to have a go after his feeble fashion, so that we have one of the rare occasions in the play where the dialogue, in an anticipation of *Much Ado About Nothing*, arrives at a kind of differentiated group wit. But only a few lines later, as Proteus has arrived and entered upon a courtesy duologue with Silvia, the function of commentator has also passed from her to Valentine:

> Leave off discourse of disability.
>
> (II iv 105)

Related to this tendency in the play, and also tied to scene rather than to character, is a reminder, which tends to crop up at key moments, of the impotency of words. Proteus' motivation of the brevity of the parting scene between him and Julia – 'For truth hath better deeds than words to grace it' (II ii 18) – may in itself be merely conventional, but Julia on her next appearance makes an ironically genuine-sounding statement of the reality of love being beyond the power of words. 'Didst thou but know', she says to Lucetta, 'the inly touch of love',

> Thou wouldst as soon go kindle fire with snow
> As seek to quench the fire of love with words.
>
> (II vii 18–20)

The irony is double here, for not only does Julia's paean to her and Proteus' love come just after we have witnessed his

decision to abandon her, but the very questioning of the power
of words is put in such an exuberant form as to question the
question. Ironically, too, Julia's argument is inverted and
perverted by Proteus as he threatens to rape Silvia:

> Nay, if the gentle spirit of moving words
> Can no way change you to a milder form,
> I'll woo you like a soldier, at arms' end,
> And love you 'gainst the nature of love – force ye.
>
> (V iv 55–8)

And significantly it is, at this point, visual and not verbal
evidence that brings about Valentine's recognition: 'nought but
mine eye / Could have persuaded me' (v iv 64–5). The
questioning of language does not loom as large, nor occupy as
thematically central a place, in *The Two Gentlemen of Verona* as it
does in *Love's Labour's Lost*, but it is in some ways still more
disturbing. In *Love's Labour's Lost* reliance on fine words and
clever patterns indicates an empty idealism, an ivory tower
knowledge of life, which collapses before real experience – be
it of love or death. The collapse can be funny, but it can also
be poignant, as when the Princess holds up the irrelevancy of
the King's diction in the final scene: 'I understand you not; my
griefs are double' (v ii 740). Berowne – for it takes the wittiest
mind to see the limits of wit – is the one to take the point:
'Honest plain words best pierce the ear of grief' (l. 741). And
so we are prepared for the play's final resting point, on good
deeds versus words. In *The Two Gentlemen of Verona*, 'honest plain
words' play little part, and the alternatives to wit are, on the
one hand, silence and, on the other, force and brutality.

SOURCE: Extract from ' "Were man but constant, he were
perfect": Constancy and Consistency in *The Two Gentlemen of
Verona*', *Shakespearian Comedy*, ed. M. Bradbury & D. Palmer
(London, 1972), pp. 31–57.

NOTES

1. Gordon S. Haight, *George Eliot: A Biography* (Oxford, 1968),
p. 178.

2. *Endimion*, III iv 124–7. Cf. M. C. Bradbrook, *Shakespeare and Elizabethan Poetry* (London, 1951), p. 150.

3. As for example in the Titus and Gisippus story in Sir Thomas Elyot's *The Governour*, Book II, Chapter XII, which Geoffrey Bullough prints as a 'possible source' of *The Two Gentlemen* (*Narrative and Dramatic Sources of Shakespeare*, vol. I (London, 1957), pp. 212–17).

4. I am not concerned here with the obvious but superficial inconsistencies of geography, timing, etc., which Clifford Leech discusses in the introduction to the new Arden edition (London, 1969), pp. xv–xxi.

5. Haight, *George Eliot*.

6. In particular, G. K. Hunter, *John Lyly* (London, 1962), chapter VI; Stanley Wells, 'The Failure of *The Two Gentlemen of Verona*', *Shakespeare Jahrbuch* 99 (1963), 161–73; Harold F. Brooks, 'Two Clowns in a Comedy (To Say Nothing of the Dog)', *Essays and Studies* (1963) 91–100.

7. Hereward T. Price, 'Shakespeare as a Critic', *Philological Quarterly*, XX (1941), 398.

8. In the absence of external evidence, scholars have varied in their opinions as to where, exactly, to place *The Two Gentlemen* among the early comedies. It could have been Shakespeare's first comedy of all.

9. Cf. Leech, new Arden edition, pp. lxix–lxx, and Bullough, *Narrative and Dramatic Sources of Shakespeare*, pp. 210–11.

10. Cf. G. K. Hunter, 'The Dramatic Technique of Shakespeare's Sonnets' *Essays in Criticism*, 3 (1953), 152–64.

11. See the helpful discussion of this point in Joan Grundy, 'Shakespeare's Sonnets and the Elizabethan Sonneteers', *Shakespeare Survey*, 15 (1962), 41–9.

12. Cf. the chapter on *Romeo and Juliet* in Nicholas Brooke, *Shakespeare's Early Tragedies* (London, 1968).

13. See the Epilogue to *The Four Seasons* (*Penguin New English Dramatists*, 9, p. 189).

RECENT PRODUCTIONS OF
THE TWO GENTLEMEN OF VERONA

THE *Two Gentlemen of Verona* has been only rarely performed this century. Reviews regularly begin by bemoaning the *play:* 'audiences never seem to like it' (*Times*, 15/1/34). The only salvation in this 'awful play' is the comedy produced by Launce and Crab who provide a 'comic oasis in this elegant desert of lovers' (*News Chronicle*, 20/4/38). Writing of the Marlowe Society production in 1951, Ivor Brown said: 'The only hope... for the *Two Gentlemen*... is a perfectly decorated stage and a production which obscures the nonsense in a veil of eye-catching masquerade' (*Observer*, 12/8/51). Dennis Carey apparently succeeded by treating the play as a masque in his 1952 Bristol Old Vic production and 'made an enchantment of the lyric comedy' (*Sketch*, 27/2/52). The success was achieved at some cost in terms of textual integrity. Crucially Valentine's notorious line ('All that was mine in Sylvia I give thee') was cut, affording him a romantic consistency, and Proteus' duplicity was glossed over. Other interesting productions include one at Nottingham Playhouse in 1953 when the play was chosen as the theatre's 100th production. John Harrison made it an actors' production with the prompter on stage. The theatrical self-consciousness was another device designed to overcome the play's perceived improbabilities. In 1957 Michael Langham trusted less 'to balletic inspiration than to carefully considered and well-invented stage effects' but nevertheless it all collapsed in 'the preposterous reconciliation scene' (*Times*, 23/1/57). In the following year there was a radio production with Frankie Howerd as Launce and Percy Edwards as Crab but Stratford had to wait until 1960 for its first major production for 27 years.

The Two Gentlemen of Verona was the play chosen by Peter Hall as his opening production in a season he devoted to the comedies. In a programme note he outlined his plan 'to trace through a sequence of six plays, the range, development and paradox of Shakespearean Comedy'. However most reviewers judged the decision a mistake, feeling that the play, Shakespeare's 'worst' (*Daily Mail*, 6/4/60) just could not sustain interest. It was condemned as boring though once again Launce (and Crab) escaped censure. Some, though, welcomed the opportunity to see the play performed alongside the more mature comedies and J. C. Trewin felt that Hall's serious treatment of the final scene showed 'how needless it is for academics to bother about points that seem to them to be mountainous difficulties on the page' (*Birmingham Post*, 6/4/60). However, the elaboration of setting and costume and the overworked stage revolve betrayed yet again an insecurity about the text.

It was ten years before the play appeared again on the Stratford stage though there was a small-scale Theatre-Go-Round production in 1969 in which Richard Pasco's Proteus shunned the habitual attempt to give him a soft centre. He was 'a gentleman who is no gentleman . . whose double-dealing. . . lurks almost from the first under his romantic protestation of eternal love' (*Financial Times*, 20/8/69). The following year Robin Phillips was determined to reveal that the play could work. He set it in modern dress on a hotel patio complete with swimming pool and the play drew to a close to the sound of the Beatles' song *All you need is love.* Helen Mirren's Julia was an 'emergent puppyish deb., sucking her thumb when distressed' (*Daily Mail*, 24/7/70) among a group of real life adolescents with time on their hands and love on their minds. There was some of the predictable resistance to updating Shakespeare but from Harold Hobson in particular strong praise for the production: 'Through modern eyes it penetrates an ancient truth . . it reaches the heart of Shakespeare's play – the rupture of its youth and the darkness of its treachery – and finds it beating fresh and strong.' Launce was redefined; 'who would have thought that this servant, usually so crude and so vulgar, could so certainly be the play's sad dark angel, harsh and sinister, yet with such depth of feeling, and so schematically beautiful as he stands framed in a panel at the back of the stage, gravely contemplating the apparent happiness of his employers?' (*Sunday Times*, 26/7/70).

In 1981 John Barton presented a cut text in a double-bill with *Titus Andronicus*. Around both he established a metatheatrical frame through the device of presenting the company as a group of Elizabethan actors (with the attendant costume skips, prop baskets, etc.). The response was mixed though the cut text gave pace to the narrative while avoiding the temptation to remove Valentine's offer of Silvia to Proteus. A leaf-strewn stage established an autumnal sadness and facilitated emotional truth. In stark contrast the 1987 Regent's Park Open Air production did nothing with the play's conclusion, prompting a reaction more of 'come off it' than belief.

Stratford had another gap of ten years before David Thacker's 1991 production exploited the greater intimacy of the Swan theatre. He set the play in the 1930s, importing not only costume and style but songs by Gershwin and Cole Porter. The songs provided apt and often moving commentary upon the action of the play. There was a permanent band on stage and the singer (Hilary Cromie) not only provided vocal musical links between scenes but more subtly she was a choric figure able to exploit a strong upstage position to good effect. For example, she took a drink of water as comment on Launce's: 'To be slow in words is a woman's only virtue.' Richard Moore was a wonderfully lugubrious Launce paired with an equally lugubrious lurcher dog (Woolly) affording the moment a genuine balance of response.

The thirties setting lent more than surface charm. It allowed the audience to see the characters as functioning within a cinematic idiom as self-conscious matinée idols. They were therefore afforded an effective correlative for the artifice of Shakespeare's text. In this world of tennis whites, silver cigarette cases, iced lemonade and gilt-framed photographs the action by and large worked. Richard Bonneville's Valentine succeeded in negotiating the fine line between naïvety and stupidity. There was a lack of both intellectual and physical agility in his scene with the Duke but the audience's laughter was stifled by the moving eloquence and emotional truth of his soliloquy: 'And why not death, rather than living torment . . .'

Barry Lynch's Proteus worked hard to keep an audience's sympathy. When the production transferred to the Barbican in 1992 he even modified his line to read: 'Were man*kind* but constant . . .' He held a long pause in the last scene to convey guilt and shame at Valentine's discovery of his perfidy. Silvia's silence here may be considered to be as much of a problem as Valentine's offer of her to his friend but the blocking of the action in this production empowered her, albeit silently. She crossed to the crouched figure of Proteus and put her hand on his shoulder. She forgave him and she paved the way for Valentine to be reconciled to his friend. The action confirmed the magnaminity of Silvia and removed any notion of Silvia as possession to be passed between the men. After the long pause which preceded Proteus' line 'My guilt and shame confounds me' and the similarly held moment for Silvia's move to Proteus before Valentine's 'Then I am paid', Julia's faint almost overlapped Valentine's controversial line.

The whole company were on stage to sing *Love is the sweetest thing* at the end of the play but the two couples fell silent, turning to face each other in a sensitive expression of the bitter-sweet mood of the play's conclusion. For many members of the audience this production rehabilitated the play. But for a few critics the weight given to the updated setting and emotive, known music confirmed the view that the play is flawed and incomplete, needing adaptation of one form or another to make it work.

PART FOUR

Love's Labour's Lost

Robert Tofte (1598)

Love's Labour Lost, I once did see a play,
Ycleped so, so called to my pain,
Which I to hear to my small joy did stay,
Giving attendance on my froward dame.
  My misgiving mind presaging to me ill,
  Yet was I drawn to see it 'gainst my will.

This play no play but plague was unto me,
For there I lost the love I liked most;
And what to others seemed a jest to be,
I, that (in earnest) found unto my cost.
  To everyone (save me) 'twas comical,
  Whilst tragic-like to me it did befall.

Each actor played in cunning wise his part,
But chiefly those entrapped in Cupid's snare;
Yet all was feigned, 'twas not from the heart;
They seemed to grieve, but yet they felt no care.
  'Twas I that grief indeed did bear in breast,
  The others did but make a show in jest.

Yet neither feigning theirs, nor my mere truth,
Could make her once so much as for to smile;
Whilst she, despite of pity mild and ruth,
Did sit as scorning of my woes the while.
  Thus did she sit to see Love lose his love,
  Like hardened rock that force nor power can move.

SOURCE: Robert Tofte, an extract from *Alba: The Month's Mind of a Melancholy Lover* (1598).

Charles Gildon   (1710)

Tho' I can't well see why the Author gave this Play this Name yet since it has past thus long I shall say no more to it but this, that since it is one of the worst of *Shakespeare's* Plays, nay I think I may say the very worst, I cannot but think it is his first . . .

SOURCE: Charles Gildon, *Notes on Shakespeare's Plays* (1710).

Samuel Johnson   (1765)

In this play, which all the editors have concurred to censure and some have rejected as unworthy of our poet, it must be confessed that there are many passages mean, childish and vulgar; and some which ought not to have been exhibited, as we are told they were, to a maiden queen. But there are scattered through the whole many sparks of genius; nor is there any play that has more evident marks of the hand of Shakespeare.

SOURCE: Samuel Johnson, *Notes on the Plays* in his edition of 1765.

George Bernard Shaw   (1886)

A performance of Love's Labor Lost is a sort of entertainment to be valued rather for Shakespear's sake than for its own. The

Dramatic Students did not tempt many people into the St James's Theatre on the sultry afternoon of 2nd July by the experiment; and it is perhaps as well that they did not, for their efforts bore the same relation to fine acting as the play does to Antony and Cleopatra . . . The play itself showed more vitality than might have been expected. Three hundred years ago, its would-be wits, with their forced smartness, their indecent waggeries, their snobbish sneers at poverty, and their ill-bred and ill-natured mockery of age and natural infirmity, passed more easily as ideal compounds of soldier, courtier, and scholar than they can nowadays. Among people of moderate culture in this century they would be ostracised as insufferable cads . . . Nothing, it seems to me, but a perverse hero-worship can see much to admire in the badinage of Biron and Rosaline. Benedick and Beatrice are better; and Orlando and Rosalind much better: still, they repeatedly annoy us by repartees of which the trivial ingenuity by no means compensates the silliness, coarseness, or malice. It is not until Shakespear's great period began with the seventeenth century that, in Measure for Measure, we find this sort of thing shown in its proper light and put in its proper place in the person of Lucio, whose embryonic stages may be traced in Mercutio and Biron. Fortunately for Love's Labor Lost, Biron is not quite so bad as Mercutio: you never absolutely long to kick him off the stage as you long to kick Mercutio when he makes game of the Nurse. And Shakespear, though a very feeble beginner then in comparison to the master he subsequently became, was already too far on the way to his greatness to fail completely when he set himself to write a sunny, joyous and delightful play. Much of the verse is charming: even when it is rhymed doggrell it is full of that bewitching Shakespearean music which tempts the susceptible critic to sugar his ink and declare that Shakespear can do no wrong. The construction of the play is simple and effective. The only absolutely impossible situation was that of Biron hiding in the tree to overlook the king, who presently hides to watch Longaville, who in turn spies on Dumain; as the result of which we had three out of four gentlemen shouting 'asides' through the sylvan stillness, No. 1 being inaudible to 2,

3, and 4; No. 2 audible to No. 1, but not to 3 and 4; No. 3
audible to 1 and 2, but not to No. 4; and No. 4 audible to all
the rest, but himself temporarily stone deaf. Shakespear has
certainly succeeded in making this arrangement intelligible; but
the Dramatic Students' stage manager did not succeed in
making it credible . . . On the whole, I am not sure that Love's
Labor Lost is worth reviving at this time of day; but I am
bound to add that if it were announced tomorrow with an
adequate cast, I should make a point of seeing it.

SOURCE: George Bernard Shaw, *Our Corner*, 1 August 1886.

Walter Pater   (1889)

The merely dramatic interest of the piece is slight enough; only
just sufficient, indeed, to form the vehicle of its wit and poetry.
The scene – a park of the King of Navarre – is unaltered
throughout; and the unity of the play is not so much the unity
of a drama as that of a series of pictorial groups, in which the
same figures reappear, in different combinations but on the
same background. It is as if Shakespeare had intended to bind
together, by some inventive conceit, the devices of an ancient
tapestry, and give voices to its figures. On one side, a fair
palace; on the other, the tents of the Princess of France, who
has come on an embassy from her father to the King of
Navarre; in the midst, a wide space of smooth grass. The same
personages are combined over and over again into a series of
gallant scenes – the princess, the three masked ladies, the
quaint, pedantic king; one of those amiable kings men have
never loved enough, whose serious occupation with the things
of the mind seems, by contrast with the more usual forms of
kingship, like frivolity or play. Some of the figures are grotesque merely, and all the male ones at least, a little fantastic.
Certain objects reappearing from scene to scene – love-letters

crammed with verses to the margin, and lovers' toys – hint obscurely at some story of intrigue. Between these groups, on a smaller scale, come the slighter and more homely episodes, with Sir Nathaniel the curate, the country-maid Jaquenetta, Moth or Mote the elfin-page, with Hiems and Ver, who recite 'the dialogue that the two learned men have compiled in praise of the owl and the cuckoo.'

SOURCE: Walter Pater, *Appreciations*, first pub. 1889, reprinted 1931.

Harley Granville-Barker (1927)

Here is a fashionable play; now, by three hundred years, out of fashion. Nor did it ever, one supposes, make a very wide appeal. It abounds in jokes for the elect. Were you not numbered among them you laughed, for safety, in the likeliest places. A year or two later the elect themselves might be hard put to it to remember what the joke was.

Were this all one could say of *Love's Labour's Lost*, the question of its staging today – with which we are first and last concerned – would be quickly answered, and Lose No Labour here be the soundest advice. For spontaneous enjoyment is the life of the theatre. . . .

Drama, as Shakespeare will come to write it, is, first and last, the projection of character in action; and devices for doing this, simple and complex, must make up three-quarters of its artistry. We can watch his early discovery that dialogue is waste matter unless it works to this end; that wit, epigram, sentiment are like paper and sticks in a fireplace, the flaring and crackling counting for nothing if the fire itself won't light, if these creatures in whose mouths the wit is sounded won't 'come alive'. To the last he kept his youthful delight in a pun; and he would write an occasional passage of word-music with a minimum of meaning to it (but of maximum emotional value, it will be found, in the character that has to speak it). His development of verse to dramatic use is a study in itself. He never ceased to develop it, but for a while the dramatist had a hard time with the lyric poet. The early plays abound, besides, in elaborate embroidery of language done for its own sake. This was a fashionable literary exercise and Shakespeare was an adept at it. To many young poets of the time their language was a new-found wonder; its very handling gave them pleasure. The amazing things it could be made to do! He had to discover that they were not much to his purpose; but it is not easy to stop doing what you do so well. Yet even in this play we may note the difference between the Berowne of

> Light seeking light doth light of light beguile;
> So ere you find where light in darkness lies
> Your light grows dark by losing of your eyes!

and of the soliloquy beginning

> And I forsooth in love . . .

Turn also from one of the many sets of wit to Katharina's haunting answer when Rosaline twits her with rebellion against Cupid:

> *Rosaline*: You'll ne'er be friends with him; he kill'd your sister.
> *Katharine*: He made her melancholy, sad, and heavy:
>   And so she died: had she been light, like you,
>   Of such a merry, nimble, stirring spirit,
>   She might have been a grandam ere she died;
>   And so may you, for a light heart lives long.

Compare it with the set of wit that follows:

> *Rosaline*: What's your dark meaning, mouse, of this light word?
> *Katharine*: A light condition in a beauty dark.
> *Rosaline*: We need more light to find your meaning out.
> *Katharine*: You'll mar the light, by taking it in snuff;
>   Therefore I'll darkly end the argument.

But Rosaline won't let her, and they manage to get five more rather spicier exchanges. It is all very charming; and a 'set of wit' describes it well. Get a knowledge of the game and it may

be as attractive to watch for a little as are a few sets of tennis.
But pages on pages of such smart repartee will not tell us as
much of the speakers as those few simple lines of Katharina's
tell us – of herself and her love for her sister, and of Rosaline
too.

SOURCE: Harley Granville-Barker, *Prefaces to Shakespeare*
(1927).

John Palmer   (1946)

The princes woo the princesses in disguise, with intricate
tributes in verse and pyrotechnical displays of ingenious wit
and pretty sentiment. Finally there is a general recantation.
Artifice is abandoned and nature carries the day.

Berowne has a very special place in this playful and satirical
design. Along with the rest he is mocked by his author and is
a target for the ladies. But he fully appreciates the comedy of
his predicament. He speaks for nature, though caught in the
toils of artifice; and, at the end, delivers the moral of the piece
in which he has, in effect, played the part of Chorus on his
author's behalf. It is as though Shakespeare had said: 'Here, if
you like, is a satire; but, if you insist on laughing at these
fantastical persons, please remember that we are all painted
with the same brush and note that, if this fellow Berowne, with
whom I am obviously on excellent terms, has my permission to
moralise the spectacle, that is only because he has been well
content to play the fool for your diversion'. . . .

The Princess of France has been unfairly neglected. Shakespeare has not yet at his command the gifts which he will
shortly bestow on his comic heroines – the music of Viola, the
voluble precision of Rosalind, the glitter of Beatrice, the
eloquence of Portia. But the Princess of France already bears
the stamp royal. She has just that commingling of good sense

and lively imagination, of quick feeling and clear thinking, of instinctive reserve and an equally distinctive candour, which distinguishes all Shakespeare's happy women who give away their hearts without losing their heads. She is the first flower upon a branch that was to bear blossoms of a deeper colour and a headier scent, all different and yet so unmistakably from the same stem; and there is a freshness in this first budding of an immortal type which has its special charm. Her first sedate challenge to the King, not without a hint of mischief, confronts him neatly with his own preposterous dilemma:

> I hear your grace hath sworn out house-keeping:
> 'Tis deadly sin, to keep that oath, my lord,
> And sin to break it.

SOURCE: John Palmer, *Comic Characters of Shakespeare* (1946).

MODERN STUDIES

Bobbyann Roesen

LOVE'S LABOUR'S LOST (1953)

IN a sense the play has ended; an epilogue has been spoken by
Berowne and that haunting and beautiful kingdom created by
the marriage of reality with illusion destroyed, seemingly
beyond recall. In the person of Marcade, the world outside the
circuit of the park has at last broken through the gates,
involving the people of the play in its sorrows and grim
actualities, the plague-houses and desolate retreats, the mourn-
ing cities and courts of that vaster country overshadowing the
tents and the fantastic towers of Navarre. Yet before the final
dissolution of that minute and once isolated kingdom of the
play, when some of the characters seem already to have
disappeared and the others are preparing sadly to journey into
the realms beyond the walls of the royal close, there is granted
suddenly a little moment of grace. In the waning afternoon, all
the people of the play return to the stage and stand quietly
together to hear the song which 'the two learned men have
compiled in praise of the Owl and the Cuckoo', a song into
which the whole of that now-vanished world of *Love's Labour's
Lost* seems to have passed, its brilliance, its strange mingling of
the artificial and the real, its loveliness and laughter gathered
together for the last time to speak to us in the form of a single
strain of music.

> When daisies pied and violets blue
> And lady-smocks all silver-white

197

> And cuckoo-buds of yellow hue
> Do paint the meadows with delight. . . .

It is the landscape of the royal park that lies outstretched before us, a little world of thickets and smooth lawns, meadows and wooded hills. In the foreground, their appearance and speech as decorative and charming as the setting in which they have met to solemnize their vows of asceticism and study, stand four young men, Berowne, Dumain, Longaville, and that ruler of Navarre whose slender kingdom of foresters and dairy-maids, courtiers, pedants, and fools seems bounded by the park and its single, rustic village. Mannered and artificial, reflecting an Elizabethan delight in patterned and intricate language, Navarre's lines at the beginning of the play are nevertheless curiously urgent and intense.

> Let fame, that all hunt after in their lives,
> Live regist'red upon our brazen tombs,
> And then grace us in the disgrace of death;
> When, spite of cormorant devouring Time,
> Th' endeavour of this present breath may buy
> That honour which shall bate his scythe's keen edge,
> And make us heirs of all eternity.

With the King's first words, an expression of that peculiarly Renaissance relationship of the idea of Fame with that of Time and Death, a shadow darkens for a moment the delicate dream landscape of the park. Touched by this shadow, affected by its reality, the four central characters of *Love's Labour's Lost* enter the world of the play.

Fantastic and contrived as they are, those absurd vows to which the four friends commit themselves in the initial scene spring from a recognition of the tragic brevity and imperm-anence of life that is peculiarly Renaissance. For the people of the sixteenth century, the world was no longer the mere shadow of a greater Reality, the imperfect image of that City of God whose towers and golden spires had dominated the universe of the Middle Ages. While the thought of Death was acquiring a new poignancy in its contrast with man's increasing sense of the value and loveliness of life in this world, Immort-ality tended to become, for Renaissance minds, a vague and even a somewhat dubious gift unless it could be connected in some way with the earth itself, and the affairs of human life there. Thus there arose among the humanist writers of Italy that intense and sometimes anguished longing, voiced by Navarre at the beginning of *Love's Labour's Lost*, to attain 'an immortality of glory, survival in the minds of men by the record of great deeds or of intellectual excellence. . . .'[1] At the very heart of the plan for an Academe lies the reality of Death, the Renaissance desire to inherit, through remarkable devotion to learning, an eternity of Fame, and thus to insure some continuity of personal existence, however slight, against the ravages of 'cormorant devouring Time'.

It is obvious, however, from the very beginning of the play, that the Academe and the idea of immortality which it embodies must fail. Less remote and docile than Dumain and Longaville, existing upon a deeper level of reality within the play, the brilliant and sensitive Berowne, a Chorus character throughout, first realizes how unnatural the vows are, how seriously they trespass, despite their three-year limit, against the normal laws of life and reality. The paradox of the Academe and the reason why its failure is not only understandable but absolutely necessary lie in the fact that this elaborate scheme which intends to enhance life and extend it through Fame even beyond the boundaries of the grave would in reality, if successfully carried out, result in the limitation of life and, ultimately, in its complete denial. In their very attempt to retain hold upon life, the King and his companions, as Berowne alone understands, are cutting themselves off from it, from love, and the beauty of women, from all those simple sensuous pleasures of the world which have prompted the establishment of the Academe in the first place by making the 'too much loved earth more lovely',[2] and the thought of its loss in Death so unbearably grim.

Long before the appearance of those two delightful but sobering characters, Holofernes and Nathaniel, Berowne has seen the barrenness of learning that is divorced from life, the tragedy of those industrious men of science who find a name for every star in the western skies and yet 'have no more profit

of their shining nights / Than those that walk and wot not
what they are.' Even in the first scene of the play, before his
love for Rosaline has made his perception deeper and more
sensitive, Berowne realizes in some sense that the only way to
deal with the bleak reality of Death and Time is to accept it,
to experience as much of life's sensory loveliness as possible
while the opportunity is still given. Implicit in his earliest lines
is the knowledge, related somehow to the first group of the
'Sonnets', that 'we cannot cross the cause why we were born',
and although he agrees at last to take the oath, it is through
him that we first sense the conviction expressed by the play as
a whole that this idea of intellectual glory is an essentially
sterile one, that the price exacted is too great to pay for a fame
and a memory on earth that will soon be lost in the unimagined
reaches of Time.

It was one of Walter Pater's most famous dictums that 'All
art constantly aspires towards the condition of music',[3] and in
his beautiful essay on 'Shakespeare's English Kings' he asserted
more particularly that 'into the unity of a choric song the
perfect drama ever tends to return, its intellectual scope
deepened, complicated, enlarged, but still with an unmistakable singleness, or identity, in its impression on the mind'.[4]
Such a unity is evident throughout *Love's Labour's Lost*, and,
indeed, the quality of the whole is very much that of a musical
composition, an inexorable movement forward, the appearance
and reappearance in the fabric of the play of certain important
themes, forcing the harmony into a series of coherent resolutions consistent with each other and with the drama as a whole.
Berowne has scarcely finished speaking before his assertion
that 'every man with his affects is born, / Not by might
mast'red, but by special grace' is echoed in the structure of the
comedy itself, with the entrance of Constable Dull and the
reluctant Costard, the first to disobey the edicts of the new
Academe.

The little episode which follows is not only significant of the
trend of future action but, in itself, one of the most delightful
moments of the play. As the King reads Armado's incredible
accusation and Costard tries feebly to avert impending doom

by making Navarre laugh, it becomes obvious for the first time how much enchantment the play holds for the ear, how subtly it combines highly individual idioms of speech into a single conversation. *Love's Labour's Lost* is a play of many voices, and much of its beauty grows from the sheer music of their rise and fall, the exploitation of their differences of quality and tone, accent and complication. Here in the first scene, the frank simplicity of Dull, the awed monosyllables of Costard, are placed by Shakespeare in a deliberate musical relationship with the studied sentences of Longaville, the fantastic style of Armado, and the more attractive elegance of Berowne, and the whole episode is given the quality of a polyphonic composition half artificial and half real.

Beyond its humour and fascination of language, the Costard scene has, of course, a more serious purpose in the play, a purpose virtually identical with that fulfilled by a scene in *Measure for Measure*. In the later comedy, Angelo appears in the opening scene of the second act in a role analogous to Navarre's in *Love's Labour's Lost*, and the old counsellor Escalus in one similar to Berowne's. The scheme of justice which Angelo would enforce in Vienna is as ridiculously inflexible, as ignorant of the nature of human beings as Navarre's Academe, and it is protested by Escalus. Not, however, until the sudden entrance of Constable Elbow, an Austrian cousin of Dull's, and Pompey, who can in some measure be compared to Costard, does it become completely obvious how impractical the system is, how helpless its high-minded idealism when forced to deal with real individuals, their private standards of morality and unpredictable human weaknesses. The fate of Angelo's justice is settled even before he himself has sinned against it, in the process of that riotous contention between Elbow, Froth, and Pompey, and in the same way, Navarre's Academe has failed before he and his friends are actually forsworn, from the moment that the real and intensely individual figures of Costard and Dull appear in their respective roles as transgressor and upholder. Among the lower social levels of the park, life itself destroys the King's scheme almost in the moment of its foundation.

Walter Pater found *Love's Labour's Lost* particularly charming in its changing 'series of pictorial groups, in which the same figures reappear, in different combinations but on the same background',[5] a composition, for him, like that of some ancient tapestry, studied, and not a little fantastic. The grouping of the characters into scenes would appear, however, to have been dictated by a purpose far more serious than the mere creation of such patterns; it is one of the ways in which Shakespeare maintains the balance of the play world between the artificial and the real, and indicates the final outcome of the comedy.

There are, of course, huge differences in the reality of the people who walk and speak together within the limits of the royal park. From the artificial and virtually indistinguishable figures of Dumain and Longaville, never really more than fashionable voices, the scale of reality rises gradually towards Berowne, in whom the marriage of a certain remote and fantastic quality with the delightful realism which first recognized the flaws in the Academe reflects the comedy as a whole, and reaches its apogee in the utter substantiality and prosaic charm of Constable Dull, who could never in any sense be accused of retreating into unreality, or affecting an elegant pose. Again and again, characters from different levels along this scale are grouped into scenes in a manner that helps to maintain the delicate balance of the play world; thus, in the first scene, with the incredible idea of the Academe and the sophisticated dialogue of Berowne and Longaville, Costard and the bewildered Dull are employed in much the same way that the mocking voice of the cuckoo is in the glowing spring landscape of the closing song, to keep the play in touch with a more familiar and real world, as well as to indicate the ultimate victory of reality over artifice and illusion.

As the first act ends, this theme is repeated again, and the inevitability of future events made even more clear with the abandonment of the edicts of the Academe by the very individual who was responsible for the deliverance of Costard into the righteous hands of Dull, the intense and serious Armado. The grave figure of the Spanish traveller is one of the most interesting and in a sense enigmatic to appear in *Love's*

Labour's Lost, and his sudden love for Jaquenetta certainly the strangest of the five romances which develop within the park. Like Berowne, Armado is a very real person who is playing a part, but in his case it is far more difficult to separate the actor from the man underneath, and the pose itself is more complex than the fashionable role of Berowne. Even in his soliloquies, Armado seems to be acting to some invisible audience, and it is only in one moment at the end of the play that we are granted a glimpse of the man without the mask.

Romantic and proud, intensely imaginative, he has retreated into illusion much further than has Berowne, creating a world of his own within the world of the park, a world peopled with the heroes of the past, Samson and Hercules, Hector and the knights of Spain. Somehow, it is among these long-dead heroes that Armado really exists, rather than among the people of the play itself, and his bizarre language, so strange and artificial when placed beside the homely speech of Costard, was created for that remote, imaginative environment and possesses there a peculiar beauty and aptness of its own. A character with some of the isolation of Jaques, always separated from the gibes and chatter of Moth, he falls in love with Jaquenetta without accepting her as the real country-wench she is, but creates a little drama about the object of his passion in which his is the central role, and Jaquenetta appears in any likeness that he pleases, Delilah or Deianira. The illusion in which the real character of Armado lives has its own beauty and charm, but as the play progresses it becomes evident that this illusion is not strong enough to withstand the pressure of reality and must in the end be destroyed.

With the coming into the King's park of the Princess of France and her companions a new stage in the development of *Love's Labour's Lost* has been reached, and a theme we have not heard before begins slowly to rise in the musical structure of the play. Before the arrival of the ladies, it has been made clear that the Academe must fail, and it is no surprise when in the opening scene of the second act we find each of the four friends stealing back alone after the initial meeting to learn the name of his love from the obliging Boyet. As life itself breaks swiftly through the artificial scholarship of the court, the vitality of the play rises to an amazing height; the Academe is kept constantly before us, the reasons for its failure elaborated and made more plain, but at the same time, while the world of the royal park becomes more and more delightful, while masque and pageantry, sensuous beauty and laughter flower within the walls, it becomes slowly obvious that more than the Academe will be destroyed by the entrance of the ladies. Not only its scholarship, but the entire world of the play, the balance of artifice and reality of which it was formed, must also be demolished by forces from without the walls.

The Princess and her little retinue represent the first penetration of the park by the normal world beyond, a world composed of different and colder elements than the fairy-tale environment within. Through them, in some sense, the voice of Reality speaks, and although they seem to fit perfectly into the landscape of the park, indulge in highly formal, elaborate skirmishes of wit with each other and with the men, they are somehow detached from this world of illusion and artificiality in a way that none of its original inhabitants are. The contrived and fashionable poses which they adopt are in a sense less serious, more playful than those of the other characters, and they are conscious all the time, as even Berowne is not, that these attitudes are merely poses, and that Reality is something quite different. With them into the park they bring past time and a disturbing reminder of the world outside, and from them come the first objective criticisms which pass beyond the scheme of the Academe to attack the men who have formed it. Maria, remembering Longaville as she saw him once before in Normandy, criticizes in her first speech the unreality with which the four friends have surrounded themselves, and points out for the first time in the play the danger of attitudes which develop without regard for the feelings of others, of wit that exercises itself thoughtlessly upon all.

In the wit of the ladies themselves, it is a certain edge of reality, an uncompromising logic, which cuts through the pleasant webs of artifice, the courtly jests and elaborations in the humour of the men, and emerges victorious with an unfailing regularity. Unlike the women, the King and his companions play, not with facts themselves, but with words, with nice phrases and antithetical statements, and when their embroidered language itself has been attacked, their courteous offers disdained as mere euphemisms, they can only retire discomfited. Even Berowne is utterly defeated when he approaches Rosaline with his graceful conceits.

> *Ber.*: Lady, I will commend you to mine own heart.
> *Ros.*: Pray you, do my commendations;
>   I would be glad to see it.
> *Ber.*: I would you heard it groan.
> *Ros.*: Is the fool sick?
> *Ber.*: Sick at the heart.
> *Ros.*: Alack, let it blood.
> *Ber.*: Would that do it good?
> *Ros.*: My physic says 'ay'.

Witty as Berowne, as agile of mind, Rosaline attacks his conventional protestations with a wit based on realism, a ridicule springing from a consciousness of the absurdity of artifice. That Berowne could be expressing a real passion in these artifical terms never enters her mind; he is merely mocking her, and she defends herself in the most effective way she can.

Berowne is, however, like the King, Dumain, and Longaville, suddenly and genuinely in love. The Academe has been thoroughly demolished and now, in the fourth act, Shakespeare introduces, in the characters of Holofernes and Nathaniel, reminders of what such a scheme might have led to, examples of the sterility of learning that is unrelated to life. As usual, Dull, surely the most delightful of that illustrious Shakespearian series of dim-witted but officious representatives of constabulary law, appears with them as the realistic element in the scene, the voice of the cuckoo which mocks, unconsciously, the intricate speech of the two pedants. Bewildered as usual, Dull shows here a quality of stubbornness we had not quite expected in him, maintaining stolidly against the fantastic perorations of Holofernes and Nathaniel that the deer killed by the Princess was 'not a haud credo; 'twas a pricket'. It is one of the most charming of his infrequent appearances, matched only by that little scene later in the play in which, utterly stupefied by the conversation which he has endured from Holofernes and Nathaniel at dinner, he sits mute and quiescent through all the arrangements for the pageant of the Nine Worthies, only at the very last, when roused by another character, entering the dialogue at all to offer us a personal performance upon the tabor, a talent as engaging and unexpected in Dull as song is in the Justice Silence of *2 Henry IV.*

Unlike Dull, the schoolmaster and the curate are in some sense mere types, elements of a satire, but Shakespeare is after all not writing a treatise, and even though their absurdity is emphasized, the two have a certain charm of their own, and their interminable quibblings a faint and grotesque beauty. On a lower, less refined level, they reflect the love of words themselves that is visible throughout the play, revelling, not like Armado in the romance and wonder of the past, but in Latin verbs and bits of forgotten erudition, spare and abstract. As Moth says, 'They have been at a great feast of languages and stol'n the scraps', and in their conversation the wisdom of ages past appears in a strangely mutilated form, the life drained from it, curiously haphazard and remote.

When in the third scene of Act Four, Berowne appears alone on the stage, we move from the two pedants to a higher level of reality, but one in which artifice is still present. Berowne's love for Rosaline is becoming increasingly intense, and although he seems at first only to be adopting another pose, that of melancholy lover, he is slowly becoming, as the play progresses, a more convincing and attractive figure, and his love more real.

By heaven, I do love; and it hath taught me to rhyme and to be melancholy; and here is part of my rhyme, and here my melancholy. Well, she hath one of my sonnets already; the clown bore it, the fool sent it, and the lady hath it; sweet clown, sweeter fool, sweetest lady.

Often, beneath ornament and convention the Elizabethans disguised genuine emotion. Berowne's love for Rosaline is as sincere as Philip Sidney's for Stella, his longing as real as that of the unknown Elizabethan lover in Nicholas Hillyarde's strangest and most haunting miniature who stands in the attitude of a familiar poetic conceit, gaunt and dishevelled, against a background of flames.

The episode which follows Berowne's introductory soliloquy is, of course, one of the finest in the entire play. It is the first of three scenes in *Love's Labour's Lost* which possess the quality of a play within the play, formal in construction, somehow contrived, always beautifully handled. Here, above the whole scene, Berowne acts as spectator and as Chorus, establishing the play atmosphere in his various asides, crying out upon the entrance of Longaville, 'Why, he comes in like a perjure, wearing papers', or in a more general affirmation,

> 'All hid, all hid' – an old infant play,
> Like a demigod here sit I in the sky,
> And wretched fools' secrets heedfully o'er-eye.

Throughout *Love's Labour's Lost*, the play is a symbol of illusion, of unreality, as it is in *A Midsummer Night's Dream*, and here it is employed to render the artificiality, the convenient but obvious device of having each of the four lovers appear alone upon the stage, read aloud the poem addressed to his lady, and step aside for the advance of the next one, not only acceptable, but completely delightful. In this play environment, a level of unreality beyond that of the comedy as a whole, the multiple discoveries are perfectly convincing, and the songs and sonnets read by the lovers the charming testimonies of a passion that is not to be questioned.

Through the comments of the spectator, Berowne, the scene is still, however, kept in touch with reality. From his wonderful, rocketing line upon the entrance of the King, 'Shot, by heaven!' to the moment when he steps from his concealment in all the splendour of outraged virtue, Berowne's role is again analogous to that of the cuckoo in the closing song, mocking the lovers 'enamelling with pied flowers their thoughts of gold',[6] maintaining the balance of the play. When he actually appears among his shamefaced friends to chide them for this 'scene of fool'ry', the play within the play ends, as the spectator

becomes actor, and we return, with his beautifully sanctimon-
ious sermon, to the more usual level of reality.

The sheer delight of the scene rises now towards its peak as,
only a few lines after the close of the play scene, another and
even more effective climax is built up. Costard appears with
Berowne's own sonnet written to Rosaline, and suddenly the
play rises into magnificence. 'Guilty, my lord, guilty. I confess,
I confess.' Berowne has become more real and brilliant than
ever before, and at the same time, his speech attains a power
and a radiance new in the comedy, an utterance still fastidious,
still choice, but less self-conscious, as he sums up for Navarre,
Dumain, and Longaville all that Shakespeare has been saying
long before, in the Costard scene, in the fall from grace of Don
Armado.

> Sweet lords, sweet lovers, O let us embrace!
> As true we are as flesh and blood can be.
> The sea will ebb and flow, heaven show his face;
> Young blood doth not obey an old decree.
> We cannot cross the cause why we were born,
> Therefore of all hands must be we forsworn.

Following these lines, there is a deliberate slackening of
intensity, and the scene descends for a moment into a completely artificial duel of wits among the King, Berowne, and
Longaville, on a somewhat hackneyed conceit. Berowne's
toying with the various meanings of dark and light is as
artificial and contrived as anything we have heard from him
earlier in the play, but from these lines the scene suddenly rises
to its final climax in that speech justifying the breaking of the
vows, which is without doubt the most beautiful in the entire
play. 'Have at you then, affection's men-at-arms.' Finally and
completely, the Academe has crumbled, and it is Berowne, as
is perfectly proper, who sums up all that the play has been
saying up to this point in his exquisite peroration upon earthly
love.

'Other slow arts entirely keep the brain, / And therefore,
finding barren practisers, / Scarce show a harvest of their
heavy toil.' Holofernes and Nathaniel are indirectly brought

before us, the symbols of learning divorced from life, and having thus disposed of scholarship, Berowne passes on to speak of Love itself, and the task of justifying his own perjury and that of his three friends. Gradually, his speech rises to a lyrical height unequalled in the rest of the play, his customary eloquence and delicacy of language transfigured and made splendid, the sincerity perfectly blended with the surviving mannerism. 'And when Love speaks, the voice of all the gods / Make heaven drowsy with the harmony.' With these two lines, the final climax of the scene has been reached, lines of an almost incredible beauty, sensuous and languid, their exact meaning a little puzzling perhaps, but communicating all that is necessary, in a realm beyond precise explanation.

After these lines, the speech loses something of its beauty, but its intensity remains and fires the King, Dumain, and Longaville. The action flares up suddenly in great, vibrant lines; 'Shall we resolve to woo these girls of France?' 'Saint Cupid, then! and, soldiers, to the field', and in a whirlwind of vitality and excitement the scene moves towards its close. 'For revels, dances, masks, and merry hours, / Forerun fair Love, strewing her way with flowers.' Yet, as is customary with Shakespeare, the scene ends quietly, with two thoughtful, foreboding lines which are prophetic of what is to come in the next act. As though he turned back for a second, musingly, in the act of going off with the others, Berowne, as Chorus, remarks more to himself and that deserted little glade which was the scene of the play within the play than to his retreating friends, 'Light wenches may prove plagues to men forsworn; / If so, our copper buys no better treasure', lines which despite their apparent gaiety are curiously disturbing.

With the beginning of that long, last act, a turning point in the action of the play has been reached. The Academe defeated by life itself on all levels of the park, one might expect that *Love's Labour's Lost* would move now, as *Much Ado About Nothing* does in its final act, into an untroubled close, a romantic ending like that of the Beatrice–Benedick plot. As we have in some sense been told by the title, and by the comments of the ladies, such an ending is, in this case, impossible. From

the Academe theme the play turns now to the destruction of
the half-real world within the royal park, a destruction which,
in the actual moment in which it is accomplished, is unexpected and shocking, and yet has been prepared for and
justified by previous events within the comedy. As we enter the
Fifth Act, shadows begin to fall across the play world. Life
within the park, its brilliance and laughter, mounts higher and
higher, yet it is the winter stanzas of the closing song that this
act suggests, and a new darkness, a strange intensity forces the
harmony of the play into unforeseen resolutions. Vanished now
are the untroubled meadows of spring, and the landscape
acquires a realism that is somehow a little harsh.

> When icicles hang by the wall,
> And Dick the shepherd blows his nail,
> And Tom bears logs into the hall,
> And milk comes frozen home in pail,
> When blood is nipp'd and ways be foul. . . .

With Act Five, the thought of Death enters the park. The
play opened, of course, under the shadow of death, the great
motivation of the Academe, but after that opening speech of
Navarre's, it vanished altogether, never appearing again even
in the imagery of the play until the entrance of the ladies.
Significantly, it is they, the intruders from the outside world of
reality, who first, in Act Three, bring death into the park itself.
In this act, the Princess kills a deer, but in the lines in which
the hunt is spoken of, those of Holofernes and the Princess
herself, the animal's death is carefully robbed of any disturbing
reality. After Holofernes has told us how 'The preyful Princess
pierc'd and pricked / A pretty, pleasing pricket', the fate of the
deer is as unreal as the wooded landscape over which it ran. It
might just as well have sprung to its feet and gambolled off
when the forester's back was turned.

Not until Act Five does the death image become real and
disturbing, and even here, until the final entrance of Marcade,
it is allowed to appear only in the imagery, or else in the
recollection by some character of a time and a place beyond
the scope of the play itself, the country of France where

Katherine's sister died of her melancholy and longing, or that forgotten antiquity in which the bones of Hector were laid to rest. Appearing thus softened, kept in the background of the comedy, it is nevertheless a curiously troubling image, and as it rises slowly through the fabric of the play, the key of the entire final movement is altered. In the mask scene, Berowne, half-serious about his love and that of the King, Dumain, and Longaville, cries to the ladies,

> Write 'Lord have mercy on us' on those three;
> They are infected; in their hearts it lies;
> They have the plague, and caught it of your eyes.
> These lords are visited; you are not free,
> For the Lord's tokens on you I do see.

and while the image is playfully treated still, it is surely a curious and grotesque figure, this marriage of love, the symbol throughout the comedy of life itself, with death. One cannot imagine such an image appearing earlier in the play, before the outside world, the echoes of its great plague bells sounding through desolate streets, the lugubrious cries of the watchmen marking the doors of the infected houses, began to filter obscurely through the little kingdom of the park.

It is the tremendous reality of death which will destroy the illusory world of Navarre as thoroughly as the gentler forces of life destroyed the Academe and the artificial scheme it represented, earlier in the play. At the very beginning of the Fifth Act, it is made apparent why this must happen, why it is completely necessary for the world of the comedy, despite its beauty and grace, to be demolished. The Princess and her gentlewomen have been discussing the favours and the promises showered upon them by the King and his courtiers, laughing and mocking one another gently. Suddenly, the atmosphere of the entire scene is altered with a single, curious comment, a kind of overheard aside, made by Katherine, upon the real nature of Love. Rosaline turns to her, and as she remembers past time and a tragedy for which the god of Love was responsible then, the scene suddenly becomes filled with the presence of death.

Ros.: You'll ne'er be friends with him: 'a kill'd your sister.
Kath.: He made her melancholy, sad, and heavy;
            And so she died. Had she been light, like you,
            Of such a merry, nimble, stirring spirit,
            She might have been a grandam ere she died.
            And so may you; for a light heart lives long.

Against such a memory of the reality of love, the Princess and her three companions place the fantastic protestations of Navarre, Berowne, Dumain, and Longaville. As we have seen, their love is genuine; it has made the character of Berowne immeasurably more attractive, caused him no little anguish of spirit, created that great speech of his at the end of Act Four. Beneath the delicate language, the elegance and the gaiety, lies a real passion, but the women from the world outside, where love has been coupled for them with death and reality, see only artifice and pose. The artificiality which has become natural to the four friends and the environment in which they live holds them from the accomplishment of their desire, for the ladies, hearing from Boyet of the masque in which their lovers intend to declare themselves, are unable to perceive in the scheme anything but attempted mockery, and in defending themselves, frustrate the serious purpose of the entertainment.

> They do it but in mocking merriment,
> And mock for mock is only my intent. . . .
> There's no such sport as sport by sport o'erthrown,
> To make theirs ours, and ours none but our own;
> So shall we stay, mocking intended game,
> And they well mock'd depart away with shame.

This masque scene is, of course, the second of the plays within the play, less delightful than the one before it, but immensely significant, the part of audience and commentator played in this instance by Boyet. As usual, the men are completely defeated by the ladies, the delicate fabric of their wit and artifice destroyed by the realistic humour of their opponents. Berowne, approaching the supposed Rosaline with a courteous request, 'White-handed mistress, one sweet word with thee', is mercilessly rebuffed by the Princess – 'Honey, and milk, and sugar; there is three' – and the charming illusion of the masque itself ruined by the satiric comments of Boyet who, unlike Berowne in the earlier play scene, actually insinuates himself into the unreal world of the entertainment, and totally upsets it.

Even when the exposure is complete and the men have asked pardon from their loves, the women think only that they have defeated a mocking jest directed against them, not that they have prevented their lovers from expressing a genuine passion. For the first time, Berowne reaches utter simplicity and humbleness in his love; his declaration to Rosaline at the end of the masque scene is touching and deeply sincere, but for her, this passion is still unbelievable, a momentary affectation, and she continues to mock her lover and the sentiments he expresses.

> *Ber.*: I am a fool, and full of poverty.
> *Ros.*: But that you take what doth to you belong,
>   It were a fault to snatch words from my tongue.
> *Ber.*: O, I am yours, and all that I possess.
> *Ros.*: All the fool mine?

More sensitive, gifted with a deeper perception of reality than his companions, Berowne seems to guess what is wrong, and he forswears 'Taffeta phrases, silken terms precise, / Three pil'd hyperboles, spruce affectation, / Figures pedantical . . .', at least to Rosaline, but the rejection itself is somewhat artificial, and he remains afterwards with more than 'a trick of the old rage'.

The masque has failed, and Berowne's more direct attempt to announce to the ladies the purpose behind the performance and detect in them an answering passion has been turned away by the unbelieving Princess. At this point, Costard enters to announce that Holofernes and Nathaniel, Moth and Armado are at hand to present the pageant of the Nine Worthies, and the third and last of the plays within the play begins. As we enter this play scene, the vitality and force of the comedy reaches its apogee, but in its laughter there rings now a discordant note that we have not heard before. The actors themselves are, after all, no less sincere than Bottom and his troupe in *A Midsummer Night's Dream*, and they are a great deal more sensitive and easy to hurt. They are real people whose intentions are of the very best, their loyalty to their King unquestioned, and although their performance is unintentionally humorous, one would expect the audience to behave with something of the sympathy and forbearance exhibited by Duke Theseus and the Athenians.

The only civil members of the audience in *Love's Labour's Lost*, however, are the ladies. The Princess cannot resist one sarcasm upon the entrance of Armado, but it is addressed quietly to Berowne, before the play itself begins, while Armado is engrossed with the King and obviously does not hear. Thereafter, every one of her comments to the players is one of interest or pity: 'Great thanks, great Pompey', 'Alas, poor Maccabaeus, how hath he been baited', 'Speak, brave Hector; we are much delighted'. The players have only the Princess to appeal to in the storm of hilarity which assails them, and it is only she, realistic as she is, who understands that a play is an illusion, that it is to be taken as such and respected in some sense for itself, regardless of its quality. Like Theseus in *A Midsummer Night's Dream*, she realizes somehow that 'the best in this kind are but shadows; and the worst are no worse, if imagination amend them',[7] and when she addresses the players she is wise and sensitive enough to do so not by their own names, which she has read on the playbill, but by the names of those whom they portray, thus helping them to sustain that illusion which is the very heart of a play.

In contrast to that of the Princess, the behaviour of the men is incredibly unattractive, particularly that of Berowne. It is difficult to believe that this is the same man who spoke so eloquently a short time ago about the soft and sensible feelings of love, and promised Rosaline to mend his ways. Costard manages to finish his part before the deluge, and Nathaniel, although unkindly treated, is not personally humiliated. Only with the appearance of Holofernes as Judas Maccabaeus and Armado as Hector is the full force of the ridicule released, and it is precisely with these two characters that the infliction of abuse must be most painful. Costard, after all, is a mere fool; he takes part in the baiting of the others with no compunction at all, and Nathaniel throughout the comedy has been little more than a foil for Holofernes, but the village pedagogue is a more sensitive soul, and not at all unsympathetic.

Holofernes has his own reality, his own sense of the apt and the beautiful which, though perverse, is meaningful enough for him, and it is exceedingly painful to see him stand here on the smooth grass of the lawn, his whole subjective world under merciless attack, a storm of personal epithets exploding about him.

> *Dum.*: The head of a bodkin.
> *Ber.*: A death's face in a ring.
> *Long.*: The face of an old Roman coin, scarce seen.
> *Boyet*: The pommel of Caesar's falchion.
> *Dum.*: The carv'd bone face on a flask.
> *Ber.*: Saint George's half-cheek in a brooch.

The laughter is unattractive, wild, and somehow discordant, made curiously harsh by the introduction of Berowne's 'death's face', and it has little resemblance to the laughter which we have heard in the play before this, delicate, sophistic-ated, sometimes hearty, but never really unkind. When Holo-fernes cries at the last, 'This is not generous, not gentle, not humble', he becomes a figure of real dignity and stature, restrained and courteous in the face of the most appalling incivility.

Meanwhile, around the pedagogue and his little audience the afternoon has been waning slowly into evening, long shadows falling horizontally across the lawn, and Boyet calls after the retreating Holofernes in a strangely haunting line, 'A light for Monsieur Judas. It grows dark, he may stumble'. A kind of wildness grips all the men, and though Dumain says in a weird and prophetic line, 'Though my mocks come home by me, I will now be merry', Armado faces a jeering throng even before he has begun to speak. Of all the players, Armado is the one for whom we have perhaps the most sympathy. He is a member of the court itself, has had some reason to pride himself upon the King's favour, and has been good enough to arrange the pageant in the first place. The people represented in it are those who inhabit that strange world of his fancy, and one knows that his anguish is not alone for his personal humiliation, but for that of the long-dead hero he portrays, when he cries, 'The sweet war-man is dead and rotten; sweet chucks, beat not the bones of the buried; when he breathed, he was a man'. A little grotesque, as Armado's sentences always are, the line is nevertheless infinitely moving in its summoning up of great spaces of time, its ironic relation to the idea of immortality through fame expressed in the opening speech of the comedy. Not since the reference to Katherine's sister have we had such a powerful and disturbing image of death brought before us, death real and inescapable although still related to a world and a time beyond the play itself.

In the remaining moments of the play scene, the hilarity rises to its climax, a climax becoming increasingly harsh. During the altercation between Costard and Armado which results from Berowne's ingenious but unattractive trick, images of death begin to hammer through the fabric of the play. The painfulness of the realism grows as Armado, poor, but immensely proud, is finally shamed and humbled before all the other characters. For the first time in the play, the mask falls from Armado's face, and the man beneath it is revealed, his romanticism, his touching personal pride, the agony for him of the confession that in his poverty he wears no shirt beneath his doublet. Still acting, he tries feebly to pass off this lack as some mysterious and romantic penance, but the other characters know the truth; Armado knows they do, and the knowledge is intensely humiliating. The illusion of the role he has played throughout *Love's Labour's Lost* is destroyed for others as well as for himself, and he stands miserably among the jeers of Dumain and Boyet while complete reality breaks over him, and the little personal world which he has built up around himself so carefully shatters at his feet.

The other people in the play are so concerned with Armado's predicament that no one notices that someone, in a sense Something has joined them. His entrance unremarked by any of the other characters, materializing silently from those shadows which now lie deep along the landscape of the royal park, the Messenger has entered the play world.

> *Mar.*: I am sorry, madam, for the news I bring
>   Is heavy in my tongue. The King your father –
> *Prin.*: Dead, for my life!
> *Mar.*: Even so; my tale is told.

There is perhaps nothing like this moment in the whole range of Elizabethan drama. In the space of four lines the entire world of the play, its delicate balance of reality and illusion, all the hilarity and overwhelming life of its last scene has been swept away and destroyed, as Death itself actually enters the park, for the first time, in the person of Marcade. Only in one Elizabethan madrigal, Orlando Gibbons' magnificent 'What Is Our Life?' is there a change of harmony and mood almost as swift and great as this one, and it occurs under precisely the same circumstances, the sudden appearance among the images of life in Raleigh's lyric of 'the graves that hide us from the searching sun'[8] the memory of the inescapable and tremendous reality of Death.[9]

Clumsy, as one always is in the presence of sudden grief, the King can think of nothing to say but to ask the Princess 'How fares your Majesty?' a question to which she, from the depths of her sorrow and bewilderment, gives no reply, but prepares with the dignity characteristic of her to leave for France. Now, the men come forward uncertainly, and first the King and then Berowne, clinging still to a world no longer existing, attempt to express their love in terms which had been appropriate to that world, terms at first still incomprehensible to the women and then, at last, understood, but not altogether trusted.

As vows had begun the play, so vows end it. The King is assigned as his symbol of reality a 'forlorn and naked hermitage' without the walls of the royal park, in the real world itself, in which he must try for a twelvemonth if this love conceived in the sunlit landscape of Navarre can persist in the colder light of actuality. For Dumain and Longaville, those shadowy figures, penances more vague but of a similar duration are assigned, and then at last, Berowne, shaken and moved to the depths of his being, inquires from Rosaline, who has been standing a little apart from the others, lost in thought,

Studies my lady? Mistress, look on me;
Behold the window of my heart, mine eye,
What humble suit attends thy answer there.
Impose some service on me for thy love.

Slowly, speaking with great care, Rosaline answers, and in
the strangest and most grotesque of the penances, Berowne is
condemned to haunt the hospitals and plague-houses of the
world outside the park, to exercise his wit upon the 'speechless
sick', and try the power of his past role, the old artificiality that
had no concern for the feelings of others, that humiliated
Armado in the play scene, the careless mocks of the old world,
upon the reality of the ailing and the dying. 'A jest's prosperity
lies in the ear / Of him that hears it, never in the tongue / Of
him that makes it.' It was this reality of actual living that
Berowne was unconscious of when he led the unthinking
merriment of the play scene just past. Yet, at the end of the
year, love's labours will be won for Berowne, and he will
receive Rosaline's love, not in the half real world of the park,
but in the actuality outside its walls. Thus the play which began
with a paradox, that of the Academe, closes with one as well.
Only through the acceptance of the reality of Death are life
and love in their fullest sense made possible for the people of
the play.

The world of the play past has now become vague and
unreal, and it is not distressing that Berowne, in a little speech
that is really a kind of epilogue, should refer to all the action
before the entrance of Marcade, the people who took part in
that action and the kingdom they inhabited and in a sense
created, as having been only the elements of a play. It is a play
outside which the characters now stand, bewildered, a little lost
in the sudden glare of actuality, looking back upon that world
of mingled artifice and reality a trifle wistfully before they
separate in the vaster realm beyond the royal park. Through
Love's Labour's Lost, the play has been a symbol of illusion, of
delightful unreality, the masque of the Muscovites, or the
pageant of the Nine Worthies, and now it becomes apparent
that there was a further level of illusion above that of the plays
within the play. The world of that illusion has enchanted us; it

has been possessed of a haunting beauty, the clear loveliness of those landscapes in the closing song, but Shakespeare insists that it cannot take the place of reality itself, and should not be made to. Always, beyond the charming, frost-etched countryside of the pastoral winter, like the background of some Flemish Book of Hours, lies the reality of the greasy kitchen-maid and her pot, a reality which must sooner or later break through and destroy the charm of the artificial and the illusory.

For us, however, knowing how Shakespeare's later work developed, and how the play image itself took on another meaning for him, there is a strange poignancy in this closing moment, with its confident assertion of the concrete reality of the world into which the characters are about to journey, the necessity for them to adjust themselves to that reality. Later, in *As You Like It* and *Hamlet* Shakespeare would begin to think of the play as the symbol, not of illusion, but of the world itself and its actuality, in *Macbeth* and *King Lear* as the symbol of the futility and tragic nature of that actuality, 'that great stage of fools'.[10] Yet he must always have kept in mind the image as it had appeared years before in the early comedy of *Love's Labour's Lost*, for returning to it at the very last, he joined that earlier idea of the play as illusion with its later meaning as a symbol of the real world, and so created the final play image of *The Tempest* in which illusion and reality have become one and the same, and there is no longer any distinction possible between them. The world itself into which Berowne and his companions travel to seek out reality will become for Shakespeare at the last merely another stage, a play briefly enacted,

> And, like the baseless fabric of this vision,
> The cloud-capp'd towers, the gorgeous palaces,
> The solemn temples, the great globe itself,
> Yea, all which it inherit, shall dissolve,
> And, like this insubstantial pageant faded,
> Leave not a rack behind. We are such stuff
> As dreams are made on; and our little life
> Is rounded with a sleep.[11]

SOURCE: '*Love's Labour's Lost*', *Shakespeare Quarterly*, 4 (1953), 411–26.

NOTES

1. Nesca Robb, *Neoplatonism of the Italian Renaissance* (London, 1935), p. 45.

2. Sir Philip Sidney, *The Defence of Poesie*, in *The Complete Works of Sir Philip Sidney*, ed. Feuillerat (Cambridge, 1923), III, 8.

3. Walter Pater, 'The School of Giorgione', in *The Renaissance* (New York, n.d.), p. III.

4. Pater, 'Shakespeare's English Kings', in *Appreciations* (London, 1901), pp. 203–4.

5. Pater, '*Love's Labour's Lost*', in *Appreciations*, p. 163.

6. Sidney, 'Astrophel and Stella, Sonnet III', in *Silver Poets of the Sixteenth Century*, ed. Bullett (London, 1947), p. 173.

7. *A Midsummer Night's Dream* V i.

8. Sir Walter Raleigh, 'What Is Our Life?', *Silver Poets of the Sixteenth Century*, p. 296.

9. Wilfrid Mellers, in a series of lectures given on 'Elizabethan and Jacobean Music', Stratford-upon-Avon, July, 1952.

10. *King Lear* IV vi.

11. *The Tempest* IV i.

James L. Calderwood

LOVE'S LABOUR'S LOST:
A WANTONING WITH WORDS (1971)

I

GIVING a rich and patterned opacity to the clear window of language is one thing Shakespeare is doing in *Love's Labour's Lost*. It is not the only thing he does, and the ending of the play modifies his doing of it very radically, but the doing deserves attention. In perhaps no other play does language so nearly become an autonomous symbolic system whose value lies less in its relevance to reality than in its intrinsic fascination. The referential role of words as pointers to ideas or things is consistently subordinated to their relational role as pointers to other words. When Maria says of Berowne 'Not a word with him but a jest' the line has as its primary object the setting up of a syntactic pattern that in the rhetorical figure called 'epanodos' can be turned inside out by Boyet's reply, 'And every jest but a word' (II i 216). When Berowne says 'The King he is hunting the deer, I am coursing myself; they have pitched a toil, I am toiling in a pitch – pitch that defiles – defile! a foul word' (IV iii 1–3), his speech is governed not by logic or conceptual intent but by purely verbal association. Such linguistic doodling here and throughout the play reminds us that words, like poems, not only mean but are. They are for instance phonic erector sets, aggregations of sound which may be built onto to produce awesomely ramshackle structures like 'honorificabilitudinitatibus' or dismantled and reduced to their basic elements, to the vowels and consonants that Moth wittily plays with (v i 47–60) or to the single letters bandied between

221

the Princess and Rosaline (v ii 38–45). The discrepancies between words as visual and as sonant objects may be revealed in the light of Holofernes's linguistic decorum – 'such rackers of orthography, as to speak *dout*, fine, when he should say *doubt*; *det*, when he should pronounce *debt* – d, e, b, t, not d, e, t . . . This is abhominable – which he would call abbominable (v i 21–8). And for a verbal mercer like Berowne the stuff of speech has surface texture so that we find 'Taffeta phrases, silken terms precise,/ Three-piled hyperboles [and] spruce affectation' contrasted with 'russet yeas and honest kersey noes' (v ii 406ff). But the major way in which *Love's Labour's Lost* bodies forth the physical character of language, promoting verbal matter at the expense of signified matter, is through its wanton use of the pun – since paronomasia no less than rhyme, rhythm, assonance, and alliteration exploits relations between words not as symbols of meaning but as sounds. In that sense it is amusingly appropriate that Dr Johnson equated the pun with seductive physicality when he called it 'the fatal Cleopatra for which [Shakespeare] lost the world and was content to lose it'.

The aesthetic pleasure generated by all this linguistic fooling is 'mirth', which in one of the play's dominant metaphors is begotten by the creative intercourse of language with wit. 'My father's wit and my mother's tongue, assist me!' – Moth's epic invocation as he girds himself to deliver a definition in song establishes the gender of wit and language, whose issue is wholly verbal. Or to pursue this metaphor a bit, the creative act engaged in by wit and language may take the form of repartee in which the mutual thrust, parry, and riposte of words are associated with hunting, dancing, combat, and most of all the sexual act:

> *BOYET*: My lady goes to kill horns; but if thou marry,
>   Hang me by the neck if horns that year miscarry.
>   Finely put on!
> *ROSALINE*: Well, then I am the shooter.
> *BOYET*:   And who is your deer?
> *ROSALINE*: If we choose by the horns, yourself; come not near.
>   Finely put on, indeed!
> *MARIA*: You still wrangle with her, Boyet, and she strikes at the brow.

BOYET: But she herself is hit lower. Have I hit her now?
ROSALINE: Shall I come upon thee with an old saying, that was a man
  when King Pepin of France was a little boy, as touching the hit it?
BOYET: So I may answer thee with one as old, that was a woman
  when Queen Guinever of Britain was a little wench, as touching
  the hit it.
ROSALINE: 'Thou canst not hit it, hit it, hit it,
    Thou canst not hit it, my good man.'
BOYET: 'An I cannot, cannot, cannot,
    An I cannot, another can.'
COSTARD: By my troth, most pleasant. How both did fit it!
                                                    (IV i 113–31)

The pleasure or mirth afforded Costard and the others here is
delivered as a result of the procreative interaction of one
person's language with another's wit, a kind of verbal copulation to which the elderly Boyet must be resigned in view of his
'I cannot, cannot, cannot'.

Berowne's generative potential both physically and verbally
is greater than Boyet's, and the first full-length portrait we get
of him exhibits his capacity for a kind of auto-conception
involving the eye, wit, and language:

> Berowne they call him; but a merrier man
> Within the limit of becoming mirth
> I never spent an hour's talk withal.
> His eye *begets* occasion for his wit,
> For every object that the one doth catch
> The other turns to a mirth-moving jest
> Which his fair tongue, conceit's expositor,
> *Delivers* in such apt and gracious words
> That aged ears play truant at his tales
> And younger hearings are quite ravished,
> So sweet and voluble is his discourse.
>   (II i 66–76)

Even Holofernes can revel in the procreative power of his wit:

This is a gift that I have, simple, simple – a foolish extravagant spirit
full of forms, figures, shapes, objects, ideas, apprehensions, motions,
revolutions. These are begot in the ventricle of memory, nourished in
the womb of pia mater, and delivered upon the mellowing of
occasion. But the gift is good in those in whom it is acute, and I am
thankful for it.
                                                    (IV ii 67–74)

And if the lowly Dull lacks wit and language unlike the devoted
academicians it is because, as Sir Nathaniel says –

> Sir, he hath never fed of the dainties that are bred in a book; he
> hath not eat paper, as it were; he hath not drunk ink; his intellect
> is not replenished; he is only an animal, only sensible in the
> duller parts;
> And such barren plants are set before us that we thankful should
> be,
> Which we of taste and feeling are, for those parts that do fructify
> in us more than he.
>
> (IV ii 24–30)

Having no father wit and no mother tongue Dull must of
necessity be barren. According to the Princess, however, even
the 'fructifying wits' are barren, for when she first hears of their
characteristic mockery and wordplay she says 'Such short-lived
wits do wither as they grow' (II i 54). With its paradox of
withering growth her statement helps bring out the basic
comment which the procreative metaphor I've been tracing
makes on the conduct of the scholars. The intercourse between
wit and words to which all their energies are devoted is
ambiguous in value and effect. On the one hand it is procreative and vital, generating through mirth and amusement a
community of feeling that goes at least partway toward binding
society together. But on the other hand it is as barren as Dull's
intellect because what could be a genuine union of words and
thoughts, language and reality, has in their practice degener-
ated to mere verbal promiscuity, to a splendid but ephemeral
dalliance between wit and words. Such a relationship is fitting
enough in a world of holiday and festive release. But in the
world of everyday toward which the drama moves, licence
whether verbal or sexual must give way to the governing forms
of social order, promiscuity to marriage. The final attitude
which the play takes toward this dalliance of wit and language
is suggested in its own punning title, for when words do duty
for realities love's labour is truly without issue and in the
metadramatics of the play literary form miscarries. But that is
to get ahead of the story.

II

So one of the things this play does is to give words the function not so much of expressing the truth of things or thoughts but of eliciting – through puns, metaphors, rhyme, alliteration, coinage, through all the devices that suggest the substantiality of language – verbal relations that are in themselves aesthetically pleasing. But if Shakespeare runs with the hares of playful speech, he hunts with the hounds of satiric sense as well. In fact most critics have found it easy to regard the hares as existing only to be coursed by the hounds. If so, Shakespeare lines up with the verbal sceptics as a kind of 'exteriorized' Berowne feeding the wormwood of burlesque to the linguistic ills of his time – gongorism, preciosity, pedantry, inkhornism, and plain ignorance. As satirist of verbal affectation and related abuses he would presumably aim to purify language, to transform the whore back into a virgin. Thus aggrandizing words as substantive entities and satirizing verbal affectation appear as twin aspects of the same desire, which is to convert the public and corrupt medium into his private and pure property, giving to transient breath a solidity in which he can carve his own enduring shapes.

The impulse to take language for one's own is most obviously figured in the opening scene of the play. To achieve eternal fame in the mouths of men the scholars create a private society by verbal fiat. They bind themselves to one another by giving their words or oaths to each other, they bind themselves to the words of the statutes that define their obligations, and they bind themselves to the study of words. As a result the court 'shall be a little Academe,/ Still and contemplative in living art' – a transfixed (still) rather than enduring (still) social unit the central feature of which is its prohibition of women. Since this academe is verbally created its integrity is primarily verbal and must be verbally guaranteed. Therefore 'no woman shall come within a mile of [the] court . . . On pain of losing her tongue' (I i 119–25), and in the only other item revealed to us from the statutes 'If any man be seen to talk with a woman within the term of three years, he shall endure such public shame as the rest of the court can possibly devise' (I i 130–3). Figured in the oaths and statutes the interdependence of language and the social order is complete; neither can exist apart from the other. Even to say that the breakdown of language precipitates the breakdown of the social order is to imply a division between the two that is simply not there. When the scholars one by one break their words, that does not *cause* their private masculine community to disintegrate; it *is* that disintegration.

The major reason for the collapse of the academic society is that the language that created it in the first place was disjoined from the truth of human nature, which is defined in the phrase of that minor lexicographer and master lover Costard – 'such is the simplicity of man to hearken after the flesh' (I i 219). In the verbal world of academe the word has been set against the word – 'will' as moral resolve against 'will' as passion and the affections. The brave conquerors who 'war against [their] own affections/ And the huge army of the world's desires' place passion under the lock and key of verbal oaths, subjecting will to will (I i 8–10). The function of both Berowne and Costard in the opening scene is to point the fact that language so divorced from realities of human nature can achieve little more than merely verbal triumphs, let alone foster an enduring social order. Thus Berowne:

> Necessity will make us all forsworn
> Three thousand times within this three years' space;
> For every man with his affects is born,
> Not by might mastered but by special grace.
> If I break faith, this word shall speak for me –
> I am forsworn on 'mere necessity.'
>
> (I i 150–5)

Costard even more bluntly reveals the disjunction between language and truth. No sooner have the 'deep oaths' been sworn than he 'is taken with a wench' in the park and brought to justice. Forecasting the scholars' later devices, he first tries to evade the facts by quibbling with the language of the statutes:

KING: It was proclaimed a year's imprisonment to be taken with a
    wench.
COSTARD: I was taken with none, sir. I was taken with a damsel.
KING: Well, it was proclaimed damsel.
COSTARD: This was no damsel neither, sir. She was a virgin.
KING: It is so varied too, for it was proclaimed virgin.
COSTARD: If it were, I deny her virginity. I was taken with a maid.
KING: This maid will not serve your turn, sir.
COSTARD: This maid will serve my turn, sir.

(I i 289–301)

In the last line Costard abandons his attempt to evade the
language of the statutes, which he has found is in its own way
perfect, an absolutely closed system without verbal loopholes.
But his last line underscores the fact that however perfect the
system may be on its own grounds it is not grounded in reality;
the word 'maid' will not serve his turn by giving him a
quibbling out, but the maid herself will 'serve' him in the
overworked sexual sense of the term. Thus when sentenced to
a week on 'bran and water' Costard can say to Berowne 'I
suffer for the truth, sir; for true it is I was taken with
Jaquenetta, and Jaquenetta is a true girl' (I i 313–14). In being
taken with a true girl Costard has revealed himself a true man
hearkening as true men do after the flesh. But separating these
masculine and feminine truths and preventing their incorpora-
tion into the social order is a repressive language in the service
of a repressive justice, or rather a language and a justice that
are mutually defining, a sterile tautology from which there is
no escape and into which reality cannot penetrate. So Costard
suffers not only 'for the truth', as he claims, but because the
truth of human nature goes unreflected in the received language of Navarre.

At his humble level Costard acts as a weathervane pointing
the way the dramatic winds blow. In demonstrating that
language can neither substitute for nor suppress reality, that
the victory of 'will' over 'will' is spuriously verbal, he exposes
more than he himself understands. Not, however, more than
the French ladies understand. At her first meeting with the
King the Princess wittily gives point to what Costard has

unwittingly demonstrated – the tenuousness of the bondage of will to will:

> KING: You shall be welcome, madam, to my court.
> PRINCESS: I will be welcome then. Conduct me thither.
> KING: Hear me, dear lady, I have sworn an oath.
> PRINCESS: Our Lady help my lord. He'll be forsworn!
> KING: Not for the world, fair madam, by my will.
> PRINCESS: Why, will shall break it – will and nothing else.
>
> (II i 94–100)

The point here is not merely to reaffirm Shakespeare's much-noted verbal scepticism in *Love's Labour's Lost*. The scepticism is of course there, and the scholars are allowed to feed so fully of the dainties that are bred in a book and to inhale so deeply of fine phrases that they threaten to suffocate on syllables. But Shakespeare's treatment of the scholars suggests not a repudiation of the power of language but an acute awareness of its limits and of the comic consequences of exceeding them. The play has yet to establish a final attitude toward the use and abuse of speech.

SOURCE: Extract from '*Love's Labour's Lost*: A Wantoning with Words', *Shakespearean Metadrama* (Minneapolis, 1971), pp. 52–84.

Philip Edwards

SHAKESPEARE AND THE CONFINES OF ART (1968)

Love's Labour's Lost, like *As You Like It*, cannot be understood at all unless we see, first, the distance between the antics of infatuation and the straightforward acknowledgement of the sexual drive; and, secondly, the inseparability of the antics and the urge towards sexual satisfaction. Nonsense has been made of the play by supposing that sweet sentimentalizing and sighing are *attacked* by Shakespeare because they do not propose the right true end of love. When Shakespeare writes his sonnets, he may wish to point out hypocrisy and self-ignorance in the distance between the protestations of a lover and the *physical* goal of his longings. But it is another matter in comedy. He is only amused at the rather extravagant and silly clothes which Desire wears. A Berowne or a Touchstone will be needed to remind the lovers in their raptures what their emotion is all about:

> If the cat will after kind,
> So be sure will Rosalind.

It may seem sometimes that as the participants go through the motions of the mating dance, each one like a peacock spreading its tail, they forget what all the pretty display is for. But they never forget for long. Eros leads them into strange capers, but I wonder if the lovers delude themselves, or fail to acknowledge the physical side of their love. Cupid's corporals are laughable, but they are fighting comedy's battle for the peopling of the world.

The sexual 'reality' in the protestations of romantic love is emphasized in the wonderful scene of the unmasking of the

229

vow-breakers in IV iii. The emblem of romantic infatuation is poetry. When Longaville threatens (to himself) to tear up his poem and 'write in prose' (57), the concealed Berowne mutters:

> Oh, rhymes are guards on wanton Cupid's hose,
> Disfigure not his shop.

There is a case, at least, for the modesty of literary soliciting. But when Berowne has heard Longaville's poem, full of 'goddess' and 'heavenly love' and 'win a paradise', he breaks out in Byronic terms:

> This is the liver vein, which makes flesh a deity,
> A green-goose a goddess. Pure, pure idolatry.
> God amend us, God amend! We are much out o' the way.
>   (72–4)

There is an unending source of humour, for Shakespeare, in the sentiments and behaviour of young people in love. They may at times be made ridiculous, as they are here. But that is a different matter from attacking them. There are various categories of absurdity as they all go the same way home, and that is about all. 'We that are true lovers run into strange capers; but as all is mortal in nature, so is all nature in love mortal in folly.'

The relations of Armado and Jaquenetta are a comic exaggeration of the comic situation of the comic lovers. Jaquenetta is the Audrey of the play, a very female wench, no more but e'en a woman. Her earthiness makes Armado's affectation all the more ludicrous – 'More fairer than fair, beautiful than beauteous, truer than truth itself, have commiseration on thy heroical vassal.' However ethereal his words, Armado is no more spiritual a wooer than the lords. Unless Costard is shifting the blame, by the end of the play Armado has got Jaquenetta with child (v ii 665).

With Berowne's self-awareness as a touchstone, Shakespeare asks us to laugh at the follies of men in love as he intones the mass to celebrate the might and the potency of love. In the end, it is his own priestly office that he attacks.

When the king and his three liegemen are revealed, each one
to himself and to the others, as men who (as Berowne
promised) cannot abjure or ostracize love, Berowne is asked to
find a solace for wounded self-esteem, 'some authority', 'some
salve for perjury'. His rationalization (IV iii 286–361) is curious
(even if we disregard the clear signs of Shakespeare's attempts
to revise the speech). He has already given the true justification
in IV iii 212–16:

> As true we are as flesh and blood can be.
> The sea will ebb and flow, heaven show his face;
> Young blood doth not obey an old decree.
> We cannot cross the cause why we were born;
> Therefore of all hands must we be forsworn.

This is a serious comment. But the long speech of rationalization ('Have at you, then, affection's men-at-arms') evaporates
into ridiculous hyperbole. It is a commonplace that Berowne
has his special depth in this play from being both the man who
participates and also the man who can see the folly of particip-
ation. He is that which he mocks. In this speech, the man who
can see the affectations of others, and of himself, lunges into a
philosophical deification of a green-goose. He really is in 'the
liver vein'. Love makes the world go round and inspires fine
spirits to fine issues. And the proof of it?

> For when would you, my liege, or you, or you,
> In leaden contemplation have found out
> Such fiery numbers as the prompting eyes
> Of beauty's tutors have enriched you with?

Unfortunately for Berowne's arguments, we have heard these
'fiery numbers' (the lords' efforts at verse) and have joined in
the laughter at them. Berowne may be a constant risk to the
security of self-deception, but he is also a constant warning that
a capacity for self-awareness is no protection against strange fits
of folly in a lover. Did Shakespeare revise this famous speech
because lines like 'Learning is but an adjunct to ourself' were
too good for the hyperbolic rant he intended?

The wooing is now to begin, and the images of war previously

used for the battle against the world's desires are now turned
in the direction of the ladies of France:

> – Saint Cupid, then! And, soldiers, to the field!
> – Advance your standards, and upon them, lords!
>
> (IV iii 363–4)

The wooing does not go well: the masque of the Muscovites is
a failure, and the lords are baited by their obdurate mistresses.
The failure of the masque seems to anticipate the final collapse
of the love-quest, but it is not a part of that final collapse. The
pattern of 'Love's Labour's Won' can easily include the pros-
tration of humiliated lovers before tyrannical mistresses. The
long, brilliant last scene of the play has many anticipations of
the reversal which brings it to a close, but none of them really
breaks the mood of the conventional love-game. Katherine has
a bitter-sweet moment when she remembers the sister who died
of love-melancholy; but this is not the real entry of death
(14–15). Rosaline promises to 'torture' Berowne, and make him
'wait the season, and observe the times' (60–6); but her relish
shows this all part of the love-play and not similar to the final
dismissal. Berowne claims to abjure rhetoric ('Taffeta phrases,
silken terms precise . . .', 396–415), but the abjuration (half-
hearted as it is) is only a stratagem in the siege and is so taken
by the ladies; it is later on that Berowne is really reduced to
'honest plain words'.

There is a real faltering in the rhythm of the play, however,
when the onlookers wilfully destroy the show of the Nine
Worthies, and then the mood of the comedy is once and for all
broken by the entry of Marcade with the news of the death of
the Princess's father. The entry of 'Death' was wonderfully
staged by Peter Brook in his production at Stratford-upon-
Avon in 1947. There *was* no perceptible entry: the lights began
to grow dim on the laughter at Armado's discomfiture. And as
the light on the general scene went low, it slowly grew stronger
on the black figure of Marcade, until he was seen and recognized. The laughter died away, and he spoke: 'God save you,
madam!' For all the audience could see, he had been standing
there for a long time.

Death comes into the play from outside: it is the impression of every observer and reader of the play. News from a 'real world' breaks in upon a world of fantasy. The brevity and simplicity of the exchange of words challenge the whole mood of the play.

> *Marcade*: I am sorry, madam, for the news I bring
>   Is heavy in my tongue. The king your father –
> *Princess*: Dead, for my life!
> *Marcade*: Even so. My tale is told.
> *Berowne*: Worthies, away; the scene begins to cloud.

The princess orders Boyet to prepare for her departure: it is the play she is leaving, as well as her embassy in Navarre. The king makes an awkward attempt to keep the play alive: in circuitous phrases, he pleads that 'the cloud of sorrow' should not hinder the wooing. 'I understand you not,' replies the princess. And she really does not understand him, finding no relation between the world of comedy and the world of grief.

Berowne comes to the rescue; he tries to save the play by bringing the world of comedy-love into the 'real' world:

> Honest plain words best pierce the ear of grief,
> And by these badges understand the king.
>
>   (743–4)

We may have been inconstant to our vows and ridiculous in our actions, he argues. But our folly is a simple consequence of falling in love. Falsehood to 'our oaths and gravities' has been a discovery of our true nature:

> And even that falsehood, in itself a sin,
> Thus purifies itself and turns to grace
>   ,
>   (765–6)

The speech seems to me wholly serious. Berowne, I said, was the spirit of comedy. We have been playing, he says, even playing the fool – but this playing is the very heart-beat of our true lives. Comedy moves men through folly towards Thalamos, the culminating YES which starts the world over again.

The princess, preoccupied with the fact of death, insists (as it were) that comedy's celebration of the power of love takes place in a false world. She refuses, without a great deal more evidence, to accept the values and actions of comedy as inhabitants of the world she has moved into. She treats the breaking of the vows (comedy's portrayal of the victory of life over sterility) as real-life offences, perjuries 'full of dear guiltiness'. The king says,

> Now, at the latest minute of the hour,
> Grant us your loves.
>
> (777–8)

'The latest minute of the hour' makes us think less of the imminent departure of the princess than of the real clock which shows us that the performance is due to end. The comedy has only a minute in which to right itself into the orthodox happy ending of love granted. But the princess replies,

> A time, methinks, too short
> To make a world-without-end bargain in.

She severs herself from the conventions of the theatre in mistaking the compressed time-scheme of comedy for the clock which actually measures men's lives. The amusing, but very important, confusion between the time-scheme of the theatre and of life is emphasized in the last words of the main characters, when the lovers are dismissed to twelve-months' hard work:

> *Berowne*: Our wooing doth not end like an old play;
> Jack hath not Jill. These ladies' courtesy
> Might well have made our sport a comedy.
> *King*: Come, sir, it wants a twelvemonth and a day,
> And then 'twill end.
> *Berowne*:   That's too long for a play.

Literally, a year is too long for a play; literally, a 'minute' is too short a time 'to make a world-without-end bargain in'. But a fictional play is not to have its time-scheme taken literally: the discourtesy of the ladies lies in challenging the value of the symbolic action of comedy. They interrupt the inevitably converging journeys of the play by an appeal to the standards of a harder kind of existence.

It is interesting that the period for which the ladies consign their lovers to the world of suffering is a complete year. Here are the princess's orders to the king:

> Your oath I will not trust, but go with speed
> To some forlorn and naked hermitage,
> Remote from all the pleasures of the world;
> There stay until the twelve celestial signs
> Have brought about the annual reckoning.
> If this austere insociable life
> Change not your offer made in heat of blood,
> If frosts and fasts, hard lodging and thin weeds,
> Nip not the gaudy blossoms of your love,
> But that it bear this trial, and last love,
> Then, at the expiration of the year,
> Come challenge me, challenge me by these deserts;
> And, by this virgin palm now kissing thine,
> I will be thine.
>
> (784–97)

A little reading of twentieth-century criticism persuades us that comedy is the advocate of spring's supremacy. In condemning a comedy-lover to a winter of endurance before she will accept his love, the princess almost in so many words asks for proof of the supremacy of spring. Can spring in fact endure winter's attack? When Rosaline forces similar orders on Berowne, neither she nor he expects that the comedy-buffoon can outlast a winter's converse with 'the speechless sick'.

> To move wild laughter in the throat of death?
> It cannot be; it is impossible.
>
> (845–6)

The characters and conventions of comedy are being rather brutally treated: they are being asked to withstand the frostiness of our ordinary experience. Canvas scenery is taken outside the theatre and asked to be real mountain and forest. This unfairness is all part of the comedy of *Love's Labour's Lost*: but the humour depends on a scepticism of a kind of comedy whose function is to despise death and belittle its power.

The play ends with music and song, reinforcing the seasonal metaphors for love and suffering, in the form of the age-old

debate between Spring and Winter. This dialogue between the
owl and the cuckoo, Armado tells us, 'should have followed in
the end of our show': Monsieur Marcade forestalled it. One
cannot help thinking that the change of mood that has come
over the play has affected the music and turned a prothalamion
into something very different. Spring comes first with an ironic
hymn to fertility: the cuckoo's voice is the voice of adultery.

> The cuckoo then on every tree
> Mocks married men, for thus sings he:
> > Cuckoo,
> Cuckoo, cuckoo: O word of fear,
> Unpleasing to a married ear!

And who has the last word in this comedy? Not spring, even
so ironically presented, but winter, 'when icicles hang by the
wall'. It is a beautiful song, of course, but winter is still winter:

> When blood is nipp'd, and ways be foul,
> Then nightly sings the staring owl:
> > Tu-who,
> Tu-whit, to-who: a merry note,
> While greasy Joan doth keel the pot.

It is easy to sympathize with those who believe that the
reversal at the end of *Love's Labour's Lost* is Shakespeare's way
of indicating his moral disapproval of an imperfect and irre-
sponsible attitude to love, delighted with itself and the sweet
flurry of words it expresses itself in, but not caring for the real
cares of love. For such a view preserves a wholeness in the play
as a love-story, and, as Barber says,[1] makes it end affirmatively,
since the ladies promise to receive the lovers when they have
purged themselves of irresponsibility in the real world. But the
characters of *Love's Labour's Lost* are simply not real enough to
permit moral judgements about the immaturity of their outlook
to apply (I am reminded of a golden remark about Touchstone:
'his lack of commitment to any way of life makes him incomplete as a man'.) The contrast in *Love's Labour's Lost* is not
between immaturity and maturity in love, but, as Miss Roesen
has made clear, between the illusion of the world of art, and
reality.[2]

By a device of art, Shakespeare tries to subject the world of art to evaluation in terms external to that world. He behaves unfairly to the creatures of comedy, not because he thought them lacking in the sagacity and maturity he might expect of people in life, but because he wished, in a jest, to protest that a certain form of comedy was not capable of showing the vicissitudes of things. It is a formal and not a moral dissatisfaction that Shakespeare shows. Comedy encourages man with an imitation of life in which love conquers its restraints, and people move from separation to union in love. But in *Love's Labour's Lost* Shakespeare challenges comedy with reminders of death, adultery and pain. A year of suffering will not go into the 'old play'. He leaves it as a challenge; there *may* be weddings at the end of a year. In later works, he pursues the question: he tries out dramatic forms which can include real pain and yet lead to real union. It is possible that his next play, after *Love's Labour's Lost*, was *Romeo and Juliet*, in which he shapes a dramatic form to bring into headlong collision a celebration of the power of love and demonstration of the power of hate.

SOURCE: Extract from *Shakespeare and the Confines of Art* (London, 1968), pp. 37–48.

NOTES

1. C. L. Barber, *Shakespeare's Festive Comedy* (1959), p. 111.
2. Compare B. Roesen (*sc.* A. Righter), '*Love's Labour's Lost*', *Shakespeare Quarterly*, IV (1953), 412.

RECENT PRODUCTIONS OF
LOVE'S LABOUR'S LOST

HARLEY Granville-Barker's essay on *Love's Labour's Lost* (published in 1927) paved the way for twentieth-century appreciation of the play's theatrical qualities. Having read the essay Tyrone Guthrie staged the play at the Westminster Theatre in 1932 and following that success directed it again at the Old Vic in 1936. Ten years later Peter Brook's production in Stratford-upon-Avon was only the fifth since the founding of the Shakespeare Memorial Theatre. Brook set the play in the world of Watteau, capturing its elegance and elegiac quality. The Princess was accompanied wherever she went by a mute, white-faced pierrot. Although only 25, Paul Scofield's Don Armado was faded and forlorn. The rustic world reflected the spirit of harlequinade but the final moments were serious. Marcade's entrance was followed by a prolonged, stricken pause. His announcement of death marked the intrusion of harsh reality upon the world of the play. In the gathering darkness relieved only by torchlight, rustics and courtiers alike stood still. It was the Princess who spoke the final line, 'You that way, we this way', signalling the divide between stage and audience. The production was so successful that it was revived the following year.

In 1949 Hugh Hunt directed the play for the Old Vic company at the New Theatre. The setting and costume were now Elizabethan and the success confirmed a theatrical vitality in the play. Paul Rogers recalled it as 'enchanted'. He wrote the introduction to the Folio Society edition which is illustrated with designs from the production by Berkeley Sutcliffe. With enthusiasm Rogers recalls: 'Redgrave, straight out of Hilliard, saying with his white-gold voice "And bright Apollo's lute, strung with his hair"; or crackling out "Have at you, then, affection's men at arms". Mark Dignam, finely pedantic, braying "Venezia, Venezia, chi non ti vede non ti pretia". Miles Malleson's perfection of Sir Nathaniel and George Benson the finest Costard: these are the stuff of superlative memories.' The designs reflected the ornamentation and beauty of the text (and perhaps also provided post-war escapism). As Rogers recalls: 'Green banks and trees, Armado's thatched lodge and a silken pavilion; a lake and Marcade arriving on a splendid barge; the barge which took the ladies away from their beloved. And drifts of autumn leaves in the dying light. All served to enrich at all times the riches of the play.' Seven years later Peter Hall's 1956 production also aspired to Renaissance elegance, but there were complaints that the text was thrown; some advocated cutting what were felt to be obscurities. In 1969 Laurence Olivier directed the play at the National Theatre. Joan Plowright's witty Rosaline prompted critics to make the connection with Beatrice. Marcade's entrance was not the usual, dramatic tableau but rather the scene was staged so as to enable him suddenly to appear, as if from nowhere, in the midst of the mingled group. The indulgent complacency was suddenly, unexpectedly and disturbingly shattered.

John Barton directed the play twice at Stratford (in 1965 and 1978). Some felt the earlier production was constrained by Barton's meticulous attention to the verse speaking, though Glenda Jackson's Princess was judged 'nicely capricious' (*Evening Standard*, 8/4/65). Thirteen years later Ralph Koltai's setting seduced. The play became 'a melancholy, mood-riven, sighful dance of words beneath a haze of autumn leaves' (*Daily Telegraph*, 12/8/78). Richard Griffiths was unusual casting for the king. He was a 'tubby, easily embarrassed monarch' who was paired with Carmen du Sautoy's 'ringletted hoyden in grannie glasses' (*Times*, 14/8/78). Both journeyed to regal authority. All the characters were immersed in 'spontaneous and muddled humanity' and the text sounded freshly minted; 'their moods veer about and conversation is punctuated by lingering, intimate silences' (*Sunday Times*, 13/8/78). Michael Hordern's Don Armado was moving, even earning the epithet

'Lear-like' (*Daily Telegraph*, 12/8/78). His was a 'sympathetic and sparing' performance, characteristic of the production as a whole.

The play was popular in the 1970s. David Jones' RSC production in 1973 offered a canopied set and elegant Edwardian costume. The women's elaborate hats and parasols granted them poise and space. The men's affectation was pointed in particular by the way, as they took their vows, they replaced their courtly dress with dull scholarly robes. At the end of the play Marcade had to struggle to make his way onstage and the awkwardness deepened the disquiet.

'Rare' and 'lyrical' are the epithets repeatedly used to describe Barry Kyle's 1984 production. Beginning as Victorian academic comedy it moved through to Edwardian romance. Roger Rees' Berowne was characterised by a lanky awkwardness exacerbated when he was in the presence of Josette Simon's cool, poised Rosaline. An isolated figure, she was a dark lady both literally and metaphorically and Berowne's journey towards a maturity to equal hers was a particularly long one. Kenneth Branagh's King was nervous of women and Emily Richard's Princess had a warmth borne of an easy authority. The role of Armado once again succeeded as a tragic cameo. Edward Petherbridge captured the loneliness of a man locked in a world apart desperately seeking someone to listen to him.

Terry Hands' 1990 production disappointed more than it satisfied. The design was felt to be fussy. The opening picnic was a slavish reconstruction of Manet's *Déjeuner sur l'herbe* which effectively established the men's mannered self-consciousness but seemed too relaxed a setting for the intensity of their self-imposed restrictions. Too often performances strained in an over-emphatic way revealing what some felt was a lack of trust in the text. Michael Billington was particularly forthright. In a review entitled *A love that's laboured* he judged it to be a production which 'looks fabulous but. . . [which] lacks heart. As a result its journey from fame-hungry seclusion to death, divorce and penance leaves one largely unmoved' (*Guardian*, 7/9/90). However, Lois Potter argued that Hands had 'sought a theatrical equivalent of Keats's urn'. The artificial snow that Armado scattered on the couples served also as confetti and the final tableau showed Jacquenetta and Armado in an passionate embrace extinguishing Marcade with the triumph and timelessness of art (*Times Literary Supplement*, 14/9/90).

Three years later the RSC staged the play again. Ian Judge found Navarre in Edwardian Oxford and his production was rich in nostalgia and visual charm. The men were elegant undergraduates beguiling in their boyish impetuosity. The women fared less well. Deirdre Clancy's costumes made them seem as vain as the men and the Princess was arch rather than astute. The director sought to fashion a romantic comedy out of Shakespeare's more complex text, allowing the men to sing their poems of love in the overhearing scene. Though an evocation of the Great War briefly brought a chilling edge to the closing sequence, the moment was dissipated in a determinedly cheerful company sing-song.

SELECT BIBLIOGRAPHY

C. L. Barber, *Shakespeare's Festive Comedy* (Princeton, NJ, 1959).

Edward Berry, *Shakespeare's Comic Rites* (Cambridge, 1984).

B. O. Bonazza, *Shakespeare's Early Comedies: A Structural Analysis* (The Hague, 1966).

Muriel C. Bradbrook, *Shakespeare and Elizabethan Poetry* (London, 1951).

J. R. Brown, *Shakespeare and his Comedies* (London, 1957; 2nd edn, 1962).

William C. Carroll, *The Metamorphoses of Shakespearean Comedy* (Princeton, NJ, 1985).

H. B. Charlton, *Shakespearian Comedy* (London, 1938).

John Danby, 'Shakespearean Criticism and *The Two Gentlemen of Verona*', *Critical Quarterly*, 2 (1960), 309–21.

Irene Dash, *Wooing, Wedding and Power: Women in Shakespeare's Plays* (New York, 1981).

Barbara Freedman, *Staging the Gaze: Postmodernism, Psychoanalysis and Shakespearean Comedy* (New York, 1991).

Northrop Frye, 'The Argument of Comedy', *English Institute Essays* 1948 (New York, 1949); reprinted in *Shakespeare: Modern Essays in Criticism*, ed. Leonard F. Dean (New York, 1957; 2nd edn, 1967), pp. 79–89.

Germaine Greer, *The Female Eunuch* (Cambridge, 1971).

Tori Haring-Smith, *From Farce to Metadrama: A Stage History of The Taming of the Shrew 1594–1983* (Connecticut, 1985).

Coppélia Kahn, *Man's Estate: Masculine Identity in Shakespeare* (Berkeley, Cal., 1981).

Alexander Leggatt, *Shakespeare's Comedy of Love* (London, 1974).

Jonathan Miller, *Subsequent Performances* (London, 1986).

Kenneth Muir, *Shakespeare's Comic Sequence* (Liverpool, 1979).

Ruth Nevo, *Comic Transformations in Shakespeare* (London, 1980).

Marianne Novy, 'Patriarchy and Play in *The Taming of the Shrew*', *English Literary Renaissance*, 9 (1979), 264–80.

Robert Ornstein, *Shakespeare's Comedies* (London, 1986).
Anne Righter [Anne Barton], *Shakespeare and the Idea of the Play* (London, 1962).
E. M. W. Tillyard, *Shakespeare's Early Comedies* (London, 1965).
D. A. Traversi, *Shakespeare: the Early Comedies* (London, 1960).

NOTES ON CONTRIBUTORS

RALPH BERRY is Lecturer in English at the University of Malaya. His publications include *Shakespeare's Comedies: Explorations in Form* (1972) and *Changing Styles in Shakespeare* (1981).

MURIEL C. BRADBROOK was Professor Emerita of English and Fellow of Girton College, Cambridge. Her publications include *Shakespeare and Elizabethan Poetry* (1951) and *The Growth and Structure of Elizabethan Comedy* (1955).

HAROLD BROOKS was Professor of English at Birkbeck College, University of London. He was one of the General Editors of the Arden Shakespeare and edited *A Midsummer Night's Dream*. He has published extensively on Shakespeare.

JAMES L. CALDERWOOD is Professor of English and Comparative Literature and Associate Dean of Humanities at the University of California, Irvine. He has published various books on Shakespeare, including *Metadrama in Shakespeare's 'Henriad'* (1979) and *Shakespeare and the Denial of Death* (1989).

DAVID DANIELL is Professor of English at University College, London. His publications include *Coriolanus in Europe* (1980) and *The Tempest: The Critics Debate* (1989).

PHILIP EDWARDS was King Alfred Professor of English at the University of Liverpool. His publications include editions of *King Lear, Hamlet* and *Pericles*.

INGA-STINA EWBANK is Professor of English at the University of Leeds. Her publications include *Their Proper Sphere* (1966) and she was joint editor (with P. Edwards and G. K. Hunter) of *Shakespeare's Styles: Essays in honour of Kenneth Muir* (1986).

ANNE BARTON [Bobbyann Roesen] is Professor of English at New College, Oxford. Her publications include *Shakespeare and the Idea of the Play (1962)* and *Ben Jonson: Dramatist* (1984).

GĀMINI SALGĀDO was Professor of English at the University of Exeter. His publications include *Eyewitnesses of Shakespeare* (1975) and *Shakespeare and Myself* (1976).

CECIL C. SERONSY was Professor of English at Bloomsburg State College. His publications include *Samuel Daniel* (1967).

STANLEY WELLS is Professor of Shakespeare Studies and Director of the Shakespeare Institute, the University of Birmingham. He is General Editor of the Oxford Shakespeare, editor of *Shakespeare Survey*, and has published extensively on Shakespeare and his contemporaries.

Index

Page numbers in bold type denote essays or extracts in this Casebook; entries in small capitals denote characters in the four plays dealt with in this volume. References to other characters have been subsumed within their individual plays.

246

17,